Maps

SAN DIEGO
INTERNATIONAL
AIRPORT

LITTLE ITALY

SEE MAP 4

W LAUREL ST

W KALMIA ST

W JUNIPER ST

W IVY ST

5

PACIFIC HWY

W HAWTHORN ST

W GRAPE ST

KETTNER BLVD

COLUMBIA ST

W HAWTHORN ST

W GRAPE ST

W FIR ST

W ELM ST

LITTLE
ITALY

Waterfront
Park

W DATE ST

W CEDAR ST

COUNTY
CENTER

INDIA ST

COLUMBIA ST

STATE ST

UNION ST

FRONT ST

5

NORTH HARBOR DR

2

W BEECH ST

1ST AVE

4TH AVE

10

MARITIME MUSEUM
OF SAN DIEGO

3
4

W ASH ST

W ASH ST

5

SEE MAP 6

W A ST

INDIA ST

COLUMBIA ST

W A ST

6

SANTA FE
DEPOT

8

11

BAYSHORE BIKEWAY

AMTRAK

AMERICA
PLAZA

9

CIVIC
CENTER

GASLAMP

GAS LAMP

CORONADO-BROADWAY PIER
FERRY

W BROADWAY

PACIFIC HWY

KETTNER BLVD

USS MIDWAY
MUSEUM
7

W F ST

W F ST

4TH AVE

1ST AVE

Tuna
Harbor
Park

W G ST

G ST

INDIA ST

SEAPORT
VILLAGE

W HARBOR DR

W MARKET ST

MARKET ST

14

19

NEW CHILDREN'S
MUSEUM

GASLAMP

H

17

CONVENTION
CENTER

J ST

San Diego Bay

15

18

CONVENTION
CENTER

K ST

HARBOR DR

16

Embarcadero
Marina Park

SEE MAP 8

San Diego

IAN ANDERSON

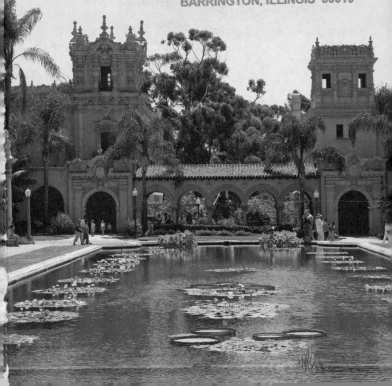

Contents

⊕ SIGHTS

3 MARITIME MUSEUM OF SAN DIEGO
7 USS *MIDWAY* MUSEUM
19 NEW CHILDREN'S MUSEUM
29 SAN DIEGO CENTRAL LIBRARY

⊕ RESTAURANTS

5 ANTHONY'S FISH GROTTO
10 EXTRAORDINARY DESSERTS
12 DONUT BAR
14 PIZZERIA MOZZA
22 NEIGHBORHOOD
23 CAFE CHLOE
24 COWBOY STAR
30 MISSION CAFÉ
32 PANCHITA'S BAKERY

⊕ NIGHTLIFE

1 THE CASBAH
20 EL DORADO COCKTAIL LOUNGE
25 BOOTLEGGER
31 MISSION BREWERY

⊕ ARTS AND CULTURE

8 MUSEUM OF CONTEMPORARY ART – DOWNTOWN
11 SAN DIEGO CIVIC THEATRE
13 COPLEY SYMPHONY HALL

⊕ SPORTS AND ACTIVITIES

2 WATERFRONT PARK
4 OCEAN ADVENTURE SAIL
6 BAYSHORE BIKEWAY
16 EMBARCADERO MARINA PARK
18 SEAFORTH BOAT RENTAL
26 EAST VILLAGE TAVERN + BOWL
28 PETCO PARK

⊕ SHOPS

15 SEAPORT VILLAGE

⊕ HOTELS

9 500 WEST HOTEL
17 MANCHESTER GRAND HYATT
21 MUDVILLE FLATS
27 HOTEL INDIGO

RESTAURANTS

1	TENDER GREENS
4	WEST BEAN
7	SPIKE AFRICA'S
16	CAFÉ 21
30	DON CHIDO
32	BERKELEY PIZZA
36	JSIX
40	BLIND BURRO
42	DONOVAN'S STEAK & CHOP HOUSE

NIGHTLIFE

12	STAR BAR
13	VIN DE SYRAH
17	TIPSY CROW
18	F6IX
19	ENCORE CHAMPAGNE BAR
22	BARLEYMASH
23	SEARSUCKER
26	PROHIBITION
27	FLUXX
37	LOUNGE SIX
39	SEVILLA NIGHTCLUB
41	MOONSHINE FLATS
43	ALTITUDE SKY LOUNGE
45	FLOAT

ARTS AND CULTURE

2	SPRECKELS THEATRE
5	CELEBRATION FINE ART GALLERY
9	LYCEUM THEATRE
10	BALBOA THEATRE
21	GASLAMP STADIUM
24	EXCLUSIVE COLLECTIONS
29	GASLAMP MUSEUM AT THE WILLIAM HEATH DAVIS HOUSE
34	HORTON GRAND THEATRE
35	SAN DIEGO CHINESE HISTORICAL MUSEUM
38	MICHAEL J. WOLF FINE ARTS
44	CHUCK JONES GALLERY

SPORTS AND ACTIVITIES

20	ANOTHER SIDE OF SAN DIEGO TOURS
31	THE BIKE REVOLUTION

SHOPS

8	BEST DAMN BEER SHOP AT KRISP
11	HORTON PLAZA

HOTELS

3	WESTGATE HOTEL
6	US GRANT HOTEL
14	GASLAMP PLAZA SUITES
15	THE KEATING HOTEL
25	HOSTELLING INTERNATIONAL SAN DIEGO, DOWNTOWN
28	HORTON GRAND HOTEL
33	HOTEL SOLAMAR
46	OMNI SAN DIEGO HOTEL

0   100 yds

0   100 m

DISTANCE ACROSS MAP
Approximate: 0.5 mi or 0.8 km

© AVALON TRAVEL

☉ SIGHTS
18 FIREHOUSE MUSEUM

Ⓡ RESTAURANTS
4   JAMES COFFEE CO
6   JUNIPER AND IVY
9   THE WATERFRONT BAR AND GRILL
11 MONELLO
13 MIMMO'S ITALIAN VILLAGE
15 IRONSIDE
19 QUEENSTOWN PUBLIC HOUSE
20 PAPPALECCO

Ⓝ NIGHTLIFE
7   SAN DIEGO CELLARS
8   BALLAST POINT BREWING

Ⓢ SHOPS
1   ARCHITECTURAL SALVAGE
2   CASA ARTELEXIA
3   ANTIQUES ON KETTNER
5   KETTNER ART & DESIGN DISTRICT
17 SATURDAY MERCATO

Ⓗ HOTELS
10 HOTEL VYVANT
12 PORTO VISTA HOTEL
14 LA PENSIONE HOTEL
16 URBAN BOUTIQUE HOTEL

W KALMIA ST
Kettner Art & Design District
W JUNIPER ST
KETTNER BLVD
INDIA ST
W IVY ST
W HAWTHORN ST
COLUMBIA ST
CALIFORNIA ST
W GRAPE ST
STATE ST
LITTLE ITALY
W FIR ST
W ELM ST
WASHINGTON ELEMENTARY SCHOOL
PACIFIC HWY
W DATE ST
Waterfront Park
W CEDAR ST
COUNTY CENTER
KETTNER BLVD
FIREHOUSE MUSEUM
INDIA ST
COLUMBIA ST
STATE ST
W BEECH ST

0   100 yds
0   100 m
DISTANCE ACROSS MAP
Approximate: 0.4 mi or 0.6 km

© AVALON TRAVEL

SEE MAP 3

SEE MAP 4

Roosevelt Middle School

Marston Hills

Marston Family

SOUTH PARK

Balboa Park

SEE MAP 6

To
5 KEATING HOUSE

SAN DIEGO ZOO 7

SAN DIEGO NATURAL HISTORY MUSEUM

BOTANICAL BUILDING

SAN DIEGO MUSEUM OF ART

8
9   10   11   12   13   14   15

EL PRADO

SAN DIEGO MUSEUM OF MAN

16   17   19   20,21
18   MODEL RAILROAD MUSEUM   22
23   REUBEN H. FLEET SCIENCE CENTER

Desert Garden

JAPANESE FRIENDSHIP GARDEN

MARIE HITCHCOCK PUPPET THEATRE
25
26

27
SAN DIEGO AIR AND SPACE MUSEUM

28

US Naval Hospital, San Diego

SEE MAP 1

STREET NAMES: 3RD AVE · IVY LN · 7TH AVE · WALNUT AVE · 4TH AVE · UPAS ST · THORN ST · SPRUCE ST · REDWOOD ST · QUINCE DR · QUINCE ST · PALM ST · OLIVE ST · NUTMEG AVE · MAPLE ST · 3RD AVE · 4TH AVE · 5TH AVE · LAUREL ST · KALMIA ST · JUNIPER ST · IVY ST · HAWTHORN ST · GRAPE ST · FIR ST · ELM ST · ASH ST · VERMONT ST · RICHMOND ST · UPAS ST · ALBERT ST · HERBERT ST · MYRTLE AVE · PARK BLVD · INDIANA ST · CRESTWOOD PL · ZOO DR · ZOO PL · PARK BLVD · VILLAGE PL · OLD GLOBE WAY · EL PRADO · PAN AMERICAN RD · PRESIDENT'S WAY · PARK BLVD · 8TH AVENUE DR · 10TH AVE · 11TH AVE · 12TH AVE · RUSS BLVD · 18TH ST

R RESTAURANTS

3   HANE SUSHI
10 PANAMA 66
18 THE PRADO AT BALBOA PARK
33 ECLIPSE CHOCOLATE BAR & BISTRO
34 MARISCOS GERMAN / NINE SEAS

N NIGHTLIFE

4   CROCE'S PARK WEST
6   THE TIN CAN
36 HAMILTON'S TAVERN

C ARTS AND CULTURE

1   MARSTON HOUSE MUSEUM & GARDENS
8   OLD GLOBE THEATRE
13 CASA DEL PRADO THEATRE
16 MINGEI INTERNATIONAL MUSEUM
20 MUSEUM OF PHOTOGRAPHIC ARTS
21 SAN DIEGO HISTORY CENTER
24 SPRECKELS ORGAN PAVILLION
26 SAN DIEGO AUTOMOTIVE MUSEUM
28 VETERANS MUSEUM AND MEMORIAL CENTER

SIGHTS

7	SAN DIEGO ZOO
9	SAN DIEGO MUSEUM OF MAN
11	SAN DIEGO MUSEUM OF ART
12	BOTANICAL BUILDING
14	SAN DIEGO NATURAL HISTORY MUSEUM
17	EL PRADO
19	MODEL RAILROAD MUSEUM
22	REUBEN H. FLEET SCIENCE CENTER
23	JAPANESE FRIENDSHIP GARDEN
25	MARIE HITCHCOCK PUPPET THEATRE
27	SAN DIEGO AIR AND SPACE MUSEUM

SPORTS AND ACTIVITIES

15	DESERT GARDEN
29	MORLEY FIELD DISC GOLF COURSE
30	BALBOA PARK CITY GOLF COURSE

SHOPS

31	PROGRESS
32	MAKE GOOD
35	SO CHILDISH

HOTELS

| 2 | INN AT THE PARK |
| 5 | KEATING HOUSE |

DISTANCE ACROSS MAP
Approximate: 2.1 mi or 3.3 km

0 — 300 yds
0 — 300 m

® RESTAURANTS

6	BLIND LADY ALEHOUSE	28	CARNITA'S SNACK SHACK
9	POMEGRANATE	31	CAFFÉ CALABRIA
10	COFFEE & TEA COLLECTIVE	32	CITY TACOS
12	GREAT MAPLE	33	EL COMAL
14	BREAD & CIE	38	WAYPOINT PUBLIC HOUSE
15	SNOOZE	43	URBN PIZZA
22	HASH HOUSE A GO GO	44	UNDERBELLY
23	100 WINES		
26	AKINORI SUSHI		

® NIGHTLIFE

1	BOURBON STREET BAR & GRILL	25	HILLCREST BREWING COMPANY
4	POLITE PROVISONS	27	BAJA BETTY'S
5	LESTAT'S WEST	29	TORONADO
7	BLIND LADY ALEHOUSE	30	COIN-OP
11	LIPS	34	SEVEN GRAND
13	URBAN MO'S	41	SPLASH WINE BAR
21	BRASS RAIL	42	MIKE HESS BREWING
24	GOSSIP GRILL	45	MODERN TIMES

® ARTS AND CULTURE

2	DIVERSIONARY THEATRE	16	HILLCREST CINEMAS
		35	NORTH PARK THEATER

® SHOPS

3	ADAMS AVENUE ANTIQUE ROW	36	BOTTLECRAFT
17	BABETTE SCHWARTZ	37	PIGMENT
18	VILLAGE HAT SHOP	39	VISUAL
19	MINT FOOTWEAR	40	RAY STREET ARTS DISTRICT
20	VINTAGE SHOPPING ON FIFTH		

® HOTELS

8	LAFAYETTE

Old Trolley Barn Park

ADAMS AVE

Spalding Place

MISSION AVE

MEADE AVE

UNIVERSITY HEIGHTS

EL CAJON BLVD

HOWARD AVE

MARYLAND ST

CLEVELAND AVE

CAMPUS AVE

PARK BLVD

NORMAL ST

JOHNSON AVE

POLK AVE

LEWIS ST

LINCOLN AVE

WASHINGTON ST

SEE MAP 4

WASHINGTON ST

LINCOLN AVE

HILLCREST

CLEVELAND AVE

HARVEY MILK ST

CENTRE ST

UPTOWN

UNIVERSITY AVE

UNIVERSITY AVE

CRESTWOOD PL

GEORGIA ST

ALABAMA ST

VERMONT ST

ESSEX ST

HERBERT ST

ROBINSON AVE

3RD AVE

4TH AVE

5TH AVE

6TH AVE

7TH AVE

8TH AVE

PENNSYLVANIA AVE

PENNSYLVANIA AVE

ROBINSON AVE

CYPRESS AVE

BROOKES AVE

RICHMOND ST

BROOKES AVE

PARK BLVD

INDIANA ST

FLORIDA ST

Marston Hills

MYRTLE AVE

Marston Family

WALNUT AVE

UPAS ST

UPAS ST

Bankers Hill

2ND AVE

3RD AVE

4TH AVE

5TH AVE

BALBOA PARK

MORLEY FIELD DR

SEE MAP 2

HOTEL CIRCLE SOUTH

C 23

PRESIDIO DR

Presidio
Park

PRESIDIO DR

24 A

PINE ST

TAYLOR ST

Presidio Hills
Golf Course

JUAN ST

MASON ST

SUNSET ST

FORT STOCKTON DR

ARISTA ST

HICKORY ST

OLD TOWN

AMPUDIA ST

PRESIDIO DR

Old Town San Diego
State Historic Park

Heritage
Park

TRIAS ST

TWIGGS ST

SAN DIEGO AVE

HARNEY ST

WITHERBY ST

JUAN ST

CONDE ST

ARISTA ST

SUNSET BLVD

JEFFERSON ST

LINWOOD ST

GUY ST

SEE MAP 6

AMPUDIA ST

25 R N 26

HORTENSIA ST

GUY ST

MOORE ST

OLD TOWN AVE

SAN DIEGO AVE

BANDINI ST

W CALIFORNIA ST

HENRY ST

TITUS ST

5

HANCOCK ST

SAN DIEGO AVE

KURTZ ST

32

S

⊙ SIGHTS

4	HERITAGE PARK VICTORIAN VILLAGE	13 CASA DE ESTUDILLO
10	OLD TOWN STATE HISTORIC PARK	20 WHALEY HOUSE MUSEUM
11	ROBINSON ROSE HOUSE	22 CAMPO SANTO CEMETERY

℞ RESTAURANTS

2	CASA GUADALAJARA	34 GELATO VERO CAFFE
25	EL AGAVE	36 EL INDIO
28	LEFTY'S CHICAGO PIZZERIA	37 BLUE WATER SEAFOOD MARKET & GRILL
33	LUCHA LIBRE	

Ⓝ NIGHTLIFE

26	EL AGAVE	35 SHAKESPEARE'S PUB & GRILLE
29	THE PATIO ON GOLDFINCH	38 57 DEGREES

Ⓖ ARTS AND CULTURE

8	SEELEY STABLE	23 JUNIPERO SERRA MUSEUM
9	OLD TOWN THEATRE	27 CINEMA UNDER THE STARS

Ⓐ SPORTS AND ACTIVITIES

3	PRESIDIO HILLS GOLF COURSE	24 PRESIDIO PARK
15	OLD TOWN TROLLEY TOURS	

Ⓢ SHOPS

1	BAZAAR DEL MUNDO	17 MINER'S GEMS & MINERALS
5	FIESTA DE REYES	18 EL CENTRO ARTESANO
6	JOHNSON HOUSE HABERDASHERY	19 CAPTAIN FITCH'S MERCANTILE
12	RACINE AND LARAMIE TOBACCONIST	21 FOUR WINDS TRADING COMPANY
14	TOLER'S LEATHER DEPOT	30 M-THEORY MUSIC
16	OLD TOWN MARKET	31 VENISSIMO CHEESE
		32 SEA JUNK

Ⓗ HOTELS

7 COSMOPOLITAN HOTEL

SEE MAP 7

La Jolla Mesa Dr
La Jolla Blvd
Turquoise St
Tourmaline St
Opal St
Loring St
Wilbur Ave
Beryl St
Law St
Chalcedony St
Missouri St
Diamond St
Emerald St
Felspar St
Garnet Ave
Hornblend St
Grand Ave
Thomas Ave
Reed Ave
Oliver Ave
Mission Blvd
Cass St
Bayard St
Daves St
Everts St
Fanuel St
Haines St
Gresham St
Jewell St
Ingraham St
Collingwood Dr
Loring St
Foothill Blvd
Los Altos Rd
Lamont St
Chalcedony St
Morrell St
Noyes St
Olney St
Balboa Ave
Kendall St
Soledad
Donaldson Dr

Kate O. Sessions Memorial Park

PACIFIC BEACH BOARDWALK

PACIFIC OCEAN

Bayside Walk

Sail Bay

Kendall-Frost Mission Bay Reserve

La Playa Ave
Moorland Dr
La Mancha Dr
La Cima Dr
Riviera Dr
Crown Point Dr

Crown Point Park

Mission Bay

San Juan Cove
Santa Clara Pl
Bayside Ln
Mission Blvd
Santa Barbara Cove

North Cove

Ski Beach Park

Vacation Rd
Vacation Isle Park

Ventura Cove
Gleason Rd

BELMONT PARK
Bonita Cove Park

Mission Beach Park

Mariner's Point Park

Mariners Basin

West Mission Bay Dr

South Cove

Perez Cove

Ingraham St

Quivira Way

Quivira Basin

SEE MAP 6

© AVALON TRAVEL

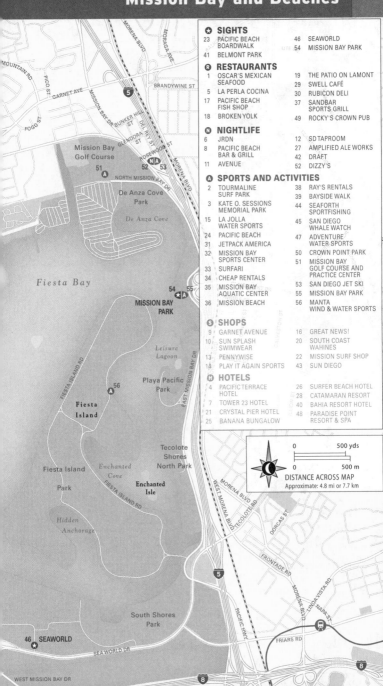

SIGHTS

23 PACIFIC BEACH BOARDWALK	46 SEAWORLD
41 BELMONT PARK	54 MISSION BAY PARK

RESTAURANTS

1 OSCAR'S MEXICAN SEAFOOD	19 THE PATIO ON LAMONT
5 LA PERLA COCINA	29 SWELL CAFÉ
17 PACIFIC BEACH FISH SHOP	30 RUBICON DELI
18 BROKEN YOLK	37 SANDBAR SPORTS GRILL
	49 ROCKY'S CROWN PUB

NIGHTLIFE

6 JRDN	12 SD TAPROOM
8 PACIFIC BEACH BAR & GRILL	27 AMPLIFIED ALE WORKS
11 AVENUE	42 DRAFT
	52 DIZZY'S

SPORTS AND ACTIVITIES

2 TOURMALINE SURF PARK	38 RAY'S RENTALS
3 KATE O. SESSIONS MEMORIAL PARK	39 BAYSIDE WALK
15 LA JOLLA WATER SPORTS	44 SEAFORTH SPORTFISHING
24 PACIFIC BEACH	45 SAN DIEGO WHALE WATCH
31 JETPACK AMERICA	47 ADVENTURE WATER SPORTS
32 MISSION BAY SPORTS CENTER	50 CROWN POINT PARK
33 SURFARI	51 MISSION BAY GOLF COURSE AND PRACTICE CENTER
34 CHEAP RENTALS	53 SAN DIEGO JET SKI
35 MISSION BAY AQUATIC CENTER	55 MISSION BAY PARK
36 MISSION BEACH	56 MANTA WIND & WATER SPORTS

SHOPS

9 GARNET AVENUE	16 GREAT NEWS!
10 SUN SPLASH SWIMWEAR	20 SOUTH COAST WAHINES
13 PENNYWISE	22 MISSION SURF SHOP
14 PLAY IT AGAIN SPORTS	43 SUN DIEGO

HOTELS

4 PACIFIC TERRACE HOTEL	26 SURFER BEACH HOTEL
7 TOWER 23 HOTEL	28 CATAMARAN RESORT
21 CRYSTAL PIER HOTEL	40 BAHIA RESORT HOTEL
25 BANANA BUNGALOW	48 PARADISE POINT RESORT & SPA

0   500 yds

0   500 m

DISTANCE ACROSS MAP
Approximate: 4.8 mi or 7.7 km

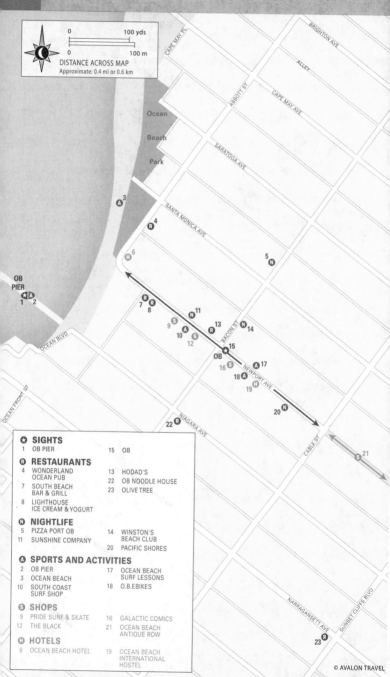

© AVALON TRAVEL

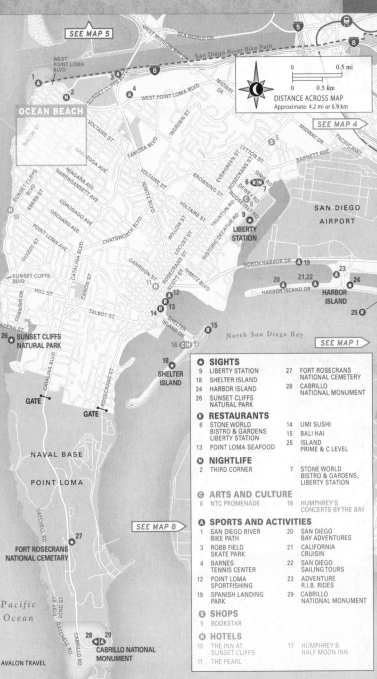

SEE MAP 5

WEST MISSION BAY DR
SEA WORLD DR
San Diego River Bike Path

WEST
POINT LOMA
BLVD

OCEAN BEACH

BACON ST

SUNSET CLIFFS BLVD
WEST POINT LOMA BLVD
MIDWAY DR

SEE MAP 4

DISTANCE ACROSS MAP
Approximate: 4.2 mi or 6.9 km

0   0.5 mi
0   0.5 km

VOLTAIRE ST
WORDEN ST
MIDWAY DR
PACIFIC HWY

SARATOGA AVE
FAMOSA BLVD
LYTTON ST
EVERGREEN ST
ROSECRANS ST
BARNETT AVE

NIAGARA AVE
NARRAGANSETT AVE
BROWNING ST
SIMS RD
DEWEY RD
ROOSEVELT RD

SAN DIEGO
AIRPORT

SUNSET CLIFFS BLVD
EBERS ST
ORCHARD AVE
CORONADO AVE
VOLTAIRE ST
NIMITZ BLVD
TRUXTUN RD
HISTORIC DECATUR RD

POINT LOMA AVE
CHATSWORTH BLVD
WILLOW ST
LOCUST ST

LIBERTY
STATION

GUIZOT ST
CATALINA BLVD
CANON ST
GARRISON ST
ROSECRANS ST
SCOTT ST
NIMITZ BLVD

NORTH HARBOR DR

SUNSET CLIFFS BLVD
HILL ST
TALBOT ST

HARBOR ISLAND DR

HARBOR
ISLAND

CORNISH DR
ADERA ST

SUNSET CLIFFS
NATURAL PARK

SHELTER ISLAND DR

North San Diego Bay

SEE MAP 1

SHELTER
ISLAND

GATE

GATE

CATALINA BLVD
ROSECRANS ST

NAVAL BASE

POINT LOMA

SEE MAP 8

GATCHELL RD

FORT ROSECRANS
NATIONAL CEMETARY

Pacific
Ocean

DIST ST
22ND ST
GATCHELL RD

CABRILLO RD

CABRILLO NATIONAL
MONUMENT

AVALON TRAVEL

SIGHTS
9   LIBERTY STATION
18 SHELTER ISLAND
24 HARBOR ISLAND
26 SUNSET CLIFFS
    NATURAL PARK

27 FORT ROSECRANS
    NATIONAL CEMETERY
28 CABRILLO
    NATIONAL MONUMENT

RESTAURANTS
6   STONE WORLD
    BISTRO & GARDENS
    LIBERTY STATION
13 POINT LOMA SEAFOOD

14 UMI SUSHI
15 BALI HAI
25 ISLAND
    PRIME & C LEVEL

NIGHTLIFE
2   THIRD CORNER

7   STONE WORLD
    BISTRO & GARDENS,
    LIBERTY STATION

ARTS AND CULTURE
8   NTC PROMENADE

16 HUMPHREY'S
    CONCERTS BY THE BAY

SPORTS AND ACTIVITIES
1   SAN DIEGO RIVER
    BIKE PATH
3   ROBB FIELD
    SKATE PARK
4   BARNES
    TENNIS CENTER
12 POINT LOMA
    SPORTFISHING
19 SPANISH LANDING
    PARK

20 SAN DIEGO
    BAY ADVENTURES
21 CALIFORNIA
    CRUISIN
22 SAN DIEGO
    SAILING TOURS
23 ADVENTURE
    R.I.B. RIDES
29 CABRILLO
    NATIONAL MONUMENT

SHOPS
5   BOOKSTAR

HOTELS
10 THE INN AT
    SUNSET CLIFFS
11 THE PEARL

17 HUMPHREY'S
    HALF MOON INN

MAP 7 La Jolla Village

✪ SIGHTS
- 6 LA JOLLA COVE
- 7 SUNNY JIM CAVE
- 14 CHILDREN'S POOL BEACH

RESTAURANTS
- 4 BROCKTON VILLA
- 16 NINE-TEN
- 23 PUESTO
- 25 WHISKNLADLE
- 26 BURGER LOUNGE
- 39 HARRY'S COFFEE SHOP
- 43 EL PESCADOR FISH MARKET

◐ NIGHTLIFE
- 8 EDDIE V'S
- 17 BARFLY
- 24 KARL STRAUSS BREWING COMPANY
- 27 HERRINGBONE
- 42 COMEDY STORE

◉ ARTS AND CULTURE
- 15 MADISON GALLERY
- 18 TASENDE GALLERY
- 19 MUSEUM OF CONTEMPORARY ART SAN DIEGO
- 22 ATHENAEUM MUSIC & ARTS LIBRARY
- 38 QUINT GALLERY

◎ SPORTS AND ACTIVITIES
- 1 ELLEN BROWNING SCRIPPS PARK
- 2 SNORKEL AND SCUBA
- 5 LA JOLLA CAVES
- 9 SAN DIEGO FLY RIDES
- 21 LA JOLLA TENNIS CLUB

⑤ SHOPS
- 10 JEWELS BY THE SEA
- 11 PROSPECT STREET ARTS AND CRAFTS
- 29 BOWERS JEWELERS
- 30 GEPPETTO'S
- 31 GIRARD AVENUE
- 32 WARWICK'S
- 33 MUTTROPOLIS
- 34 ASCOT SHOP
- 35 LE CHAUVINIST
- 36 ECHOES TOO
- 37 LA JOLLA DESIGN DISTRICT
- 40 DG WILLS BOOK SHOP
- 41 SPOILED ROTTEN BOUTIQUE
- 44 MITCH'S SURF SHOP

⊕ HOTELS
- 3 LA JOLLA COVE SUITES
- 12 LA VALENCIA HOTEL
- 13 PANTAI INN
- 20 THE BED & BREAKFAST INN AT LA JOLLA
- 28 LA JOLLA VILLAGE LODGE

Ellen Browning
Scripps Park

LA JOLLA
COVE

SUNNY
JIM CAVE

CHILDREN'S
POOL BEACH

Pacific

Ocean

Whispering
Sands Beach

La Jolla
Park

COAST BLVD

OCEAN BLVD

PROSPECT ST

ROSLYN LN

CAVE ST

PROSPECT PL

SILVERADO ST

EXCHANGE PL

PARK ROW

WALL ST

IVANHOE E AVE

EADS AVE

SILVERADO ST

GIRARD AVE

HERSCHEL AVE

IVANHOE E AVE

TORREY PINES RD

BLUEBIRD LN

VIRGINIA WAY

CUVIER ST

DRAPER AVE

KLINE ST

FAY AVE

HERSCHEL AVE

HIGH AVE

SILVER ST

PROSPECT ST

COAST BLVD

LA JOLLA BLVD

CUVIER ST

PEARL ST

OLIVETAS AVE

MARINE ST

SEA LN

GENTER ST

DRAPER AVE

| 0 | 200 yds |
| 0 | 200 m |

DISTANCE ACROSS MAP
Approximate: 0.9 mi or 1.4 km

© AVALON TRAVEL

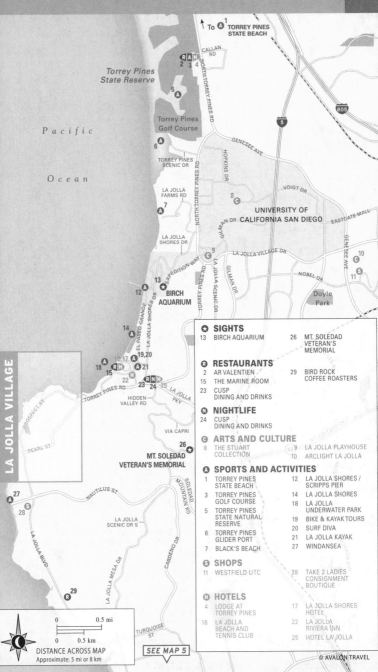

Torrey Pines State Reserve

Torrey Pines Golf Course

Pacific

Ocean

LA JOLLA FARMS RD

TORREY PINES SCENIC DR

LA JOLLA SHORES DR

BIRCH AQUARIUM

LA JOLLA VILLAGE

MT. SOLEDAD VETERAN'S MEMORIAL

PROSPECT ST

PEARL ST

NAUTILUS ST

LA JOLLA SCENIC DR S

LA JOLLA MESA DR

LA JOLLA BLVD

TORREY PINES RD

HIDDEN VALLEY RD

VIA CAPRI

SOLEDAD MOUNTAIN RD

CARDENO DR

TURQUOISE ST

UNIVERSITY OF CALIFORNIA SAN DIEGO

GENESEE AVE

HOPKINS DR

VOIGT DR

EASTGATE MALL

GENESEE AVE

NOBEL DR

Doyle Park

LA JOLLA VILLAGE DR

GILMAN DR

LA JOLLA SCENIC DR

EXPEDITION WAY

EL PASEO GRANDE

LA JOLLA SHORES DR

NORTH TORREY PINES RD

CALLAN RD

To **①** TORREY PINES STATE BEACH

SIGHTS
13 BIRCH AQUARIUM
26 MT. SOLEDAD VETERAN'S MEMORIAL

RESTAURANTS
2 AR VALENTIEN
15 THE MARINE ROOM
23 CUSP DINING AND DRINKS
29 BIRD ROCK COFFEE ROASTERS

NIGHTLIFE
24 CUSP DINING AND DRINKS

ARTS AND CULTURE
8 THE STUART COLLECTION
9 LA JOLLA PLAYHOUSE
10 ARCLIGHT LA JOLLA

SPORTS AND ACTIVITIES
1 TORREY PINES STATE BEACH
3 TORREY PINES GOLF COURSE
5 TORREY PINES STATE NATURAL RESERVE
6 TORREY PINES GLIDER PORT
7 BLACK'S BEACH
12 LA JOLLA SHORES / SCRIPPS PIER
14 LA JOLLA SHORES
18 LA JOLLA UNDERWATER PARK
19 BIKE & KAYAK TOURS
20 SURF DIVA
21 LA JOLLA KAYAK
27 WINDANSEA

SHOPS
11 WESTFIELD UTC
28 TAKE 2 LADIES CONSIGNMENT BOUTIQUE

HOTELS
4 LODGE AT TORREY PINES
16 LA JOLLA BEACH AND TENNIS CLUB
17 LA JOLLA SHORES HOTEL
22 LA JOLLA RIVIERA INN
25 HOTEL LA JOLLA

0   0.5 mi
0   0.5 km
DISTANCE ACROSS MAP
Approximate: 5 mi or 8 km

SEE MAP 5

© AVALON TRAVEL

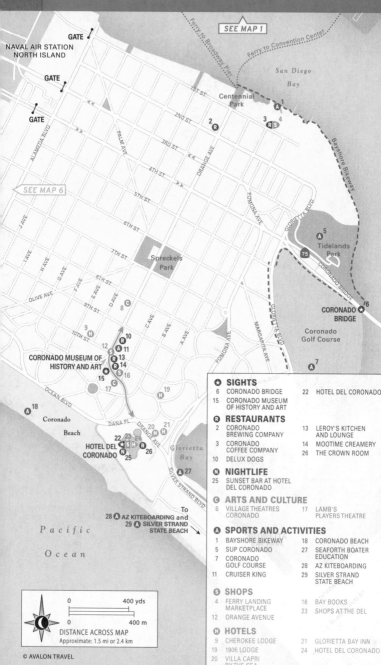

SEE MAP 1

San Diego Bay

Ferry to Broadway Pier
Ferry to Convention Center

NAVAL AIR STATION NORTH ISLAND

GATE
GATE
GATE

Centennial Park

Bayshore Bikeway

Tidelands Park

SEE MAP 6

Spreckels Park

CORONADO BRIDGE

Coronado Golf Course

CORONADO MUSEUM OF HISTORY AND ART

Coronado Beach

HOTEL DEL CORONADO

Glorietta Bay

To
AZ KITEBOARDING and
SILVER STRAND STATE BEACH

Pacific Ocean

SIGHTS
- 6 CORONADO BRIDGE
- 15 CORONADO MUSEUM OF HISTORY AND ART
- 22 HOTEL DEL CORONADO

RESTAURANTS
- 2 CORONADO BREWING COMPANY
- 3 CORONADO COFFEE COMPANY
- 10 DELUX DOGS
- 13 LEROY'S KITCHEN AND LOUNGE
- 14 MOOTIME CREAMERY
- 26 THE CROWN ROOM

NIGHTLIFE
- 25 SUNSET BAR AT HOTEL DEL CORONADO

ARTS AND CULTURE
- 8 VILLAGE THEATRES CORONADO
- 17 LAMB'S PLAYERS THEATRE

SPORTS AND ACTIVITIES
- 1 BAYSHORE BIKEWAY
- 5 SUP CORONADO
- 7 CORONADO GOLF COURSE
- 11 CRUISER KING
- 18 CORONADO BEACH
- 27 SEAFORTH BOATER EDUCATION
- 28 AZ KITEBOARDING
- 29 SILVER STRAND STATE BEACH

SHOPS
- 4 FERRY LANDING MARKETPLACE
- 12 ORANGE AVENUE
- 16 BAY BOOKS
- 23 SHOPS AT THE DEL

HOTELS
- 9 CHEROKEE LODGE
- 19 1906 LODGE
- 20 VILLA CAPRI BY THE SEA
- 21 GLORIETTA BAY INN
- 24 HOTEL DEL CORONADO

0   400 yds
0   400 m
DISTANCE ACROSS MAP
Approximate: 1.5 mi or 2.4 km

© AVALON TRAVEL

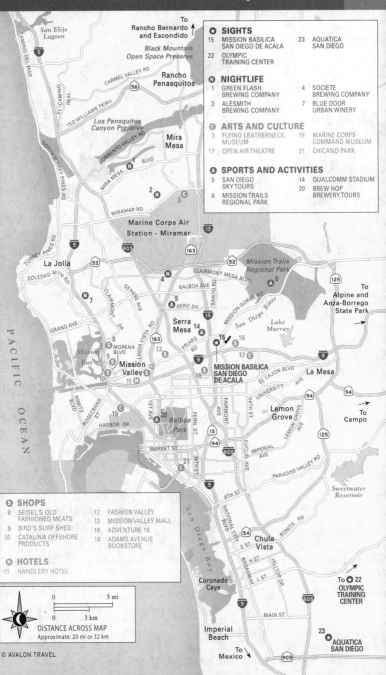

SIGHTS
- 15 MISSION BASILICA SAN DIEGO DE ACALA
- 22 OLYMPIC TRAINING CENTER
- 23 AQUATICA SAN DIEGO

NIGHTLIFE
- 1 GREEN FLASH BREWING COMPANY
- 2 ALESMITH BREWING COMPANY
- 4 SOCIETE BREWING COMPANY
- 7 BLUE DOOR URBAN WINERY

ARTS AND CULTURE
- 3 FLYING LEATHERNECK MUSEUM
- 17 OPEN AIR THEATRE
- 19 MARINE CORPS COMMAND MUSEUM
- 21 CHICANO PARK

SPORTS AND ACTIVITIES
- 5 SAN DIEGO SKY TOURS
- 6 MISSION TRAILS REGIONAL PARK
- 14 QUALCOMM STADIUM
- 20 BREW HOP BREWERY TOURS

SHOPS
- 8 SEISEL'S OLD FASHIONED MEATS
- 9 BIRD'S SURF SHED
- 10 CATALINA OFFSHORE PRODUCTS
- 12 FASHION VALLEY
- 13 MISSION VALLEY MALL
- 16 ADVENTURE 16
- 18 ADAMS AVENUE BOOKSTORE

HOTELS
- 11 HANDLERY HOTEL

DISTANCE ACROSS MAP
Approximate: 20 mi or 32 km

0   3 mi
0   3 km

© AVALON TRAVEL

DISCOVER
San Diego

San Diego is a golden-hued playground beckoning thrill-seekers, revelers, and soul searchers with its magnificent sunsets, sparkling waters, and promise of the good life. A typical weather forecast is 70°F and sunny, and pretty much everybody wears sunglasses all the time.

On the beaches, locals sport board shorts, wetsuits, and bikinis, and the air carries the mingled scents of surf wax, suntan lotion, and salt water. On a clear day, sailboats traverse the bay, scuba divers explore underwater canyons, golfers tee up, and bicyclists cruise from beach to beach.

San Diego offers 80 miles of coastline, but with the resources of a major metropolitan city. For all its leisurely appearance, the city supports thriving industries—a vibrant performing arts scene, an emerging culinary identity, the finest craft brewing, and research institutions that attract some of the world's brightest scientific minds.

With a southern border and a western edge, San Diego collects people from every direction. Some come for the sunshine and the beaches, then stay to form a community of friendly, optimistic, and relaxed individuals who love and appreciate the natural resources of "America's Finest City." To make the most of your time in San Diego, all you need is a laid-back approach and a gentle push in the right direction.

Clockwise from top left: La Jolla Cove; Balboa Park; the *HMS Surprise*; Oceanside Pier

Planning Your Trip

Where to Go

Downtown

San Diego's urban Downtown was built around its huge, naturally protected harbor. Mere blocks from the city's skyscrapers are ships, bayside parks, and pleasant ocean breezes.

Within Downtown are pocket neighborhoods with their own appeal and personalities. The embarcadero is where the city meets the harbor; it's home to the tall antique ships of the San Diego Maritime Museum, the USS Midway Museum, San Diego Convention Center, and plenty of visitor-friendly businesses. The Gaslamp is filled with bars and clubs that attract revelers to blow off steam. South of the Gaslamp, the East Village is a hip area home to Petco Park and the San Diego Public Library. On the northern border of Downtown is Little Italy. While traditional Italian restaurants still populate this ethnic quarter, lately the design-savvy neighborhood has become a top destination for California cuisine as well as craft beer, artisanal coffee, and urban wine.

Balboa Park

Balboa Park's 1,200 acres are home to some of the city's best museums and gardens, as well as the famous San Diego Zoo. The heart of the park is El Prado, a Spanish colonial plaza that hosted an exposition celebrating the opening of the Panama Canal. The neighborhoods surrounding the park are among the oldest in the city, including upscale Banker's Hill and the quiet enclave South Park on its eastern border.

Spanish Village in Balboa Park

Downtown's Gaslamp Quarter

Uptown

Uptown actually comprises several neighborhoods, almost all of which abound with great food and craft beverages. Hillcrest has been an LGBT hub since the 1970s and stays lively with great bars and restaurants. In North Park, the city's tastemakers and creatives find a community among the area's century-old Craftsman homes.

Old Town and Mission Hills

Before Old Town was a town, it was a pueblo. The original Mexican village of San Diego has been faithfully restored within Old Town State Historic Park, preserving the city's adobe origins with plenty of gift and souvenir shops. Among the historical museums, you'll find homage to the city's Mexican origins and influence.

Mission Bay and Beaches

The Mission Beach boardwalk's rides and attractions make family forays an adventure. The beach can be fantastic, while adjacent Pacific Beach provides a raucous playground for young adults both day and night. The real action takes place in Mission Bay, which can put you on a fishing boat, Jet Skis, wakeboards, or other watercraft that don't need a good swell to be a blast.

Ocean Beach and Point Loma

Ocean Beach (better known as OB) offers a wild blend of hippies, surfers, bikers, and sailors that must be experienced to be believed. The character of the community extends to a sometimes hilarious nightlife. Or enjoy a quiet evening at Sunset Cliffs Natural Park watching the sun dip into the ocean each night.

the Hotel del Coronado

The Point Loma peninsula sits across the bay from Coronado. On the bay side of the peninsula, seafood lovers have access to the morning's fresh catch at Shelter Island, home to many of the area's yachts and fishing boats. At the tip of the peninsula, the Cabrillo National Monument commands the widest panoramic view of all of San Diego.

La Jolla

La Jolla is the city's most upscale neighborhood, with fine dining, high-end shopping, and multimillion-dollar homes. The views are just as rich below the ocean surface in protected La Jolla Underwater Park. La Jolla Shores is one of the county's best beaches for relaxing and splashing in the waves. Just to the north, the cliffs at Torrey Pines State Natural Reserve offer scenic hiking opportunities and undeveloped beaches, as well as a famous golf course.

Coronado

Just across the harbor from Downtown, Coronado actually connects to a long sliver of peninsula, but the sleepy upscale beach community feels like an island. Coronado's claim to fame is the Hotel del Coronado, which made a starring appearance alongside Marilyn Monroe in the film *Some Like It Hot.*

Greater San Diego

Some sights are worth the drive, whether it be the Mission Basilica San Diego de Alcalá in Mission Valley, beer-vana at Green Flash Brewing Company in Mira Mesa, or SeaWorld's Aquatica San Diego in Chula Vista.

When to Go

Spring

March and April see occasional spring showers with partly sunny days, small to medium crowds, and fluctuating surf. May and June are notoriously socked in with the marine layer (called "May Gray" and "June Gloom"). Days are warm, but cloudy with smaller crowds and surf.

Summer

July and August are peak season, with hot sunny days, very large crowds, and small to occasionally medium surf. July consistently provides the year's best weather, but the crowds can be outrageous, especially during the long weekend around the immeasurably popular Comic Con (usually the second week of July). Hotel prices go through the roof that week, often triple the standard rate.

Fall

September and October are the "local's summer," with warm, sunshiny days, medium crowds, and a mix of surf conditions.

Winter

In November and December, morning fog gives way to mild, partly cloudy afternoons. Crowds are small, with the exception of the last two weeks of December. Surfers can expect medium to very large waves.

Historically, January and February are the rainy months, though it's just as likely to have 90-degree days as it is three inches of rain. Considering most climes experience snow, 65°F with a chance of rain might seem pretty worthwhile. Crowds are small and surfers can expect large (sometimes very large) waves.

Lifeguards love it here, too.

a lifeguard stand on Ocean Beach

The Best of San Diego

Day 1

▶ Get an early start and head up to the San Diego Zoo, where the animals are always livelier in the morning. Watch the pandas cuddle and the polar bears swim, then go next door to Balboa Park for lunch at Panama 66, a sculpture garden-restaurant with hot sandwiches and a terrific tap list.

▶ Your first stop for an afternoon of museum-hopping is to peruse the minor masterpieces at the San Diego Museum of Art. Study humankind at the San Diego Museum of Man, marvel at aeronautic engineering in the San Diego Air and Space Museum, then catch your breath in the Botanical Building.

▶ Head up to North Park for happy hour at Polite Provisions; their beautiful cocktail lounge may hook you up with some small plates if you're hungry. Save the appetite, though—North Park's Restaurant Row is nearby.

▶ Slurp ramen and savor yakitori at Underbelly gastropub, a great first stop for the local beer scene. The slick Modern Times tasting room is next door, or walk up the street to Coin-Op for vintage video games with your brews.

the Botanical Building in Balboa Park   San Diego Museum of Man

Best Beaches

Coronado Beach

Choosing the best beach for you depends upon whether you have children to entertain or are on your own looking for entertainment.

- **Mission Beach** (page 143) has Belmont Park, a seaside amusement park with a roller coaster and an artificial wave where surfing performances are regularly staged throughout the day. Bikes and skateboards roll past on the boardwalk, giving even older children plenty to see and do.

- **Pacific Beach** (page 143) offers fun surf and athletic beach games, but much of its character stems from the bars and cantinas fronting the boardwalk. The party vibe starts early and sometimes makes for a rowdy scene.

- **La Jolla Shores** (page 153) offers a wealth of water sports, a playground, more than a mile of gorgeous sand, and a large parking lot at that fills quickly in summer.

- **Ocean Beach** (page 149) is a popular spot for young adults, who come here regularly to surf, swim, play volleyball, run their dogs, and gather around summer bonfires.

- **Coronado Beach** (page 158) is long a stretch of sand that starts at historic Hotel del Coronado and runs north to a dog-friendly beach. In between are families and couples quietly appreciating its beauty.

the USS *Midway* Museum

Day 2

▶ Take the ferry to Coronado and wander the impressive Hotel del Coronado. Spend some time on Coronado Beach, then grab lunch at Coronado Brewing Company before heading back on the ferry.

▶ Stroll up the Embarcadero and visit the Maritime Museum of San Diego and USS *Midway* Museum. After gazing at ships both antique and modern, walk north to Little Italy, where you can sample some reds from urban winery San Diego Cellars before dining at one of the neighborhood's fantastic restaurants, such as Juniper and Ivy.

▶ After dinner, stroll through the charming neighborhood to reach decadent Extraordinary Desserts. The sugar rush should get you started for a night out in the Gaslamp District club scene; if you prefer something chill, the swanky retro cocktail bar Prohibition is a great way to finish the night.

Day 3

▶ Start the day with doughnuts and coffee from The Donut Bar, which will fuel you without leaving you too full for a day of action.

▶ Catch a morning surf lessons from Surfari at north Mission Beach, and enjoy some prime people-watching on the Pacific Beach Boardwalk while you catch your breath. You'll have worked up quite an appetite, so sate it the way a local surfer would—with fish tacos from Oscar's Mexican Seafood.

Best Craft Breweries

San Diego is crazy for beer and has dozens of small breweries. Beer drinkers come from all over to taste their wares.

Stone World Bistro & Gardens Liberty Station

- **AleSmith** (page 114): In Miramar, next to the Marine Corps Air Station, AleSmith may have the greatest international reputation. The brewery shows off its stellar lineup of flagship beers and some rarely seen special issues.

- **Ballast Point** (page 98): The length of the tap list at the restaurant and tasting room in Little Italy makes its central location a benefit.

- **Green Flash** (page 116): The brewery doubles as one of the better tasting rooms in town, turning an industrial park drinking patio in Mira Mesa into a hoppy party, sometimes serving the rare beers of brew-buddy Alpine Brewing.

- **Lost Abbey** (page 228): Lost Abbey is a California outpost of brewing that's been handed down by Belgian monks for centuries. As far as West Coast beers go, they've nailed it, with excellent craft beers in an unlikely location—a San Marcos business park.

- **Societe** (page 116): Societe is taking the region by storm with a deep roster of ales ranging from hoppy West Coasters to British and Belgian styles. Located in Kearny Mesa, it's not easy to find, but the beer is worth it.

- **Stone World Bistro & Gardens Liberty Station** (page 110): This location may not have the cachet of its Escondido sibling, but it has plenty of space to serve up a huge variety of beers.

- **Stone World Bistro & Gardens** (page 225): Located in Escondido, this gorgeous brewery sports indoor and outdoor bars, a restaurant, a desert garden, and an illuminating brewery tour. Many Stone beers are served here, as are some of the brewery's favorite craft beers.

Family-Friendly San Diego

Whatever your kids are into, there's probably a little something to keep *them* entertained. The question you need to ask yourself as a parent is: how much can you handle?

See the Animals
The San Diego Zoo is a no-brainer. However, it's sister park, San Diego Zoo Safari Park, offers the opportunity to ride along in an off-road vehicle to see lions, tigers, and elephants in something closer to their natural habitats. SeaWorld delivers dolphins and killer whale shows where you're likely to get doused with water, while the smaller, drier Birch Aquarium exhibits fish that actually live in the region.

Lion cubs play at the San Diego Zoo Safari Park.

Ride the Rides
For action-packed theme-park experiences, check out the rides and games at Belmont Park, right by beautiful Mission Beach. Or make the drive north to Legoland, which smaller kids will especially love. In the summer, bigger kids will enjoy the water slides and wave pool at SeaWorld's Aquatica San Diego.

Water Sports Camps
If your kids are ready to go beyond the wave pool, sign them up for surf camp days with Surf Diva in La Jolla or Ocean Beach Surf Lessons. To really get 'em going, sample the wakeboarding, kayaking, windsurfing, or sailing at camps offered by Mission Bay Sports Center.

Planes, Boats, and Trucks
To see life-size versions of the toys kids love to play with, start at the San Diego Air and Space Museum and USS ˙Midway Museum. The ships of the San Diego Maritime Museum skew older, though kids are just the right size to squeeze through a submarine. The Firehouse Museum offers fire trucks galore to explore.

Learn Something Fun
The Reuben H. Fleet Science Center teaches science lessons in the most fun way imaginable. Across the courtyard is the San Diego Natural History Museum, where the learning often involves dinosaurs. The New Children's Museum engages kids with interactive art installations that stimulate different parts of the brain.

► Next up is Mission Bay, where you choose your speed: kayak, Jet Ski, wakeboard, or sail. (Hint: there's time to do two.) After playing all day, you'll need serious nourishment.

► Roll up to La Jolla for sustainable ingredients perfectly prepared at Whisknladle. If you still have energy, nourish your mind with a destined-for-Broadway show at La Jolla Playhouse.

Day 4

► Spend a long morning in Old Town State Historic Park, exploring the adobe buildings and browsing the many gift shops. You'll be tempted to sit down for a Mexican lunch at one of the tourist restaurants, but save your appetite for a more genuine experience at El Indio, just up the street in Mission Hills.

► After lunch, ride over to Ocean Beach for a walk along the lengthy Ocean Beach Pier, a great vantage point for watching surfers. Grab your own spot of sand and enjoy the local color while you soak up some sun.

► Hit happy hour at Wonderland Ocean Pub when you get thirsty, then sit at the window to wait for an incredible sunset. Or, make your way up to Sunset Cliffs Natural Park to stroll the cliffs and experience the panoramic pink, purple, and bright-orange majesty as the sun goes down.

► Finish off the day over the hill at Stone World Bistro & Gardens Liberty Station. The local brewer celebrates beer from all over (as well as its own) and raises the gastropub bar with an excellent local, organic menu.

Old Town State Historic Park

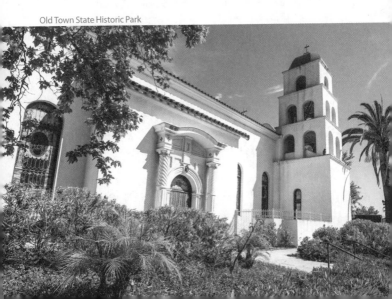

La Jolla Cove

Day 5

▶ Beat the crowds into La Jolla and grab a cup of local coffee at Bird Rock Coffee Roasters.

▶ Take advantage of the calm morning conditions to snorkel or scuba off La Jolla Cove and experience the vibrant below-sea-level nature reserve of the La Jolla Underwater Park. This will prime your appetite for some of the city's best Mexican food with a taco plate at Puesto, in the center of La Jolla Village.

▶ Walk it off along the famous shoreline, then spend the afternoon exploring neighborhood shops and art collections, including the Madison Gallery and Museum of Contemporary Art.

▶ Pick up a couple of sashimi plates at the excellent fresh seafood counter El Pescador Fish Market and take them with you up the hill to Kate O. Sessions Memorial Park. Snack while lounging on a grassy hillside with a wraparound view of the city's bays, beaches, and skyline.

▶ At night, dine on prime steak dinner at Cowboy Star in the East Village, then celebrate a terrific trip with something sparkling at Encore Champagne Bar.

Sights

Look for ★ to find
recommended sights

Highlights

★ **Oldest Fire Trucks:** The retired station hosting the **Firehouse Museum** still has a fire pole, but you can't ride down it. You'll forget all about that though when you see the old-time fire trucks and hose wagons (page 38).

★ **Most Historical Ships:** It's just a short walk from the **Maritime Museum of San Diego** to the USS *Midway* **Museum** to see amazing sea vessels, including an aircraft carrier, clipper ships, and two submarines (pages 38 and 40).

★ **Most Culturally Rich Landmark:** Balboa Park's **El Prado** is an ornate Spanish Revival promenade lined with many of the city's best museums, gardens, and theaters (page 41).

★ **Best Kid-Friendly Attraction:** There's no topping the **San Diego Zoo,** where millions of parents bring their children to view lions, tigers, and pandas (page 44).

★ **Best Historic Birthplace:** Old Town State Historic Park preserves the surviving structures that made up the original Mexican pueblo of San Diego, but it's the colorful, uniquely designed wooden houses in **Heritage Park Victorian Village** that you'll ooh and aah over (page 46).

★ **Best Watery Playground:** Designed for visitors to boat, swim, and play, **Mission Bay Park** has long lived up to the task with sailing, kayaking, and stand-up paddleboarding along this 4,200-acre waterway (page 49).

★ **Best Views:** On the Point Loma Peninsula, **Cabrillo National Monument** looks west across the ocean, south past Coronado into Mexico and east facing the bay and city skyline (page 51).

★ **Best Place to Watch Surfers Strut Their Stuff:** Walk out a little ways on the **Ocean Beach Pier** and you'll find yourself looking down on the local lineup, who aren't above showing off a little if the waves are up (page 52).

★ **Best Place to Catch a Sunset:** The sandstone cliffs at **Sunset Cliffs Natural Park** face a western sky known to put on a show when the sun drops behind scattered clouds (page 54).

★ **Most Historic Building:** The original, all-wood **Hotel del Coronado** may not be considered the modern resort it was in 1888, but it's still gorgeous and one of a kind (page 57).

What should people see in San Diego while they're here? It's not a question every visitor thinks to ask.

To be fair, there are plenty of people who've lived here for years who are far too distracted by the great weather and beaches to explore many of the city's interesting historic or culturally significant sights.

There are exceptions. Many of your fellow explorers in Balboa Park and Old Town are residents visiting or revisiting a favorite museum or historic home. Some locals maintain annual memberships to the San Diego Zoo so they may visit often. And hey—anything involving a beach? We're all over it.

San Diego's actually a fairly old city, at least as far as the West Coast is concerned—a frontier town first settled by boat rather than overland passage, a desert by the sea, with an undercurrent of both sailor and cowboy cultures, built on indigenous and Mexican foundations, with strong military ties and millions invested in tourism. There's a lot to see and do once you've had your fill of the beach.

Previous page top: the Botanical Building in Balboa Park **bottom:** Casa de Estudillo

★ Firehouse Museum

Also known as the Pioneer Hook and Ladder Museum, this former home of San Diego Fire Station No. 6 offers a stunning visual history of firefighting, including antique gear, the fire badges of several nations, and a glimpse into the living quarters of on-call firefighters. While you can't slide down the fire pole, you will be impressed by the museum's collection of vintage fire trucks, wagons, and hose carts, some dating back to the mid-19th century. The museum is staffed by former and current firefighting volunteers and includes a 9/11 memorial. While fascinating to fire truck-loving kids, adults will also find plenty to marvel at.

Map 1: 1572 Columbia St., Little Italy, 619/232-3473, www.sandiegofirehousemuseum. com; Thurs.-Fri. 10am-2pm, Sat.-Sun. 10am-4pm; $3 adults, $2 children, $2 seniors

★ Maritime Museum of San Diego

Cruising down Harbor Drive, it's tough to miss the *Star of India*, canvas unfurled from its 127-foot top mast. After all, how many 19th-century merchant sailing vessels do you see on a daily basis? The striking ship is the oldest active clipper of its type, and just one of many boats that make up the Maritime Museum. Beside it is the *HMS Surprise*, a replica 17th-century British frigate best known for its role in the film *Master and Commander*. Nearby is the *Berkeley*, a steamboat that once served as a ferry in early-20th-century San Francisco. Museum guests board each ship to explore the deck and cabins, and stand where the captain once stood.

Perhaps none of these vessels are more intriguing than the pair of Cold War-era submarines. The USS *Dolphin* holds the distinction of diving deeper than any other operational sub, and its compact decks and sailors' quarters aren't for the claustrophobic. More confining still is the B-39 Soviet sub, which cannot be traversed end-to-end walking upright. History is alive within these boats, providing one of San Diego's most memorable museum experiences.

Map 1: 1492 N. Harbor Dr., 619/234-9153, www.sdmaritime.org; Daily 9am-8pm; $16 adults, $8 ages 3-12, $13 seniors, $13 ages 13-17, $13 military

New Children's Museum

Interactive artwork stokes the imagination of kids who engage with educational pieces by touching and climbing, or playing with art supplies. Various permanent and revolving exhibits are based on a specific educational theme, which shifts every two years (previous themes have included Animal Art, Child's Play, and Feast, devoted to teaching kids about food and nutrition). Parents will enjoy watching their kids' brains light up, and

top to bottom: the Maritime Museum of San Diego; the Firehouse Museum

may even have occasion to marvel at the ingenuity behind some of the hands-on pieces in this stylish glass-and-steel space.

Map 1: 200 W. Island Ave., 619/233-8792, www.thinkplaycreate.org; Mon. 10am-4pm, Wed.-Sat. 10am-4pm, Sun. noon-4pm; $10 adults, $10 children, $5 seniors, $5 military

San Diego Central Library

San Diego's public library opened in late 2013 as one of the most ambitious new libraries in the nation, and it's certainly not your traditional stuffy institution. At 500,000 square feet, it boasts more than 1.25 million books and roughly 1,200 comfortable places to sit down and read, with panoramic windows and modern architectural flourishes such as a rooftop deck with a killer view of the Coronado Bridge and the south bay. Information technology runs throughout, with adaptive computer devices for those with special needs, media editing suites, and a 3-D printing lab for those with more advanced know-how (most likely the students of the high-tech high school housed on the sixth and seventh floors of the nine-story building). Terrific (and separate) kid and teen sections make it a great family stop on a rainy day, or you may want to stop by just to redefine in your mind's eye what a library can be. Validation at an information desk nets you two hours free parking in the underground lot.

Map 1: 330 Park Blvd., 619/236-5800, www.sandiego.gov/public-library; Mon. noon-8pm, Tues. 9:30am-5:30pm, Wed. noon-8pm, Thurs.-Fri. 9:30pm-5:30pm, Sat. 9:30am-2:30pm, Sun. 1pm-5pm; free

★ USS *Midway* Museum

The museum tag almost does a disservice to this 64-ton historical artifact— a true-to-life aircraft carrier. Commissioned at the end of World War II, the USS *Midway* was the world's largest ship when it was built, and served as a temporary home to more than 200,000 sailors before retiring to its current location after nearly half a century in service. Each year, one million visitors explore the close confines experienced by those service members, inspecting their bunks, examining the bulwarks, and comparing them to the relative luxury of the captain's quarters.

Complimentary audio tours offer insights to the inner workings of the sonar and engine rooms. When it gets too claustrophobic, head up to the massive flight deck, where many of the museum's 29 vintage military aircraft have been restored to original condition. To gain an even more dynamic understanding of just how vital a role behemoths like this play in our nation's military defenses, check out one of the ship's flight simulators, where you may experience the vertigo of aerial combat, and discover just how much skill it takes to land planes on an ocean vessel.

Map 1: 910 N. Harbor Dr., 619/544-9600, www.midway.org; Daily 10am-5pm; $20 adults, $10 children, $17 seniors, $15 students, $10 retired military

Botanical Building

The domed, rust-colored lath Botanical Building stands as a striking departure from the ornate stucco Spanish architecture surrounding it on Balboa Park's El Prado. Fronted by a large reflecting pool populated by lily pads, the building hosts a tropical oasis of more than 2,000 flowers and fronds, including orchids, ferns, and palms. Take a brief stroll through the lush, shady rooms; these gorgeous plants are well tended, and for many, this stop turns out to be a highlight.

Map 2: 1549 El Prado, 619/239-0512, www.balboapark.org; Fri.-Wed. 10am-4pm; free

★ El Prado

Balboa Park houses a number of museums, theaters, and gardens, but the central promenade known as El Prado (translated as "the meadow") serves as a sight in itself. Locals regularly stroll the 0.5-mile-long Prado just for the pleasure of wandering its fountains, plazas, and ponds and appreciating the Spanish Revival architecture throughout the park. Others hop on and off a circling tram that shuttles between parking lots and popular attractions. During the park's December Nights events (usually the first weekend in December), thousands arrive to enjoy the park's holiday decorative light show.

Map 2: El Prado between Cabrillo Bridge and Park Ave.

Japanese Friendship Garden

The Japanese made gardening an art form, and the small but growing Japanese Friendship Garden tucked between El Prado and the Spreckels Organ Pavilion demonstrates this art with elegance. A winding path leads past bonsai trees, a koi pond, and a rock garden. A small exhibition house features culturally relevant artwork with picture windows overlooking the garden's manicured grounds and the canyon beyond.

Map 2: 2215 Pan American Rd., 619/232-2721, www.niwa.org; Daily 10am-4:30pm; $6 adults, $5 seniors, students, and military, free under age 7

Marie Hitchcock Puppet Theatre

The oldest continuously active puppet theater in the country stages puppet shows of all types, with marionettes and hand puppets (both glow-in-the-dark and life-size). Kid-friendly plays and musicals are adapted from folklore, or written specifically to take advantage of the production company's talent pool and venue. Weekend performances run year round, with Wednesday-Friday shows during the summer.

Map 2: 2130 Pan American Rd. W., 619/544-9203, www.balboaparkpuppets.com; $5 adults, $4 seniors, $4 military, $5 children, free under age 2

One Day at Balboa Park

There's more to see and do at Balboa Park than can comfortably be accomplished in one day. If you're only going to make one pass through the treasured cultural center of San Diego, here's how to prioritize your visit with kids and without.

- **San Diego Museum of Art.** It doesn't have the most outstanding collection of paintings, but it's always reliable for enchanting visual moments, and the visiting exhibitions tend to be quite good.

- **San Diego Museum of Man.** It can be thought of as a museum of anthropology, and you may learn a lot about our biological and cultural origins.

- **Mingei International Museum.** This museum doesn't get enough credit for bringing in unusual exhibits involving artisanal handiwork. Some objects are baffling in the sense that you can't believe it came out of someone's imagination; others baffle for different reasons altogether (page 124).

- **Botanical Building.** The flora inside is as lovely as the building, and while you may not remember their Latin names, some flowers may create a lasting image.

- **San Diego Air and Space Museum.** A stealth bomber is on display in front; inside there is much more.

Children will get pretty bored if you try to fill a whole day with museums. Bring them to these Balboa Park sights and they'll have fun despite themselves.

- **Reuben H. Fleet Science Center.** Blow everybody's mind with hundreds of learning stations that trick you with optical illusions or turn common sense on its ear.

- **Marie Hitchcock Puppet Theatre.** If there's not a puppet theater in your town, expose your child to this sort of culture with the theater's puppet shows, sometimes involving very large puppets.

- **San Diego Natural History Museum.** Frankly, some parts of this museum on the natural history of San Diego are kind of ho hum, but there's a mastodon skeleton, a 3-D theater, and some pretty engaging temporary exhibits.

- **San Diego Model Railroad Museum.** Children love miniatures and trains, and this exhibit is huge and remarkably well detailed.

- **San Diego Air and Space Museum.** On this point, kids and parents may agree: Everybody's going to have fun here.

Reuben H. Fleet Science Center

Interactive exhibits at the Reuben H. Fleet Science Center offer kids hands-on instruction about electricity, space, optical illusions, and the human body, including a video program that predicts what you might look like at age 70. More relaxed entertainment includes planetarium shows, magic shows, and IMAX screenings of documentaries that virtually place you in the middle of a black hole, at the bottom of the ocean, or on the top of

Mount Everest. Performances and screening schedules vary, and may include an additional entry fee.

43

Map 2: 1875 El Prado, 619/234-8291, www.sandiegoairandspace.org; Daily 10am-4:30pm;
$18 adults, $15 seniors and students, $15 retired military, $9 ages 3-11, free for active-duty
military

San Diego Air and Space Museum

You can't miss this museum devoted to flight—just look for the giant SR-71
stealth bomber out front. Inside are more thrills, with a close-up of the
Apollo 9 space capsule, the World War II carrier-based Hellcat fighter,
and a full-size replica of Lindbergh's *Spirit of St. Louis*. Rotating exhibitions offer a taste of different technologies and wonders, but you can always
count on the myriad aircraft built from years of humankind looking at the
sky and thinking, "I can go there." Try out one of the flight simulators on
hand to see if you've got the right stuff.

Map 2: 2001 Pan American Plaza, 619/234-8291, www.sandiegoairandspace.org;
Daily 10am-5pm; $18 adults, $15 seniors and students, $9 ages 3-11, free under age 3

San Diego Model Railroad Museum

This museum contains a small universe built around one of America's best-
loved hobbies. Vast, incredibly detailed model towns and landscapes are
on display, with working vintage trains chugging through them. Marvel at
the craftsmanship behind these toys elevated to the status of collectibles,
including some pristinely preserved vintage models.

Map 2: 1649 El Prado, 619/696-0199, www.sdmrm.org; Tues.-Fri. 11am-4pm,
Sat.-Sun. 11am-5pm; $8 adults, $6 seniors, $3 students, $4 military, free under age 13

San Diego Museum of Art

San Diego doesn't boast one the greatest art collections in the world, but
this Balboa Park favorite certainly houses its share of minor masterpieces.
Paintings by such luminaries as Monet, Degas, Dalí, O'Keeffe, Modigliani,
and Matisse are on permanent display, along with work by some of their
lesser-known contemporaries. Ongoing museum highlights include East
and South Asian pieces, and an Art of the Americas exhibit that illustrates
colonial through Civil War-era portraiture and frontier landscapes. Check
out the ground-floor western gallery for visiting exhibitions, and pause to
enjoy the building's entryway, with its ornately festooned Plateresque facade depicting famous statues, ships, and coats of arms.

Map 2: 1450 El Prado, 619/232-7931, www.sdmart.org; Mon.-Tues. 10am-5pm, Thurs.-Sat.
10am-5pm, Sun. noon-5pm; $12 adults, $9 seniors, $8 students, $9 military, $4.50 ages 7-17,
free under age 7

San Diego Museum of Man

The study of humankind covers a lot of ground, so this anthropologi-
cal museum continually finds captivating ways to keep people coming
back. Recent exhibits have focused on the history of brewing beer and

instruments of torture, while more permanent exhibits include castings of Mayan monoliths and displays of the ancient civilization's hieroglyphics, a comparable collection of ancient Egyptian artifacts, and the illuminating *Footsteps through Time*, which traces four million years of evolution from primates to humans and beyond (think cyborgs). Here you'll see such diverse items as fossil records, Neanderthal skulls, and a life-size C-3PO.

Map 2: 1350 El Prado, 619/239-2001, www.museumofman.org; Sun.-Wed. 10am-5pm, Thurs.-Sat. 10am-7:30pm; $12.50 adults, $10 over age 62, $8 students, $10 military, $6 ages 3-12, free under age 3

San Diego Natural History Museum

"The Nat," as it's sometimes known, focuses on the natural history of San Diego. Exhibits feature fossils and dinosaur bones of animals that once lived in and around Southern California and the Baja Peninsula, including mastodons, whales, and a giant shark, all of whom are depicted in 3-D films throughout the day. As you wander amid all this history, gaze at a large animated globe as it visualizes the continental shifts that have defined and redefined the Earth's landscape over the past 600 million years.

Map 2: 1788 El Prado, 619/232-3821, www.sdnhm.org, Daily 10am-5pm; $17 adults, $15 over age 62, $12 students and military, $11 ages 3-17, free under age 3

★ San Diego Zoo

With more than 600 species covering 100 acres smack in the middle of Balboa Park, the "World Famous" San Diego Zoo covers a lot of ground, both literally and figuratively. Popular beasts include massive polar bears (occasionally known to wrestle in their aquarium-like tank), gorgeous tigers, charming elephants, majestic lions, and no shortage of monkeys, chimps, and gorillas. But the zoo's pride and joy is its family of pandas. Technically on loan from China, the pandas have been actively breeding, and park visitors line up for the chance to see panda cubs doing their thing (which is almost always cute).

Most of the zoo grounds are built into canyons, which means lots of walking—often up and down hills—which can be especially tiring on sunny days. Fortunately, the zoo operates an aerial tram that offers gondola rides from the lower zoo level to its top, as well as bus tours with a quick overview of the park. Mornings are the best time to visit by far, offering easier parking, cooler weather, and livelier animals, though late hours in summer offer a chance to see the zoo at night. During the winter holidays, special decorative lighting makes evening visits a real treat.

Map 2: 2920 Zoo Dr., 619/231-1515, www.sandiegozoo.org; July-Aug. daily 9am-9pm, Mar., May-June, and Sept.-Oct. daily 9am-6pm, Apr. daily 9am-7pm, Jan.-Feb. and Nov.-early Dec. daily 9am-5pm, Dec. holidays daily 9am-8pm; $46 adults, $36 ages 3-11, free parking

clockwise from top left: a giant panda at the San Diego Zoo; San Diego Museum of Man; the lily pond in Balboa Park

Campo Santo Cemetery

Is it really haunted? Some say it is, but you won't find out unless you've got the nerve to visit at night. San Diego's original graveyard attracts its share of visitors during daylight hours. Wooden crosses and burial markers of the 447 San Diegans buried here between 1850 and 1880 include Yankee Jim Robinson, an accused boat thief hung at nearby Whaley House while still proclaiming his innocence. The 2,000-square-foot "holy field" used to be much larger, but many graves were moved or paved over to create the shopping district now surrounding it. Now *that's* scary.

Map 4: 2410 San Diego Ave.

Casa de Estudillo

Nearly two centuries ago, this Spanish colonial home was considered among the grandest in northern Mexico. Times have changed, but the restored adobe hacienda remains both a state and a U.S. historic landmark. Beneath a pointed bell tower and lined with terra-cotta ceramic tile rooftops, the building's 13 rooms are decorated with period furniture that illustrates how the family of a presidio commandant may have lived—from table settings to sitting rooms, including household tools and accessories available at the turn of the 19th century.

Map 4: 4002 Wallace St., 619/220-5422, www.parks.ca.gov; Daily 10am-5pm; free

★ Heritage Park Victorian Village

Just southeast of Old Town's historic park are seven unique Victorian structures that were moved here from their original locations in order to preserve their historic architecture. The vibrant avocado-green Sherman-Gilbert House arrived first; the delicate stick structure of its mid-19th-century turret survived the truck ride from Banker's Hill. These gorgeous brightly colored buildings have been faithfully restored but sit quiet and closed up; they can only to be admired from outside. One exception is the Temple Beth Israel, San Diego's first synagogue, built in 1889. It was moved here in 1978 from its original location in the Downtown neighborhood of Cortez Hill, and it remains open during park hours and for occasional private events.

Map 4: 2454 Heritage Park Row, 858/565-3600, www.co.san-diego.ca.us; Daily 9am-5pm; free

Old Town State Historic Park

The name San Diego once referred to this small strip of land tucked under a hill next to where the I-5 and I-8 freeways now meet. Most of its residents left more than a century ago, though many of the original buildings remain. The city's oldest standing structures are now historic landmarks preserved within Old Town State Historic Park. A visit here gives a sense of what the

clockwise from top left: Heritage Park Victorian Village; the Wells Fargo Museum in Old Town; Casa de Estudillo

original settlement must have been like, a combination of Spanish colony and the American Old West.

Built between the 1820s and the 1850s, most buildings are old family residences, including the homes of Spanish soldiers who came here to fortify the presidio just up the hill. The restored adobe buildings are furnished to their period; each tells a story about daily life here in the early 19th century. Dining tables in the **Commercial Kitchen** are set with old-fashion plates and utensils, as if dinner were about to be served.

Strolling around the park, you can bear witness to how the city matured. Later generations of wood and eventually brick buildings reflect the influx of American settlers from the East Coast. The **Mason Street Schoolhouse** depicts a reconstructed 19th-century classroom complete with desks and chalkboards. The **San Diego Union Building** features the typesetting tables and a printing press of the city's first newspaper. The Colorado House, site of the **Wells Fargo Museum,** invites guests inside an old bank vault.

Many of the old structures now house shops and restaurants, turning the park into a mall of sorts. The overall experience retains its historical character, though, with Mexican food and crafts commemorating the decades San Diego belonged to what was then a Spanish colony. A visit here is a must for anyone keen on gaining a sense of local history.

Map 4: 4002 Wallace St., 858/220-5422, www.oldtownsandiegoguide.com; Daily 10am-5pm; free

Robinson Rose House

Now the Old Town State Historic Park's **visitors center,** this replica of the original 1853 Robinson Rose House primarily consists of one very functional room open to the public. But it's worth a visit if only for one reason: the large scale-model of Old Town as it looked in 1872. This mesmerizing reference point will flesh out your imagination as you explore the park. It's also the starting point for the free and educational walking tours that begin daily at 11am and 2pm.

Map 4: 4098 Mason St., 619/220-5422, www.parks.ca.gov; Daily 10am-5pm; free

Whaley House Museum

In 1857, the Whaley House was the first of its kind in town, built with bricks and the addition of a second story. The former home of Thomas Whaley, it would go on to serve as a general store, a courthouse, and a theater after the Whaley's move to a newer residence in New Town, better known today as Downtown. Inside, the rooms are decorated with period furniture and include detailed histories of the house—ghost stories long associated with murders and untimely deaths that took place here, as well as public hangings staged on the front steps during its time as a courthouse. The Whaley House's reputation as one of the most haunted houses in the country makes nighttime visits especially spooky and popular among ghost hunters.

Map 4: 2482 San Diego Ave., 619/297-7511, www.sohosandiego.org; Memorial Day-Labor Day daily 10am-9:30pm, Labor Day-Memorial Day Sun.-Tues. 10am-5pm, Thurs.-Sat. 10am-9:30pm; admission: 10am-5pm $6 adults, $4 ages 3-12, $5 over age 65; 5pm-9:30pm $10 adults, $5 ages 3-12

49

Mission Bay and Beaches   Map 5

Belmont Park

For 90 years there has been an amusement park on Mission Beach. While the amusements may change, there are still plenty of bells and whistles attempting to lure visitors from the gorgeous beach right next door. One of the park's biggest attractions is the **Wave House,** an outdoor beachfront restaurant and lounge built around a pair of wave machines. The standing waves are always up at the push of a button; would-be surfers can try it on the beginner-friendly **FlowRider.** The bigger and faster **FlowBarrel** rides are reserved for the seasoned pros who stage acrobatic surfing shows on the hour. Belmont Park also features a small roller coaster, bumper cars, a laser maze, an arcade, and a carousel. Parking and admission are free; prices for rides and other amusements vary.

Map 5: 3146 Mission Blvd., 858/228-9283, www.belmontpark.com; Mon.-Thurs. 11am-9pm, Fri. 11am-10pm, Sat. 11am-midnight, Sun. 11am-11pm; free

★ Mission Bay Park

While surfing reigns up and down the coast, Mission Bay is the undeniable epicenter of all action water sports—from Jet Skis and wakeboard-toting powerboats to sailboats, kite-surfers, and kayaks. This artificial bay is really a network of parks and peninsulas, which split the 4,200-acre park into a couple of bays, six or seven small coves, and at least one "basin." For every small waterway filled with rowdy pontoons speeding along, there is a tranquil cove for stand-up paddleboarding or a romantic cruise in a pedal boat. If you prefer to stay on dry land, there are plenty of beaches, picnic areas, and playgrounds, and a scenic bike path that circles the entire bay.

Map 5: 2688 E. Mission Bay Dr., 619/525-8213, www.sandiego.gov; Daily 4am-midnight

Pacific Beach Boardwalk

Technically called Ocean Front Walk, this concrete bike, skate, and pedestrian path actually begins at the south end of Mission Beach and continues north between the sand and oceanfront homes to the Crystal Pier and Pacific Beach Park. All along are people riding beach cruisers, men flexing tattoos, and women parading in bikinis. The party starts somewhere around Pacific Beach Drive, as beachfront restaurants serve drinks on patios and decks overlooking the action on the beach. Pacific Beach's "PB" party reputation begins here, usually pretty early in the day, and it's a place where young adults tan and preen, drink and flirt, and generally live it up

The SeaWorld Controversy

In 2013 a documentary titled *Blackfish* investigated the circumstances of the death of a SeaWorld trainer who was killed by a captive orca she was working with at SeaWorld Orlando. The film prompted a nationwide discussion about the practice of keeping killer whales and other large aquatic mammals in captivity, posing questions about its impact on the animals' psychological health and life spans. Amid the backlash stirred up by the film's publicity, a number of popular performing artists cancelled scheduled appearances at SeaWorld parks, which also became the sites of frequent demonstrations by animal welfare activists calling for a boycott.

SeaWorld San Diego was not immune to this. While the company initially insisted ticket sales were up in the wake of the movie's widespread release, it later admitted that attendance figures did decline as potential visitors were turned off by the prospect that the captive animals—and main attractions—at many of its parks were sensitive to the conditions of their confinement. (SeaWorld's Aquatica park in Chula Vista features only turtles and flamingos.)

Since the film came out, SeaWorld has announced plans to improve their captive habitats and to continue to contribute money to animal research and conservancy organizations, though it's too early to tell whether these efforts will bring back visitors in the long run.

from ocean to bar. It may not always be family-friendly, but it rarely fails in the people-watching department.

Map 5: Ocean Front Walk, between Pacific Beach Dr. and Garnet Ave.

SeaWorld

Combine the most popular parts of a zoo, aquarium, and circus and you'll get something a lot like SeaWorld. The aquatic mammal theme park features thousands of sea creatures in observable habitats as well as trained performances, none more famous than the killer whale Shamu. While several of the iconic black-and-white whales have donned the Shamu mantle over the years, the idea behind the shows remains the same: Spectators watch as four-ton orcas leap athletically out of the water, creating massive splash waves that soak large sections of the delighted audience. Plenty of other attractions may be found in the park, including dancing dolphins and a couple of hilarious vaudevillian sea lions.

Map 5: 500 Sea World Dr., 800/257-4268, www.seaworldparks.com; Daily 10am-6pm; peak summer and winter holidays: Daily 10am-9pm; $84 adults, $78 ages 3-9

Ocean Beach and Point Loma

Map 6

★ Cabrillo National Monument

Named for the first European explorer to sail into San Diego Bay, the monument to Juan Rodríguez Cabrillo is only a small part of what draws people to the "most southwesterly spot in the contiguous United States." Comprising 144 acres at the tip of the long, narrow Point Loma Peninsula, the monument centers on a statue of Cabrillo that commands a breathtaking panorama with views of the Pacific Ocean, San Diego, and on a clear day, all the way to county's eastern mountain ranges.

At the peninsula's highest point stands the historic **Old Point Loma Lighthouse,** a preserved 19th-century structure that only ceased operation because low clouds and fog too often obscured its signal (it was retired in favor of a newer lighthouse down the hill).

A series of trails crisscross the monument, including the **Bayside Trail** (2.5 miles), a scenic trek overlooking the bay while traversing rare coastal sage scrub habitat on the peninsula's eastern side. It's just a short drive down the hill to the new lighthouse and the 0.5-mile **Coastal Tidepool Trail,** which winds past a series of protected tide pools. These play home to entire ecosystems of starfish, anemones, and other exotic sealife that has evolved to survive within the shallow pools of seawater left behind at low tide. Time your visit by consulting a daily tide schedule.

Map 6: 1800 Cabrillo Memorial Dr., Point Loma, 619/557-5450, www.nps.gov/cabr; Daily 9am-5pm; $5 per vehicle, $3 per walk-in

Fort Rosecrans National Cemetery

A worthy view commends this 77.5-acre burial ground for fallen service men and women, dating back to the Mexican-American War. It was first established in 1882, when remains of the American casualties of the 1846 Battle of San Pasqual were transferred here, and it continued to be a final resting place for fallen troops through World War II. With the bay, the ocean, and the city skyline, there's plenty of beautiful backdrop for grave markers and several memorials built to commemorate specific battles, including Guadalcanal and the Battle of Leyte Gulf. Notable service members interred here include Major Reuben H. Fleet (after whom the Balboa Park science museum is named) and Major General Joseph H. Pendleton, a career marine and eventual mayor of Coronado who advocated for a major marine base in the San Diego area.

Map 6: 1800 Cabrillo Memorial Dr., Point Loma, 619/553-2084, www.cem.va.gov; Mon.-Fri. 8am-4:30pm, Sat.-Sun. 9:30am-5pm

Harbor Island

Harbor Island is an artificial peninsula designed to form long, protected yacht basins for the thousands of boats that moor here. It's home to a couple of hotels and restaurants boasting excellent city views across the bay, as well as a few boating and sailing charters. The easiest way to enjoy Harbor Island is to walk or bike along the path through the park on its outer edge.

Map 6: south of N Harbor Dr., across from San Diego International Airport

Liberty Station

What used to be a naval training base has been reclaimed as a burgeoning commercial arts district. The once Spartan military buildings now host creative workshops and spacious restaurants, with new and interesting organizations moving in on a seemingly monthly basis. On its eastern edge is grassy NTC Park, and along its western border is a shopping center with familiar food and drink franchises. The place gets most lively on the first Friday of the month, when a regular arts event brings people out to explore various studios, galleries, and special performances.

Map 6: bounded by Barnett Ave., N. Harbor Dr., Rosecrans St., and Chauncey Rd., www.libertystation.com

OB

Ocean Beach may be called a lot of strange things (and most are true), but the name that sticks is "OB." Backpackers, teenagers, bikers, surfers, service members, yoga adepts—all types congregate on this stretch of coastal unreal estate, which began its days amid the carnival atmosphere of a beachfront amusement park built in the early 1900s. The park closed 100 years ago, but the vibe remains. Visitors will find ocean-themed souvenirs, bead shops, swimwear boutiques, and plenty of countercultural businesses kept alive by wave after wave of the wild diversity this little beach town with a quirky reputation tends to attract.

Map 6: 4800-5000 block of Newport Ave., between Abbott St. and Cliffs Blvd., Ocean Beach, www.oceanbeachsandiego.com

★ Ocean Beach Pier

It's said that the concrete Ocean Beach Pier is the longest on the West Coast. Whether or not that's true, its 1,971 feet make a perfect distance for a scenic stroll. Where the waves break, stop for an unbeatable view of surfers practicing their moves directly below. Along the way you'll pass promenading families, the occasional romantic couple on a sunset walk, and a lot of recreational anglers trying their hand at a different kind of catch (usually herring). A café bravely does business in the middle of the pier, which isn't impervious to occasional waves in winter months.

Map 6: west of the 5000 block of Niagara Ave., Ocean Beach

Shelter Island

When it comes time to berth their vessels, members of the active boating community have a number of options up and down the coast, but the most desirable may be found on this inside leg of Point Loma. Though not far on a map from the wildness of Ocean Beach, this side of the hill is decidedly

Clockwise from top left: Children's Pool Beach in La Jolla; statue of Cabrillo on Point Loma; Belmont Park on Mission Beach

more peaceful, with pretty houses peppering the hillside above, and gorgeous sailboats and pleasure craft in the Shelter Island Yacht Basin and America's Cup Harbor. However, restaurants top the list of reasons to visit, particularly when it comes to fresh-catch seafood that comes directly off some of the fishing boats that call this area home.

Map 6: southeast of Rosecrans St. between Nimitz Blvd. and Talbot St.

★ Sunset Cliffs Natural Park

Sunset Cliffs delivers gorgeous, unobstructed Pacific views from the top of eroding sandstone cliffs. On the east side of Sunset Cliffs Boulevard are rows of beautiful homes built to appreciate the scenery. The west side is reserved for the rest of us: a narrow strip of trails that wind along the waxing and waning cliffs' edge, overlooking the rocky outcroppings below. More than a mile of walking offers plenty of opportunities to stop and watch the surfers who consider this long stretch of waves their greatest local resource.

At the southern end of the road, the park opens up to a wider embankment of short hiking trails and desert foliage, as well as a large parking lot. The lot fills up in spring and fall evenings, when partly cloudy days culminate in vibrant orange and electric pink sunsets, and onlookers flock to the cliffs hoping to spot the elusive green flash, rumored to appear the moment the sun finally touches below the horizon.

A word of caution: These sandstone cliffs are in a perpetual state of decay, and while many ledges are fenced off for safety, that's not to say the unfenced areas are safe. Lives have been lost and many injuries attained by people trying to enter or exit the water. Stay back from the edge and don't attempt to surf or navigate the tricky goat trails to the water.

Map 6: 700-1300 block of Sunset Cliffs Blvd., between Adair St. and Ladera St., and extending south of Ladera St., www.sunsetcliffs.info; free

La Jolla

Map 7

Birch Aquarium

The Birch Aquarium is overseen by the Scripps Institution of Oceanography and includes plenty of interesting exhibits devoted to local aquatic life— reef ecosystems, kelp forests, lagoons, and underwater canyons. A great deck features touchable tide pools and boasts a fantastic view of La Jolla below. Jellyfish, anemones, and leopard sharks are always fascinating, but it's tough to imagine another creature as marvelous as the leafy sea dragon.

Map 7: 2300 Expedition Way, 858/534-3474, www.aquarium.ucsd.edu; Daily 9am-5pm; $17 adults, $14 ages 13-17, $12.50 ages 3-12, $13 over age 60, $12 students, $15 military

Children's Pool Beach

It may sound like a place for children to swim, but it's not. It used to be, however: In 1931 Ellen Brown Scripps commissioned construction of a seawall to create a wave barrier along the beach so that small children could

Scenic Walks

shoreline at Sunset Cliffs Natural Park

These leisurely walks can be a great way to notice the understated sights of the city.

- **The Harbor Walking Path,** Downtown, extends north from Marina Park (500 Kettner Blvd.) and leads along the waterfront past boats, parks, and monuments as well as San Diego Bay.

- The **Mission Bay Trail** (850 W. Mission Bay Dr.), in Mission Bay, offers a biking and walking path that circles almost the entire inside edge of Mission Bay, though you can always stick to a fraction of the 27-mile loop.

- **Sunset Cliffs Natural Park,** in Ocean Beach, passes between big homes and sandstone cliffs rising above the ocean. It's an easy mile-long scenic walk along Sunset Cliffs Boulevard that can be extended into a 0.5-mile circuit of light trails once the road ends at Ladera Street.

- **The Coast Walk Trail,** in La Jolla, picks up just left of the Sunny Jim Cave Shop (1325 Coast Blvd.) and winds along the ocean toward La Jolla Shores, passing some ridiculous oceanfront properties in a mere 0.3 miles.

- For quainter, less modern homes, try a couple of circles through the **North Park Historic Craftsman District,** beginning at Upas and 28th Streets in Uptown. Walk a few blocks south for an idea what sort of properties local renters wish they could afford. Continue a couple of blocks north to see refurbished Craftsman cottages.

play safely at the water's edge. Over time, the local seal population decided to start bringing their pups here, to the point that bacteria levels in the water became too high for humans. Today, a rope barrier keeps people off the beach and the seawall serves as a perfect vantage point to stand and watch the seals belly along and roll around in the sand.

Map 7: 850 Coast Blvd.

La Jolla Cove

It's a wonder how so many folks flock onto this little stretch of sand just a few steps from La Jolla Village. The cove teems with underwater life, making it a popular spot for scuba divers and snorkelers, often seen floating just a few dozen yards off shore. Sea lions lounge on the large rocks sitting on either side of the beach, lolling on top of each other, barking, and catching some sun. Most of the year, waves are small or nonexistent, making for a fun swimmers' beach. But in the winter, uncommonly large swells may kick up a wave known as the Sleeping Giant, and local big-wave surfers flock to the cove to give onlookers an exhilarating show.

Map 7: 1100 Coast Blvd.

Mount Soledad Veteran's Memorial

A 29-foot cross stands atop Mount Soledad, La Jolla's highest point, which boasts a panoramic view that surveys the entire county on a clear day. It's currently the centerpiece of a Korean War memorial enumerating the names of thousands of veterans who served their country during that conflict. However, ownership of the cross has changed hands several times over the years as legal battles were waged to have it removed from government land. At the moment it remains, and the memorial isn't going anywhere. Bring something to eat, picnic in the grass, and enjoy the beauty of greater San Diego.

Map 7: 6905 La Jolla Scenic Dr. S., 858/459-2314, www.soledadmemorial.com

Sunny Jim Cave

One of seven La Jolla smugglers caves, Sunny Jim allegedly received its name from L. Frank Baum, author of *The Wizard of Oz*. Apparently the shape of the cave mouth reminded Baum of the original cartoon serial cereal box mascot, Sunny Jim, who first appeared on a box of Force Wheat Flakes in 1903.

There are two ways to see the cave: from the ocean, or through the Cave Store (which rents snorkeling gear and sells souvenirs). A steep, slippery set of stairs leads into the cave from above and through a tunnel carved by immigrant laborers to smuggle more immigrant laborers and, during Prohibition, booze. Daily kayak tours are also available.

Map 7: 1100 Coast Blvd., 858/459-0746, www.cavestore.com; Daily 10am-5:30pm; $5 adults, $3 under age 16

Coronado Bridge

If there is a signature piece of San Diego architecture, the bridge connecting Coronado to Downtown is it. The Coronado Bridge arches up to a 200-foot clearance (high enough for tall ships to pass under) before curving hard upon approaching Coronado, forming a swoop of blue steel and gray concrete that appears far less rigid than the sum of its parts. The views from the top are equally majestic, but check them out from the passenger seat; stopping on the bridge nets you a steep fine.

Map 8: 1825 Strand Way, www.coronado.ca.us

Coronado Museum of History and Art

How did Coronado come to be and why? This museum tells the story of the island that's really the tip of a peninsula. View pictures of early vacationers at Tent City, a canvas resort built beside the Hotel del Coronado as a friendly option for budget travelers. Examine vintage military costumes while learning how the Navy's presence has impacted the community. The small museum packs a lot Coronado in its three exhibits—it's certainly not a full-day or even half-day activity, but it's great for establishing context on the area.

Map 8: 1100 Orange Ave., 619/435-7242, www.coronadohistory.org; Mon.-Fri. 9am-5pm, Sat.-Sun.10am-5pm; $5 adults, $3 seniors, $3 military, free under age 17

★ Hotel del Coronado

It's rare that a hotel can be considered a sight in its own right, but then few carry the panache of Hotel Del. Built in 1888, the all-wood Victorian construction of the original building can take your breath away, particularly the grandly furnished lobby and the iconic dome over its historic **Crown Room,** which hosts a lavish Sunday brunch. Once the world's largest resort, the Del has been a popular destination among Hollywood VIPs for nearly a century; movie buffs will remember it as the location of Billy Wilder's comedy classic *Some Like It Hot.* Much of the luxury resort is open to the public: sip a drink at the outdoor **Sunset Bar** or enjoy the outdoor ice-skating rink set up between Thanksgiving and New Year. Of course, the main attraction is what inspired the hotel's construction—just outside is one of the nation's finest beaches. Rent a cabana for the day and enjoy cocktail service on the sand as you watch sailboats, Navy ships, and the occasional breaching whale enhance the panoramic Pacific view.

Map 8: 1500 Orange Ave., 619/435-6611, www.hoteldel.com

top to bottom: a view of Coronado Bridge from Glorietta Bay; Mission Basílica San Diego de Alcalá

Aquatica San Diego

This SeaWorld water park doesn't rely on splashing dolphins or whales to get you sopping wet. A series of individual and group water slides, a wave pool, an inner-tube float, and an interactive area with geysers and jets and a few other tricks offer excuses to dump water on the unsuspecting. Though not open year round (or even weekdays most of the year), hot summer days see a lot of slippery sliding and splashing action in Chula Vista.

Map 9: 2052 Entertainment Circle, Chula Vista, 619/661-7373, www.aquaticabyseaworld.com; June-Aug. daily 10am-6pm, Apr.-May and Sept.-Oct. Sat.-Sun. 10am-6pm; $40 adults, $34 ages 3-9

Mission Basilica San Diego de Alcalá

When the first California mission was established in 1769, it was originally to sit on the hill above Old Town. However, in 1774 this site was chosen in part to distance the mission from the garrison of Spanish soldiers, whose presence intimidated the indigenous people the mission meant to convert. In 1775, hundreds of indigenous people sacked and burned the mission; it has been rebuilt three times since. The current building has stood since 1931, and still holds regular Roman Catholic masses at 7am, 8am, and 9am on Sunday morning. The whitewashed adobe structure is instantly recognizable by its unique stacked bell tower, which features five bells. The large lower right bell is original, dating to 1802 and notably topped by a crown representing the King of Spain.

Map 9: 10818 San Diego Mission Rd., Mission Valley, 619/283-7319, www.missionsandiego.com; Mon.-Fri. 8am-4:30pm

Olympic Training Center

No, you don't get to work out at this complex built to train world-class athletes for the Olympics, but you can walk an established mile-long path past those facilities for BMX, rugby, archery, and track-and-field hopefuls. For self-guided phone tours, you only need to show up, call 619/215-9070, and walk the Olympic Path, which passes by the mostly outdoor training fields. You may learn a lot about how the athletes work leading up to competition, and may feel a little closer to the team when the next summer games take place. For more in-depth information, come at 11am on Saturday for a free tour with a tour guide who can answer any questions.

Map 9: 2800 Olympic Pkwy., Chula Vista, 619/656-1500, www.teamusa.org; Daily 9am-5pm; free

60

Restaurants

PRICE KEY

$ Entrées less than $10

$$ Entrées $10–20

$$$ Entrées more than $20

San Diego may not be the most diverse metropolis around, but you can typically find quality samplings of any notable cuisine. For the best dining experience, stick to what we do best: seafood or Mexican.

The city's Mexican restaurants range from delicious little taco trucks to restaurants where someone makes fresh guacamole at your table. Avoid the tourist traps along San Diego Avenue in Old Town, and you'll be hard-pressed to find one that doesn't at least taste good.

The local fishing industry provides all manner of fresh catch, and our taste for it means we get some pretty great fish flown in from out of town as well. Most local sushi restaurants have been declared "best in town" by enthusiastic customers, but more unique to the region are the fresh-catch fish counters. Customers line up at a well-stocked glass counter to choose whichever cut of fish looks best that day. These popular, casual spots have popped up all over town—if you love grilled fish, make visiting one a priority.

California's farm-to-table movement has also caught on locally. Thanks to the state's year-round growing season, locally sourced meat and produce is a rich prospect and a growing number of talented chefs have embraced locavore principles. The result: some of the best restaurants in town are places you'll enjoy and feel good about eating.

Of course, there are classic staples. Burger lovers debate a number of places that do them well, Sunday brunch spots have some of the longest wait times in town, and starting a dessert bar has become a legitimate

---

Previous page top: Downtown's Fifth Avenue **bottom:** Juniper and Ivy

Look for ★ to find
recommended restaurants

Highlights

★ **Best Celebrity Chef Restaurant:** *Top Chef All-Stars's* Richard Blais chose San Diego as the location of his "left coast cookery." His **Juniper and Ivy** turns out creative and delicious dishes, including secret menu items you should definitely ask your server about (page 64).

★ **Best Dessert:** Want to justify dessert? Make it one at **Extraordinary Desserts.** Cakes, pastries, and more are made with artistic integrity and decadently great taste (page 64).

★ **Best Steak House:** An unlikely combination of American steak house with the French fine dining experience, **Cowboy Star** works across the board, serving prime cuts of meat with gourmet sides and appetizers. It's fancy, but just rugged enough (page 69).

★ **Best Burger:** You might call it ironic that pork specialist **Carnita's Snack Shack** turns out the area's best burger. But the North Park street spot does everything well, drawing a line each night till midnight (page 74).

★ **Best Pizza:** San Diego loves its pizza pies, especially those of **URBN Pizza** in North Park, which also features a great tap list and terrific craft cocktails (page 76).

★ **Top Farm-to-Table:** The farm-to-table ethos is fantastic for the planet and foodies alike. Rarely is it done so well as at **Whisknladle,** where the talent of chef Chris Powell truly stands out in fantastic tasting dishes (page 88).

★ **Best Mexican Food:** You don't have to spend much money for amazing Mexican food in this town, and that's even true for the all-sustainable, high-quality ingredients used by **Puesto.** It captures all the flavors of our beloved hole-in-the-wall taco shops taken up a notch (page 89).

★ **Freshest Catch:** For decades, **El Pescador Fish Market** has provided La Jolla with simple fresh fish done right, usually grilled, often on sandwiches or in tacos. With its new larger location, it does more of the same, but with more comfort (page 89).

★ **Finest Dining:** Though the ocean laps against the windows of this French-inspired seafood spot, it's not just about the views at **The Marine Room.** It's an elite dining experience (page 89).

★ **Best Brunch:** You won't believe your eyes when you see the extravagant Sunday brunch buffet in the **Crown Room** at Hotel del Coronado. Every craving you could imagine will be fulfilled (page 91).

Downtown

Map 1

BREAKFAST

Donut Bar $

The real beauty of the Donut Bar folks is their willingness to push the boundaries of donut-dom. There's the standard maple bacon bar, and they'll take a stab at the cronut hybrids, but they also incorporate flavors by creating fruity sandwiches or turning the concept of a PB&J into a dough-nut. Go early, because they always sell out.

Map 1: 631 B St., 619/255-6360, www.donutbarsandiego.com; Daily from 8am until sold out

Mission Café $

The Mission Café's menu draws heavily from Mexican and American tra-ditions, and has become a favorite among locals for its pancakes and egg dishes as well as breakfast burritos and *chilaquiles* (sort of like breakfast nachos). The Mission bakes its own bread, and does so rather well, so ex-pect outstanding sandwiches and the best cinnamon-bread french toast in town. You'll find the same menu at its other locations in North Park (2801 University Ave.) and Mission Beach (3795 Mission Blvd.), with paintings by local artists on the walls and Southwestern decorative motifs throughout.

Map 1: 1250 J St., East Village, 619/232-7662, www.themissionsd.com; Daily 7am-3pm

CAFÉS

James Coffee Co. $

With a rock-and-roll approach to specialty coffee, this local artisanal roaster in Little Italy occupies a large garage space, conducive to motorcycle parking as well as sipping terrific espresso and pour-over brews. Popular among musicians, graphic designers, software developers, and tattooed creative types, the shop manages to feel like a workspace without losing street cred in the process.

Map 1: 2355 India St., Little Italy, 619/756-7770, www.jamescoffeeco.com; Daily 7am-6pm

West Bean $

Choose between a fruity bean or a chocolaty roast, and enjoy some of the most balanced local coffee within the bar's slick modern-rustic interior. If tea's your thing, try the shop's offering by Mad Monk, a local tea purveyor that keeps it simple and sensuous.

Map 1: 240 Broadway, Gaslamp, 619/324-9915, www.thewestbean.com; Mon.-Fri. 6am-6pm, Sat.-Sun. 7am-3pm

★ **Juniper and Ivy** ⑤⑤⑤

Top Chef All-Stars winner Richard Blais found a receptive audience when he opened this "Refined American Food with Left Coast Edge" eatery in Little Italy, and San Diego foodies have enthusiastically embraced his creative approach. Blais's liquid nitrogen tricks come into play while crafting the horseradish "pearls" that top oysters with a melon mignonette. Blais and his team constantly redraft the imaginative menu with dozens of intriguing dishes. When making reservations, request one of the few circle booths for the best seats in the house. The lively and comfortable industrial dining room is a place to be seen, so dress casually cool and enjoy excitedly discussing your meal.

Map 1: 2228 Kettner Blvd., Little Italy, 619/269-9036, www.juniperandivy.com; Sun.-Thurs. 4pm-10pm, Fri.-Sat. 4pm-11pm

DESSERT

★ **Extraordinary Desserts** ⑤

This sweets specialist offers the best desserts in town. You'll have trouble choosing, but you'll definitely be singing its praises if you order a slice of cake with some of the handcrafted small-batch ice cream. Lines always seem to be out the door, but you'll want to stand in this one to get a good look at each of the daily offerings, whether you're grabbing dessert to go or eating in the spacious modern dining room. If all that's too daunting, you may try the stellar bakery's smaller location in nearby Banker's Hill (2929 5th Ave.).

Map 1: 1430 Union St., 619/294-7001, www.extraordinarydesserts.com; Mon.-Thurs. 8:30am-11pm, Fri. 8:30-midnight, Sat. 10am-midnight, Sun. 10am-11pm

Panchita's Bakery ⑤

Mexican pastries, or *pan dulce,* are a departure from those found in most bakeries. Depending on the source, many vary in quality and simply aren't worth trying. If you happen by Panchita's, make the effort. Grab a pair of tongs and a self-serve tray and browse shelves filled with the city's best, which often range from cookies to shortbreads. Look for sugar-crusted conchas, glazed *campechanas,* and pineapple-stuffed empanadas, which are especially worth remembering.

Map 1: 2519 C St., 619/232-6662, www.panchitasbakery.com; Mon.-Sat. 5:30am-9:30pm

Pappalecco ⑤

Pappalecco's gelato is made on the premises daily, and there are usually dozens of creamy and delicious flavors. Choose a regular hazelnut or Nutella, which adds a ribbon of the popular hazelnut spread to the melt-in-your-mouth frozen treat, or marvel over the refreshing fruitier options. There's not much seating, so on crowded evenings it may be best to grab a cup or cone to go for a walk around Little Italy. Or try their larger second location in Hillcrest (3650 5th Ave.).

FARM-TO-TABLE
Café 21 ⑤⑤⑤

Avocado fries, duck wings, and lamb ribs paired with a tasting flight of six different sangrias make this a great happy-hour spot. For dinner, the kitchen turns out great dishes featuring a rotating selection of local and sustainable ingredients. Live music sometimes accompanies the grass-fed steak or fresh catch of the day in this stylish restaurant, which boasts a warm brick bar, a colorful dining room, and a bank of large windows looking out onto the lively Gaslamp sidewalk.

Map 1: 802 5th Ave., Gaslamp, 619/795-0721, www.cafe-21.com; Sun.-Thurs. 8am-11pm, Fri.-Sat. 8am-midnight

J Six ⑤⑤⑤

Seasonal local cuisine and matching craft cocktails are the hallmark of this hotel restaurant near the ballpark, though on pleasant days its most remarkable feature may be the beautiful rooftop lounge just a quick elevator ride away. Service upstairs may not match the promptness and enthusiasm found within the brick and brass dining room, but either way you'll enjoy cleverly conceived meat, fish, and vegetable dishes made by kitchen staff who seem genuinely interested in pleasing customers.

Map 1: 616 J St., 619/531-8744, www.jsixrestaurant.com; Sun.-Fri. 7am-10pm, Sat. 8am-10pm

Tender Greens ⑤⑤

Technically a fast food chain, this California franchise breaks the mold by practicing farm-to-table principles. Each restaurant is overseen by a pedigreed executive chef who works to make the most out of seasonal ingredients and natural meats, including cured-in-house salami, marinated steak, and buttermilk fried chicken. You won't get fries with that; instead, enjoy assorted grilled vegetables and some of the best salads available Downtown.

Map 1: 110 W. Broadway, Gaslamp, 619/795-2353, www.tendergreens.com; Mon.-Fri. 11am-9pm, Sat.-Sun. 11:30am-9pm

FRENCH
Café Chloe ⑤⑤⑤

Nestled pleasantly in the sweet spot between casual and fine dining, this local favorite serves up Parisian embellishments and quality French cuisine. Start the day with a *croque madame* or bistro salad on the dog-friendly patio, or swing by late for a romantic meal in the quaint dining room. Enjoy traditional dishes like *steak frites* or pan-roasted duck breast, expertly paired with a *vin rouge*, of course.

Map 1: 721 9th Ave., East Village, 619/232-3242, www.cafechloe.com; Mon.-Thurs. 7:30am-10:30pm, Fri.-Sat. 8:30am-10:30pm, Sun. 8:30am-9:30pm

RESTAURANTS
DOWNTOWN

ITALIAN

Berkeley Pizza $

Stuffed, deep-dish Chicago pies have a home in San Diego thanks to Berkeley Pizza. The pizza is the real deal, thick with toppings and a delicious chunky marinara—a single slice will fill most. Berkeley started as a farmers market booth, then opened a storefront to keep up with the high demand caused by excellent word of mouth. Its small barebones Gaslamp location may lack ambiance, but things look a little better at the North Park location (3934 30th St.).

Map 1: 539 Island Ave., Gaslamp, 619/937-0808, www.berkeleypizza.net, Sun.-Thurs. 11am-11pm, Fri.-Sat. 11am-3am

Monello $$

Northern Italian cuisine is the calling card of this Little Italy eatery, specifically the street food of the owners' hometown of Milan. This translates to light calzone-like *panzerotti*, fresh-cut prosciutto, flaky *raspa dura* cheese, polenta, and a variety of sauces topping the homemade pasta. Pizza lovers won't go wrong here, and any drink made with the house-made sweet vermouth is sure to be tasty.

Map 1: 750 W. Fir St., Little Italy, 619/501-0030, www.lovemonello.com; Tues.-Fri. 11:30am-close, Sat.-Sun. 10am-close

Mimmo's Italian Village $$

Mimmo's dining room literally resembles a small Italian village, with a traditional Italian menu and dining experience. Feast on pasta, olives, and *caprese,* then choose from cannoli, tiramisu, or mascarpone for dessert. A sidewalk dining patio proves a popular spot to eat and people-watch.

Map 1: 1743 India St., 619/239-3710, www.mimmos.biz; Mon.-Wed. 10am-3pm and 5pm-9pm, Thurs. 10am-3pm and 5pm-10pm, Fri. 10am-3pm and 5pm-11pm, Sat. 5pm-11pm, Sun. noon-9pm

Pizzeria Mozza $$

A centerpiece of the recently opened dining complex "The Headquarters" at Seaport Village, Mozza belongs to a small chain of restaurants opened by *Food Network* chef Mario Batali. While the terrific pizza gets the spotlight, Batali's Italian cooking acumen shines throughout the menu, with mainstays like *burrata caprese* setting the stage for a mastery of tomato-based dishes. It's tough to beat the marinara, often recommended by a smiling service staff who work hard to earn their full tips.

Map 1: 789 W. Harbor Dr., 619/376-4353, www.pizzeriamozza.com; Daily 11am-10pm

MEXICAN

Blind Burro $$

Though its dishes may be steeped in Baja tradition, the modern Mexican cuisine of this East Village bar and grill isn't overly confined by the notion

of authenticity. A lengthy taco menu includes coffee-rubbed salmon with
tomatillo-avocado kale slaw, Maine lobster scampi, and a surprisingly good
cauliflower veggie option. Other dishes incorporate lamb shank or rib eye,
while sides like corn off the cob or chorizo guacamole starters legitimately
add to the experience, as does the extensive tequila bar.

Map 1: 639 J St., East Village, 619/795-7880, www.theblindburro.com;
Sun.-Mon. 11am-11pm, Tues.-Thurs. 11am-midnight, Fri.-Sat. 11am-1:30am

Don Chido $$

A custom red oak-burning Santa Maria grill and Caja-China-style subter-
ranean roasting oven ensure this Mexican spot in the Gaslamp serves up
succulent, perfectly cooked meat dishes, ranging from a skirt steak carne
asada to braised pork *carnitas*. A tortilla station ensures that all the sustainable ingredients show up at your table with warm, handmade corn tortillas.

Map 1: 527 5th Ave., Gaslamp, 619/232-8226, www.donchido.com;
Sun.-Mon. 11am-midnight, Tues. 11am-2am, Wed. 11am-midnight, Thurs.-Sat. 11am-2am

PUBS

Neighborhood $

Burgers are the specialty of this minimalist gastropub near the ballpark,
with a number of well-crafted sauces to top them, including cranberry habanero aioli and cumin mayo. The only caveat worth mentioning is that
you won't find ketchup, so if that's an all-American deal-breaker, stick
to the beer-braised short ribs, meatball pita, or steak tacos. Local drafts
are featured, although the rotating selection always has a few out-of-town
gems as well.

Map 1: 777 G St., East Village, 619/446-0002, www.neighborhoodsd.com;
Sat.-Wed. 11:30am-midnight, Thurs.-Fri. 11:30am-1:30am

Queenstown Public House $$

Featuring a mostly local tap list and British comfort food by way of
New Zealand, this converted Craftsman home offers unique decor, a
dog-friendly patio, and an overall enjoyable dining experience. You
can't go wrong with perennial favorites like fish-and-chips or the pot
pie, which has a roasted Cornish game hen in the middle of the crust.
The staff is always willing to recommend standouts from the current
spate of beers.

Map 1: 1557 Columbia St., Little Italy, 619/546-0444, www.queenstownpublichouse.com;
Mon.-Thurs. 11am-11pm, Fri. 11am-midnight, Sat. 9am-midnight, Sun. 9am-11pm

The Waterfront Bar and Grill $

The Waterfront opened back in 1933, just as Prohibition ended, making
it San Diego's oldest continually operating bar. Known for its burgers, the
menu also includes a Mexican brunch with classic salsa and egg dishes such
as *chilaquiles* (served over tortilla chips) and huevos rancheros (served with

Gastropubs

A happy consequence of the city's romance with all things beer, San Diego's dining scene has witnessed an increase in gastropubs: restaurants built around the idea that drinking and eating well should go hand in hand.

You may find traditional pub fare like fish-and-chips, sausages, and burgers at **Queenstown Public House** (1557 Columbia St., Little Italy, 619/546-0444, www.queenstownpublichouse.com; Mon.-Thurs. 11am-11pm, Fri. 11am-midnight, Sat. 9am-midnight, Sun. 9am-11pm), **Waypoint Public House** (3794 30th St., 619/255-8778, www.waypointpublic.com; Mon.-Fri. 4pm-1am, Sat.-Sun. 10am-1am), and **Neighborhood** (777 G St., East Village, 619/446-0002, www.neighborhoodsd.com; Sat.-Wed. 11:30am-midnight, Thurs.-Fri. 11:30am-1:30am), but these restaurants go the extra mile to ensure their menus appeal to foodies and even—

dare I say it—health-conscious beer drinkers.

Spots like **Underbelly** (3794 30th St., 619/255-8778, www.godblessunderbelly.com; Mon.-Fri. 4pm-1am, Sat.-Sun. 10am-1am) and **OB Noodle House** (4993 Niagara Ave., Ocean Beach, 619/255-9858, www.obnoodlehouse.com; Mon.-Thurs. noon-11pm, Fri.-Sun. 11am-11pm) buck the pub tradition, offering Asian favorites to pair with their terrific tap lists. The way San Diegans have responded suggests that ramen and IPA are meant to go together.

Stone World Bistro & Gardens Liberty Station (2816 Historic Decatur Rd., Suite 116, 619/269-2100, www.stonelibertystation.com; Mon.-Sat. 11:30am-10pm, Sun. 11am-9pm) takes it all the way, pairing sustainable, made-from-scratch, farm-to-table world cuisine with local and far-flung world-class beers. Beer snobs can now maintain high drinking standards without missing out on a good meal.

fresh tortillas). The bar opens to a dining patio and serves enough beer to keep it lively and easy to spot from the sidewalk, all day long.

Map 1: 2044 Kettner Blvd., Little Italy, 619/232-9656, www.waterfrontbarandgrill.com; Daily 6am-2am

SEAFOOD

Anthony's Fish Grotto ⑤⑤

Large, tiled arch windows offer expansive views of San Diego bay that have made Anthony's a visitor favorite for nearly seven decades. Conveniently located beside the Maritime Museum and close to Little Italy, Anthony's works especially well as a lunch option on clear day. Shellfish and filleted fish are fried, grilled, charbroiled, steamed, or seared on plates, in sandwiches, or in chowder. There are even a few nonseafood options available for those only here for the view.

Map 1: 1360 N. Harbor Dr., Little Italy, 619/232-5103, www.gofishanthonys.com; Sun.-Thurs. 11am-9:30pm, Fri.-Sat. 11am-10pm

Ironside $$

Mermaids, fish skulls, and brass tables set the tone in this design-savvy raw bar and seafood restaurant. Start with oysters, mussels, clams, or ceviche, then move on to San Diego's best lobster roll or a whole roasted fish. This place knows seafood—cold or cooked—so you could even try the "fries with eyes" while marveling at mermaid statues and a wall made from barracuda skulls.

Map 1: 1654 India St., Little Italy, 619/269-3033, www.ironsidefishandoyster.com; Mon.-Fri. 11:30am-2:30pm and 5pm-10pm, Sat.-Sun. 10am-10:30pm

Spike Africa's $$

This Gaslamp seafood restaurant thinks global, whether it's Scottish salmon, Fiji tuna, Alaskan cod, or Maine lobster. Of course, some of the farthest-flung dishes come at a premium, but the menu is fairly balanced between comfort seafood, low-calorie, and gluten-free dishes. A great selection of starters is worth noting, including freshly shucked oysters, beer-braised mussels, clam chowder, and a daily ceviche.

Map 1: 411 Broadway, Gaslamp, 619/795-3800, www.spikeafricas.com; Mon.-Thurs. 11am-10pm, Fri.-Sat. 11am-11pm, Sun. 10am-10pm

STEAK HOUSE

★ Cowboy Star $$$

Combine a Western steak house with sustainable principles and European fine dining standards and you'll have a fair approximation of Cowboy Star. Enjoy prime-grade rib eye or "intensely marbled" *wagyu* beef while comfortably seated in a leather booth beneath a painting of John Wayne. Impeccable service comes from a supremely knowledgeable waitstaff prepared to suggest a wine pairing for the exquisite filet mignon steak tartare (complete with a quail egg). Everything—from the cocktails to the wine list to the long list of hormone- and antibiotic-free meats—is top-shelf, with several selections cured or dry-aged in the restaurant's own butcher shop. The menu varies with the whims of the French-trained chef, though you'll always find seafood and game selections in addition to a variety of steaks. This may well be the future of prime steak houses.

Map 1: 640 10th Ave., East Village, 619/450-5880, www.thecowboystar.com; Mon. 4pm-10pm, Tues.-Thurs. 11:30am-2:30pm and 4pm-10pm, Fri. 11:30am-2:30pm and 4pm-10:30pm, Sat. 5pm-10:30pm, Sun. 5pm-9pm

Donovan's Steak & Chop House $$$

USDA prime steak reigns supreme at Donovan's. It's the sort of restaurant professional athletes might eat at following a game, where bartenders wear tuxedoes and captains of industry drop tips that could singlehandedly change the lives of the waitress. Everything here is top-shelf all the way,

clockwise from top left: Queenstown Public House, Downtown; Cowboy Star, Downtown; Mariscos German/Nine Seas food truck, South Park

with dark wood paneling and an enormous glass wine vault filled with superb bottles of the good stuff.

Map 1: 570 K St., Gaslamp, 619/237-9700, www.donovanssteakhouse.com; Mon.-Thurs. 4pm-10pm, Fri.-Sat. 4pm-11pm

Balboa Park
Map 2

ASIAN

Hane Sushi $$$

One of the best sushi chefs in town is behind this Banker's Hill restaurant, which means that some of the best raw fish in town is consumed here daily. It's the sort of place where you can take a chance on *omakase*—chef's choice. Locals tend to evangelize Hane's sister restaurant, Sushi Ota (4529 Mission Bay Dr.), but this menu is just as authentic and delicious while in a more spacious, central location, where it's easier to get a table.

Map 2: 2760 5th Ave., 619/260-1411; Tues.-Fri. 11:30am-2pm, Tues.-Sun. 5:30pm-10pm

BREAKFAST

Eclipse Chocolate Bar & Bistro $$

A terrific artisanal chocolatier, Eclipse turns concepts like burned-chili caramel into tantalizing reality. Stop in for a box of chocolates, then stick around to devour one of the sweet and savory meals (especially brunch). Incorporating chocolate into just about every dish is accomplished with complexity and grace: maple-bacon blueberry pancakes with toasted white chocolate shavings will start your day brilliantly. The clean, mid-century-style bistro sports a menu of rich drinking chocolates that can be enjoyed with a shot of espresso.

Map 2: 2145 Fern St., 619/578-2984, www.eclipsechocolate.com; Mon.-Thurs. 8am-10pm, Fri.-Sat. 8am-11pm, Sun. 8am-6pm

CALIFORNIA

The Prado at Balboa Park $$

When exploring the El Prado, many visitors stop here for lunch, happy hour, or dinner for one good reason: the dining patio overlooks a particularly verdant section of the park. The layout makes it tough on waitstaff, who probably log more miles per shift than any park visitor, so don't expect to rush through the menu's California comfort food items. Instead, order a drink at the bar and choose from a menu of tacos, sandwiches, and large salads.

Map 2: 1549 El Prado, 619/557-9441, www.cohnrestaurants.com/theprado; Mon. 11:30am-3pm, Tues.-Thurs. 11:30am-10pm, Fri. 11:30am-11pm, Sat. 11am-11pm, Sun. 11am-10pm

FARM-TO-TABLE
Panama 66 ⑤⑤

Tucked in a courtyard beside the Museum of Art's sculpture garden sits the latest addition to Balboa Park's dining scene. This locally sourced gastropub features a rotating selection of San Diego's best beers to help wash down tasty sandwiches, salads, and charcuterie pates. Dine at one of the shady tables, or ask for a blanket and picnic among the artwork.

Map 2: 1549 El Prado, 619/557-9441, www.panama66.blogspot.com; Mon. 11:30am-3pm, Tues.-Thurs. 11:30am-10pm, Fri. 11:30am-11pm, Sat. 11am-11pm, Sun. 11am-10pm

MEXICAN
Mariscos German/Nine Seas ⑤

A truth peculiar to fish tacos is that some of the tastiest in town come off the back of a truck. Most days, one of these Mariscos trucks is parked in the Target parking lot in South Park, serving ridiculously good fried and grilled fish tacos as well as soups, ceviche, and other seafood delights.

Map 2: 3030 Grape St., 619/279-0010; Mon.-Sat. 10am-sunset

Uptown

Map 3

ASIAN
Akinori Sushi ⑤⑤

Chef Akinori Sato practices 14th-century Edomae preparation methods, which gives his modest Hillcrest establishment a bit of distinction. Fish is sometimes cured with vinegar or other interesting marinades, while the *nigiri* reflects 700 years of tradition. Old it may be, but the creativity behind the counter flows so that everything winds up tasting incredibly fresh in a dining room that feels as contemporary as the neighborhood around it.

Map 3: 1417 University Ave., 619/220-4888, www.akinorisushi.com; Sun.-Thurs. 5:30pm-10pm, Fri.-Sat. 5:30pm-10:30pm

Underbelly ⑤⑤

Ramen is having a moment, and its best local representation might just be this beer drinker's haven. Underbelly offers a succulent take on pork marrow *tonkatsu*, and its soy and mushroom-based broths also do well to flavor perfectly cooked noodles with add-ons such as *char siu* pork belly, hoisin short rib, and charred kimchi. Be prepared to order before you take a seat, and don't forget to explore the yakitori menu. Grab a seat on the spacious street-side patio, which dazzles even when the fire tables aren't lit.

Map 3: 3794 30th St., North Park, 619/255-8778, www.godblessunderbelly.com; Mon.-Fri. 4pm-1am, Sat.-Sun. 10am-1am

BREAKFAST

Hash House a Go Go $$

Heaping portions of farm-style breakfasts keep this eatery busy during breakfast and brunch, especially on weekends when locals line up for pancakes, waffles, benedicts, and meaty hashes. The simple farmhouse interior will do, but for the best experience, hold out for patio seating. Consider splitting a meal, or be prepared to walk away with a full belly as well as leftovers.

Map 3: 3628 5th Ave., Hillcrest, 619/298-4646, www.hashhouseagogo.com; Mon. 7:30am-2pm, Tues.-Thurs. 7:30am-2pm and 5:30pm-9pm, Fri. 7:30am-2pm and 5:30pm-10pm, Sat. 7:30am-2:30pm and 5:30pm-10pm, Sun. 7:30am-2:30pm and 5:30pm-9pm

Snooze $

Pancake lovers will find the wait at Snooze worth it. The variety of specialty flavors includes sweet potato, strawberry malted, and pineapple upside-down cakes, with a rotating selection of daily specials. Savory eaters will find solace in traditional and experimental egg dishes, including benedicts with lox, prosciutto, or pulled pork. Be ready to share, because you will want to try everything. Despite a large dining room, wait times can be long.

Map 3: 3940 5th Ave., Hillcrest, 619/500-3344, www.snoozeeatery.com; Mon.-Fri. 6:30am-2:30pm, Sat.-Sun. 7am-2:30pm

CAFÉS

Caffé Calabria $

Fresh-roasted beans make superior coffee, and if you already know this you'll want to check out this Italian-style roaster. A variety of dark roasted, single-origin beans and blends can be purchased in bulk or brewed into your preferred coffee drink, and they'll taste great, because they were recently roasted on the premises. Inside, TV screens show Italian league soccer or cycling races, or opt for parklet seating outside.

Map 3: 3933 30th St., North Park, 619/291-1759, www.caffecalabria.com; Mon.-Tues. 6am-3pm, Wed.-Fri. 6am-11pm, Sat.-Sun. 7am-11pm

Coffee & Tea Collective $

Third-wave coffee popped up in San Diego with this dedicated artisanal coffee roaster and tea crafter. The minimalist white space and stylish baristas project a cool quotient few coffee shops in the area can match. Their pour-over brewing skills make a visit worthwhile, and they take their reputation as a source of quality beverages quite seriously.

Map 3: 2911 El Cajon Blvd., 619/564-8086, www.coffeeandteacollective.com; Daily 7am-6pm

RESTAURANTS

UPTOWN

CONTEMPORARY

Bread & Cie $

It's no accident you'll come across Bread & Cie baked goods in restaurants and markets all over town; the French-style bakery bakes some of the best bread in San Diego. Stop in for sandwiches, either to dine in or take out for a picnic, and grab some desserts while you're here—you'll have to have one once you see them. The *macarons* in particular deliver a decadently sweet dose of Parisian nostalgia, perfect for nibbling on the restaurant's bistro-style dining patio.

Map 3: 350 University Ave., Hillcrest, 619/683-9322, www.breadandcie.com; Mon.-Fri. 7am-7pm, Sat. 7am-6pm, Sun. 8am-6pm

★ Carnita's Snack Shack $

You don't need to dig swine to enjoy Carnita's, but you'll sure love this street-side casual outdoor eatery if you do. Between the braised pork belly appetizer, pulled pork tacos, and fries served with bacon ketchup, hog heaven becomes a delectable possibility. Other regular menu items include a cheese bread and sliced rib-eye steak sandwich; one of the city's best burgers; and a terrine made from beets, spinach, and goat cheese (in case there's a vegetarian in your group). Local carnivores line up all day for this, even when the überdecadent *poutine* isn't on the menu.

Map 3: 2632 University Ave., North Park, 619/294-7675, www.carnitassnackshack.com; Daily noon-midnight

Great Maple $$

With a cobbled stone exterior and polished interior, this slick and welcoming restaurant feels like the contemporary version of a mountain town diner. Hardwood floors, green vinyl booths, and white marble countertops give it a clean look that matches its impeccable menu, which strikes an unusually good balance between meat and vegetable dishes. You may choose between steak tartare and beet tartare, and for every succulent grass-fed burger there's a creatively assembled salad. Nevertheless, keep reading; the list goes on and includes occasional surprises like Maine lobster *poutine*. Also, save room for dessert—the place is known for its pies as well as a decadent take on the maple-bacon doughnut.

Map 3: 1451 Washington St., 619/255-2282, www.thegreatmaple.com; Sun.-Thurs. 8am-2pm, 5pm-9:30pm, Fri.-Sat. 8am-2pm and 5pm-10pm

Waypoint Public House $$

With 30 rotating taps, including two nitro, you won't have trouble finding fantastic beer at Waypoint, but if you need pointers, the menu always recommends a couple of worthy beer pairings for each dish. The corner restaurant's a lot brighter and airier than the name might suggest, with huge rows of windows open on warm days, which are, of course, most of them. The breezy contemporary decor matches the playful menu, which bounces creatively between comfort food and light California cuisine.

EUROPEAN

100 Wines ⑤⑤

A lengthy list of bottles is only one of this restaurant's distinctions. The mostly French-influenced dishes of chef Miguel Valdez also stand out, whether it's the lightness of walnut-crusted market fish, or the savory perfection of a grilled *coulotte* steak. And if you don't think he's bringing a local perspective, try his grandmother's strawberry rhubarb cobbler. A comfy Mediterranean vibe extends through the dining room and out to a secluded courtyard in back.

Map 3: 1027 University Ave., 619/491-0100, www.cohnrestaurants.com/100wines; Mon. noon-3pm and 5pm-10pm, Tues.-Thurs. 5pm-10pm, Fri.-Sat. 4pm-11pm, Sun. 5pm-midnight

Pomegranate ⑤⑤

The Georgian cuisine served here has nothing to do with the American South; instead, this Georgia refers to the former Soviet state, now an independent republic bordering the Black Sea. An array of pickled vegetables and barbecued meats satisfy a loyal customer base, while the stewed lamb and roasted chicken dishes prove most tender. Handwritten positive reviews line the white walls; bring a felt-tip pen and add your own. Cash only.

Map 3: 2312 El Cajon Blvd., 619/298-4007, www.pomegranatesd.com; Sun.-Thurs. 5pm-10pm, Fri.-Sat. 5pm-11pm

MEXICAN

City Tacos ⑤

Eating tacos must be done in San Diego, and there are a number of places that serve them, whether authentic Baja street tacos or some traditional local take on fried fish. Then there's City Tacos, which turns tradition on its head for foodies looking to enjoy traditional flavor profiles in creative new ways. The chile relleno taco invokes the classic dish with mid spice and a gloriously melted cheese blend. The mahimahi adobo sears a lovely piece of fish and pairs it with mango salsa. Then there's the Borrego taco—lamb, mushroom, and fried leeks. You won't find the likes of it elsewhere, much to the detriment of elsewhere.

Map 3: 3028 University Ave., North Park, 619/294-8292, www.citytacossd.com; Mon.-Thurs. 11am-11pm, Fri.-Sat. 11am-2am, Sun. noon-10pm

El Comal ⑤⑤

If you're ready to experience homemade Mexican food, this family-owned restaurant offers a delicious and down-to-earth experience. *Comal* translates to "griddle," a reference to the restaurant's *antojitos*, traditional small dishes built around the ground hominy dough masa, used to make tamales and the best corn tortillas you'll ever taste. Consequently, any taco on the menu is a go, especially the goat *barbecoa*. To see what else masa can do, try the *mulitas*, gorditas, huaraches, or the green mole enchiladas, if they're available. And if you see a soup you like, just order it—they're all fantastic.

Map 3: 3946 Illinois St., 619/294-8292, www.elcomalsd.com; Mon.-Wed. 10am-3pm and 5pm-9pm, Thurs.-Fri. 10am-10pm, Sat. 9am-10pm, Sun. 9am-9pm

PIZZA
Blind Lady Alehouse $$

Tasty Napolitano pizza and 26 craft beers on tap would probably be enough to keep this place popular. But a comfortable wood dining room filled with community tables elevates this to a joy-filled space where families and friends bond over great ales. Whether you order a pie with house-made chorizo and sausage toppings, *moules frites,* or a charcuterie board, it's tough to go wrong, especially if you try one of the beers brewed in-house by Automatic Brewing Co.

Map 3: 3416 Adams Ave., 619/255-2491, www.blindladyalehouse.com; Daily 11:30am-midnight

★ URBN Pizza $$

The best crust in town hails from the coal-fire ovens of this chic pizza spot—and yes, pizza spots can be chic. A full bar turns out tasty cocktails as well as local craft beer, so the place often fills up with thirsty pretty things, hipsters, and cocktail connoisseurs. But excellent pizza is the root of URBN's success, with toppings like sausage-stuffed peppers, fresh clams, and mashed potatoes. Great happy hour specials make a visit worth your while.

Map 3: 3085 University Ave., 619/255-7300, www.urbnnorthpark.com; Sun.-Mon. noon-10pm, Tues.-Thurs. noon-midnight, Fri.-Sat. noon-2am

Old Town and Mission Hills Map 4

DESSERT
Gelato Vero Caffe $

Holding down its little corner for more than 30 years, this gelato shop is a great place to for dessert after indulging in one of the block's many good restaurants. Classic Italian flavors include *gianduia* (chocolate hazelnut) and spumoni (cherry chocolate amaretto) as well as a fruit-flavored *sorbettos.*

Map 4: 3753 India St., Mission Hills, 619/295-9269, www.gelatoverocaffe.com; Mon.-Thurs. 6am-midnight, Fri. 6am-1am, Sat. 7am-1am, Sun. 7am-midnight

top to bottom: Waypoint Public House in Uptown; Stone World Bistro & Gardens Liberty Station

Must-Try Mexican Food

a classic Baja fish taco from Oscar's Mexican Seafood

To make the most of San Diego's local specialties, look for these menu items at their recommended restaurants, along with other mainstays like enchiladas, chiles rellenos, shredded pork *carnitas,* and the curry-inspired pork *al pastor.* Don't forget to hit the salsa bar and use it generously.

- **Baja-style fish tacos** consist of beer-battered fish fillets deep-fried and served on corn tortillas with cabbage and a white *crema* sauce. Add-ons like *pico de gallo,* onions, and guacamole are great, but eat them with just a little Cholula or Valentina hot sauce instead. Try them at **Oscar's Mexican Seafood** (703 Turquoise St., Pacific Beach, 858/488-6392, www.oscars-mexicanseafood.com; Sun.-Thurs. 8am-9pm, Fri.-Sat. 8am-10pm) or **Mariscos German/Nine Seas** (3030 Grape St., 619/279-0010; Mon.-Sat. 10am-sunset).

- **Antojitos** are like Mexican tapas: small plates, usually dishes made

MEXICAN

Casa Guadalajara 💲💲

Old Town's historic park has no shortage of "authentic" Mexican restaurants vying for tourist attention. If you're intent on finding the classic Mexican margarita and Latin music dining patio experience, do as the locals do and head to Casa Guadalajara, the best of the bunch. Dishes like *chile colorado* and carne asada *tampiqueña* offer all the flavors you seek, though tacos, enchiladas, and fajitas always prove popular. Sit on the patio, order some chips and guacamole, and savor the experience.

Map 4: 4105 Taylor St., 619/295-5111, www.casaguadalajara.com; Mon.-Thurs. 11am-10pm, Fri. 11am-11pm, Sat.-Sun. 11am-10pm

El Agave 💲💲💲

El Agave creates a "Mexican Gastronomy," crafting a menu of authentic dishes that range from the usual to the exotic, including an appetizer called *tlacoyos cuitlacoche* (a rarely found delicacy of blue masa and corn fungus). For the less adventurous, the menu's safest bets include any of its 10 moles, with masa, a corn dough commonly associated with tamales and corn tortillas. The handmade tortillas at **El Comal** (3946 Illinois St., 619/294-8292, www.elcomalsd.com; Mon.-Wed. 10am-3pm and 5pm-9pm, Thurs.-Fri. 10am-10pm, Sat. 9am-10pm, Sun. 9am-9pm) are phenomenal, and their *sopes*, *mulitas*, and gorditas incorporate beans, cheese, and other ingredients that resemble tiny pizzas, grilled sandwiches, and empanadas, respectively.

- **California Burritos** or **Carne Asada Fries:** California's great contribution to Mexican food? French fries. The Cali burrito adds fries to a beefy carne asada burrito, with melting cheddar cheese, and maybe a little sour cream or guacamole. Carne asada fries pile all the same ingredients on a plate, resulting in a nachos-like dish with fries instead of chips. Try them at **La Perla Cocina** (745 Emerald St., Pacific Beach, 858/274-3038; Mon.-Sat. 8:30am-9pm, Sun. 8:30am-8:30pm).

- **Mole** is a smooth sauce made from chilies and other ingredients, including almonds, ground pumpkin seeds, and chocolate. Moles are usually ordered by color—brown, green, white, or red (aka *colorado*). With 10 moles to choose from, ordering one from **El Agave** (2304 San Diego Ave., 619/220-0692, www.elagave.com; Daily 11am-10pm) may be a little more complicated, but entirely worth it.

- *Taquitos* are rumored to have been invented at **El Indio** (3695 India St., 619/299-0333, www.el-indio.com; Daily 8am-9pm). Their rolled tacos are available with shredded beef, chicken, or potato, and garnished with cheese and guacamole for the proper effect. The flautas are prepared the same way as a *taquito*, but with flour tortillas instead of corn.

each a worthy excuse to dine here. The restaurant doubles as a tequila museum, and its walls are lined by more than 2,000 bottles that add a beautiful brightness to the rustic decor.

Map 4: 2304 San Diego Ave., 619/220-0692, www.elagave.com; Daily 11am-10pm

El Indio $

For 75 years this *tortilleria* has been churning out homemade tortillas and tortilla chips. During most of that time, it has also been serving up beloved and authentic Mexican food to a loyal following of locals and visitors. The founder of the family-owned mainstay is said to have invented the term *taquito*, so the little tacos are worth a try. Sit down in the busy casual dining room, the patio, or order to go.

Map 4: 3695 India St., Mission Hills, 619/299-0333, www.el-indio.com; Daily 8am-9pm

Lucha Libre $

If you like your Mexican food with a side of extreme kitsch, dive into this campy masked wrestling-themed taco and burrito shop. Wrestler murals and a mask gallery liven up the bright pink walls, and old matches and movies usually run on TV screens, playing up the wild vibe. You'll find some pretty authentic San Diego-style Mexican food here, as well as a few modern takes along the lines of a lettuce-wrapped taco and creamy cilantro salsa. It's a kooky way to eat like a local while still living like a traveler. With 24 hours' notice, you can even reserve the Champion's Booth, which must be seen to be believed.

Map 4: 1810 W. Washington St., 619/296-8226, www.tacosmackdown.com; Sun.-Thurs. 8am-11pm, Fri.-Sat. 8am-2:30am

PIZZA
Lefty's Chicago Pizzeria ⑤

Chicago may be a far cry from our sun-drenched beach lifestyle, but who doesn't love deep-dish pizza, Polish sausage, and Italian beef sandwiches? The family behind Lefty's came straight from the windy city with authenticity on their mind. Both this Mission Hills outpost and their original North Park location (3448 30th St.) have become standbys for Chicago expatriates and longtime locals, who keep coming back for the eatery's thin- or thick-crust pizzas and excellent char-grilled burgers.

Map 4: 4030 Goldfinch St., Mission Hills, 619/299-4030, www.leftyspizza.com; Sun.-Thurs. 11pm-9pm, Fri.-Sat. 11am-10pm

SEAFOOD
Blue Water Seafood Market & Grill ⑤⑤

The secret got out about Blue Water when the beloved fresh-catch seafood spot was covered on TV's *Diners, Drive-Ins and Dives,* but the line out the door always existed near lunchtime. That line moves quickly, though, guiding you past the market counter where you can linger over the different cuts of fish available. Decide which looks best and then order it as a sandwich, a salad, a taco, or on a plate with your choice of seasoning. The place always looks packed, but tables open up frequently; grab one on the patio if you can.

Map 4: 3667 India St., 619/497-0914, www.bluewaterseafoodsandiego.com; Mon.-Thurs. 11am-9pm, Fri. 11am-10pm, Sat. 11:30am-10pm, Sun. 11:30am-9pm

Mission Bay and Beaches   Map 5

AMERICAN
Rocky's Crown Pub ⑤

Pacific Beach's legendary local burger bar doesn't need special toppings or gimmicky burgers in its recipe for success, just tried and true burger fixings that have earned it decades' worth of devoted clientele, *Food Network* accolades, and a spot on many San Diegan's best burgers list.

Daily 11am-midnight

BREAKFAST

Broken Yolk $$

If you can stand the wait, hold out for rooftop seating at this PB brunch institution. The massive menu includes classic Mexican egg dishes like *chilaquiles* and *huevos con chorizo;* a griddle menu of pancakes and waffles; and a litany of benedicts and massive omelets. Gather your friends, order a couple rounds of mimosas, and feast. Other locations include Gaslamp (355 6th Ave.) and Point Loma (3577 Midway Dr.).

Map 5: 1851 Garnet Ave., Pacific Beach, 619/270-9655, www.thebrokenyolkcafe.com;
Daily 6am-3pm

Swell Café $

Steamed bagels and house-roasted coffee make this patio restaurant an excellent first stop for a day in Mission Beach, just a block away. Breakfast options include waffles, crepes, and french toast as well as regional classics such as breakfast burritos and huevos rancheros. Whatever you choose, try not to rush. Take a deep breath and appreciate a friendly scene that perfectly encapsulates the SoCal beach lifestyle.

Map 5: 3833 Mission Blvd., Mission Beach, 858/539-0039, www.theswellcafe.com;
Daily 7am-4pm

CONTEMPORARY

Sandbar Sports Grill $$

Sandbar is not just a nice piece of real estate on Mission Beach—though it is that. Set on the boardwalk just north of Belmont Park, its windows capture the beach vibe, the ocean breeze, and plenty of people watching. Order a drink while you wait for tasty tacos or burgers.

Map 5: 718 Ventura Pl., Mission Beach, 858/488-1274, www.sandbarsportsgrill.com;
Daily 9am-2am

The Patio on Lamont $$$

What's better at the Patio: the food or the decor? It's a tough call. The menu features braised short ribs, braised octopus, seafood risotto, and a 21-day-aged bone-in rib eye. Seating options include a romantically lit interior dining room, or a bright spot beneath the living wall of plants that adorn the eatery's namesake covered patio. If you think these decisions are tough, wait until you see the cocktail list! Of course, first you've got to decide between this and a possibly more gorgeous Mission Hills location (4020 Goldfinch St.).

Map 5: 4445 Lamont St., Pacific Beach, 858/412-4648, www.thepatioonlamont.com;
Daily 9am-midnight

DELI

Rubicon Deli $

This local sandwich chain lays a solid foundation for its subs with a variety of house-baked breads, including pesto, jalapeño jack, and Dutch crunch. All the favorite lunch meats are available, or opt for one of the more intriguing house specials such as the Whale's Veg—spinach, kale, cabbage, carrot, bell pepper, avocado, tomato, onion, cucumber, hummus, tarragon Dijon mustard, balsamic vinaigrette, and jack cheese. You'll find a second location in Mission Hills (3715 India St.).

Map 5: 3819 Mission Blvd., Mission Beach, 858/488-3354, www.therubicondeli.com; Mon.-Thurs. 11am-7pm, Fri.-Sun. 10am-7pm

MEXICAN

La Perla Cocina $

There's not much to look at within this beach-adjacent Mexican dive; it's the lamb tacos and one of the city's best California burritos (marinated carne asada, grated cheddar cheese, and french fries) that keeps people coming back. This staple street food proves tasty and filling, but if you want to take it further, try the Oaxacalifornia burrito—a California burrito wrapped inside a quesadilla.

Map 5: 745 Emerald St., Pacific Beach, 858/274-3038; Mon.-Sat. 8:30am-9pm, Sun. 8:30am-8:30pm

Oscar's Mexican Seafood $

Why do lines of people keep forming beside the taco truck mural of that hole in the wall in north PB? Because the fish tacos demand it. Oscar's excels at the classic Baja-style battered fish, available for $1 on weekday afternoons. Smoked fish, shrimp, and steak tacos also go great with the house ceviche or fish stew. There's a less charming central Pacific Beach location (746 Emerald St.) and another in Hillcrest (646 University Ave.).

Map 5: 703 Turquoise St., Pacific Beach, 858/488-6392, www.oscarsmexicanseafood.com; Sun.-Thurs. 8am-9pm, Fri.-Sat. 8am-10pm

SEAFOOD

Pacific Beach Fish Shop $$

Line up for grilled fish, sandwiches, or tacos at the counter of this local's favorite that's easy to spot thanks to a marlin trophy out front. Order your choice of fish based on what looks good that day accompanied by marinades such as blackened lemon-butter or chipotle. Or keep it *crudo* with ceviche, oysters, a shrimp cocktail, or sashimi of the day. Take it to the patio with a draft beer and relish where you are.

Map 5: 1775 Garnet Ave., Pacific Beach, 858/483-4746, www.thefishshoppb.com; Daily 11am-10pm

AMERICAN

Hodad's ⓢ

The *Food Network* inexorably changed the face of Ocean Beach a few years back when it named Hodad's among the nation's best burgers. Now lines run half a block long on sunny days. Whether the basic burger selection here is worth the hype or just another greasy beneficiary of TV fame, you're in for a wait. Hold out for the prime people-watching real estate at the counter overlooking the sidewalk. Otherwise, prepare to spend your meal deciphering the hundreds of quirky personalized license plates that cover the walls.

Map 6: 5010 Newport Ave., Ocean Beach, 619/224-4623, www.hodadies.com; Sun.-Thurs. 11am-10pm, Fri.-Sat. 11am-11pm

ASIAN

OB Noodle House ⓢⓢ

The popularity of this gastropub and noodle house led to its recent expansion into a larger location a mere block from the OB Pier. Locals love the place and seek out their favorite dishes among *udon, pho,* lo mein, and other pan-Asian pastas, as well as a fine rotation of local craft brews to drink with them. It's never a bad place to be on a warm evening; enjoy a beer on the outdoor patio as the neighborhood's nightlife starts to pick up.

Map 6: 4993 Niagara Ave., Ocean Beach, 619/255-9858, www.obnoodlehouse.com; Mon.-Thurs. noon-11pm, Fri.-Sun. 11am-11pm

Umi Sushi ⓢⓢ

For gorgeous sushi boats and shoji decor, give this Shelter Island sushi joint the nod. You can eat your fill of clean, beautifully cut fish, or order from the impressive list of rolls. Try the Mountain Roll, spicy tuna topped by baked salmon, or opt for more standard fare with the Crazy Boy, a tempura-fried California roll. Umi offers a traditional feel, yet welcomes novice sushi eaters looking to try delicious raw seafood.

Map 6: 2806 Shelter Island Dr., Shelter Island, 619/226-1135, www.umisushisandiego. com; Mon.-Sat. 11:30am-2:30pm and 5pm-10pm, Sun. 5pm-10pm

CONTEMPORARY

Bali Hai ⓢⓢⓢ

This bay-view restaurant opened during the 1950s Polynesian craze, so you'll still spot some tiki decor and catch live Hawaiian tunes some evenings. The menu covers a variety of Pacific Rim dishes, including seafood, meat, vegetarian, and gluten-free options. There's something for everyone, especially if everyone enjoys potent cocktails. Share a scorpion bowl or add another to the tally of 2.3 million mai tais served in this warm and

Dining with a View

Whether you're looking for a romantic dinner with a sunset view or just want to gaze out the window, a number fine establishments offer excellent views, especially if you call ahead to reserve a good table.

For the most up-close interaction with the Pacific Ocean, try **The Marine Room** (2000 Spindrift Dr., 866/644-2351, www.marineroom. com; Sun.-Thurs. 4pm-9:30pm, Fri.-Sat. 4pm-10pm), which boasts reinforced windows that keep the water out during high tide. Waves crashing against a dining room window isn't likely something you'll experience elsewhere.

Cusp Dining & Drinks (7955 La Jolla Shores Dr., 858/551-3620, www. cusprestaurant.com; Mon.-Thurs. 7am-10:30am and 5pm-9pm, Fri. 7am-10:30am and 5pm-10pm, Sat. 8am-2pm and 5pm-10pm, Sun. 8am-2pm and 5pm-9pm) near La Jolla Shores offers another glassed in ocean view—this one from the 11th floor. Sunsets from this perspective can be everything and more than you'd imagined, and when it's good, a round of champagne livens the room.

Wonderland Ocean Pub (5083 Santa Monica Ave., Ocean Beach, 619/255-3358, www.wonderlandob. com; Mon.-Fri. 11am-close, Sat.-Sun. 9am-close) also gives good sunset by the pier in lower-brow OB, though the best seats are reserved for those looking to kick up their feet and drink.

To check out the city skyline, look into the confusing coupling of **Island Prime & C Level** (880 Harbor Island Dr., 619/298-6802, www. cohnrestaurants.com/islandprime; C Level: Daily 11am-close, Island Prime: Daily 5pm-close) on Harbor Island. The two separate restaurants share a bar and occasional menu items. Island Prime is the fancier of the

the view from Island Prime

two, with a glamorous dining room and picture windows. At C Level you don't get the prime streaks, but you do get outdoor lounge seating with the same view, and bay water almost within reach.

Bali Hai (2230 Shelter Island Dr., 619/222-1181, www.balihairestaurant. com; Mon.-Thurs. 11:30am-9pm, Fri.-Sat. 11:30am-10pm, Sun. 9:30am-9pm) has a broader perspective of the bay, including a glimpse at some of the naval vessels coming out of Coronado, which aren't always pretty, but can be fascinating.

The greenest views come courtesy of the golf course at Torrey Pines. Check it out from the deck of the terrific **AR Valentien** (11480 N. Torrey Pines Rd., 858/777-6635, www.arvalentien.com; Mon.-Fri. 11:30am-2:30pm and 5:30pm-10pm, Sat.-Sun. 7am-11:30am, noon-2:30pm, and 5:30pm-10pm), one of the most pleasant lunch spots in town. It also happens to face west, delivering golf course greenery, an ocean sunset, and incredible food: the trifecta.

welcoming space. Reserve in advance for a window seat, so you can catch an up-close glimpse of Navy vessels traversing the harbor.

Map 6: 2230 Shelter Island Dr., 619/222-1181, www.balihairestaurant.com; Mon.-Thurs. 11:30am-9pm, Fri.-Sat. 11:30am-10pm, Sun. 9:30am-9pm

Island Prime & C Level ⑤⑤⑤

Built around a shared bar, these two restaurants pose a simple question: How much are you willing to spend to enjoy this extraordinary view? Drop in for the outdoor lounge seating at C Level, which sits right on top of the bay facing the entirety of the Downtown skyline, and enjoy specialty cocktails to go with steaks, sandwiches, and seafood specialties such as lobster bisque, shrimp Louie, and macadamia-crusted sea bass.

For upscale indoor dining with the same view, Island Prime delivers prime-grade steak in a decidedly swankier dinner atmosphere. Rumors are that a third restaurant will soon be added to the space.

Map 6: 880 Harbor Island Dr., Harbor Island, 619/298-6802, www.cohnrestaurants.com/ islandprime; C Level: Daily 11am-close, Island Prime: Daily 5pm-close

Wonderland Ocean Pub ⑤⑤

Offering the best view in OB, Wonderland sits on the second floor facing the beach and pier serving up hearty soups and stews, contemporary spins on Thai and Hawaiian dishes, robust burgers, and a variety of tacos, all reliable quality at reasonable prices. When the surf is up, you can watch local wave riders from the bay windows. Time it right and enjoy a few more beers while watching the reliably thrilling sunsets.

Map 6: 5083 Santa Monica Ave., Ocean Beach, 619/255-3358, www.wonderlandob.com; Mon.-Fri. 11am-close, Sat.-Sun. 9am-close

DESSERT

Lighthouse Ice Cream & Yogurt ⑤

You'll smell this ice cream and frozen yogurt shop before you see it, specifically the made-on-site waffle-ice cream sandwiches. If you come within sniffing distance, you will wind up standing in line trying to decide between an apple-cinnamon waffle sandwich filled with sea salt-caramel ice cream or a cone of huckleberry topped with bacon. Or keep it simple with a blueberry-cheesecake ice cream banana split.

Map 6: 5059 Newport Ave., Ocean Beach, 619/222-8600; Daily 11am-10pm

FARM-TO-TABLE

Stone World Bistro & Gardens Liberty Station ⑤⑤

Stone reigns as the biggest and most successful craft brewer in town. It's also a 40,000-square-foot organic farm-to-table restaurant with 40 taps of Stone special releases, collaborations, and dozens of handpicked guest beers. The huge outdoor patio is the place to be on warm days; half the taps are out here, along with bocce ball courts and outdoor movie screenings. Amid such amenities, it's easy to forget about the food, which is made from scratch, often with produce grown at Stone's very own farm. Asian-inspired dishes include *yakisoba* and Korean barbecued ribs, plus intriguing takes on duck tacos, a corned lamb Reuben, and a *jidori* chicken schnitzel.

Map 6: 2816 Historic Decatur Rd., Suite 116, Point Loma, 619/269-2100, www.stonelibertystation.com; Mon.-Sat. 11:30am-10pm, Sun. 11am-9pm

MARKETS

Olive Tree $

This small market and deli, with an adjacent beer tasting room, proves indispensable for those who want to take a break from eating tacos to exhibit more refined tastes. Everybody stops by eventually for a sandwich, fine wine, gourmet foodstuffs, or rotisserie chicken. Craft beer aficionados also consistently heap praises on its value as a bottle shop. It may not have the largest selection of beer in town, but as with most things in the shop, any brew you pick up is likely to taste great.

Map 6: 4805 Narragansett Ave., Ocean Beach, 619/224-0443, www.olivetreemarket.com; Daily 8am-9pm

MEXICAN

South Beach Bar & Grill $

With windows overlooking the pier, OB's always-bustling South Beach Bar & Grill is the fish taco destination for locals and out-of-town guests. Choices range from traditional Baja battered-and-fried tacos to grilled options, including wahoo, mahimahi, lobster, and shark; wash these down with one of the local beers on tap. You're on your own finding an open table amid the constant rush, but once you've claimed your spot, you've earned the right to enjoy it awhile.

Map 6: 5059 Newport Ave., Ocean Beach, 619/226-4577, www.southbeachob.com; Daily 11am-2am

SEAFOOD

Point Loma Seafood $

When do you know the seafood's truly fresh? When you pass a fleet of fishing boats outside the restaurant. Point Loma Seafood has achieved cultlike status over the years, with a glass deli counter displaying your choice of the latest catch. Line up at the counter and choose your fresh catch for fish tacos, seafood salad, sushi, or plates with fries and slaw. The best-known option may be the simplest: a piece of fish on fresh-baked sourdough with tartar sauce—that's it. The freshness of the fish is all the frills this sandwich needs.

Map 6: 2805 Emerson St., Point Loma, 619/223-1109, www.pointlomaseafoods.com; Mon.-Sat. 9am-7pm, Sun. 10am-7pm

AMERICAN

Burger Lounge ⑤

This cleanly designed local chain offers grass-fed hamburgers, free-range turkey burgers, organic quinoa veggie burgers, big salads, and gluten-free buns with fries and onion rings cooked in "100% refined peanut oil." Thing is, all of this stuff tastes great, granting an affordable meal that's relatively good for you. Other locations include Hillcrest (406 University Ave.) and the Gaslamp (528 5th Ave.).

Map 7: 1101 Wall St., 858/456-0196, www.burgerlounge.com; Sun.-Thurs. 10:30am-9pm, Fri.-Sat. 10:30am-10pm

BREAKFAST

Brockton Villa ⑤⑤

Three things make Brockton Villa a favorite in La Jolla: a patio with views overlooking La Jolla Cove, the quaint 1894 beach bungalow setting, and the french toast. The soufflé-style toast is a fluffy, moist-in-the-middle treat that draws rave reviews decade after decade. A friendly warning: When the wind is blowing in from the cove, the scent of local animal life can take a few minutes to ignore.

Map 7: 1235 Coast Blvd., 858/454-7393, www.brocktonvilla.com; Daily 8am-9pm

Harry's Coffee Shop ⑤

Hidden among the high-end boutiques and trendy restaurants is this anachronistic coffee shop embodying the classic American diner, complete with vinyl booths and a breakfast counter. The menu offers eggs dishes galore, from a list of omelets to eggs with bacon, sausage, chicken-fried steak, or corned beef hash. Order refills on that mug of joe, which is made from a special blend of beans roasted by local coffee mainstay Café Moto.

Map 7: 7545 Girard Ave., 858/454-7381, www.harryscoffeeshop.com; Daily 6am-3pm

CAFÉS

Bird Rock Coffee Roasters ⑤

This celebrated local roaster favors light-roasting its single-origin beans, which are usually the product of direct agreements between Bird Rock and a network of farmers around the globe. Bird Rock puts a lot of thought and craft into its coffee, and the staff welcomes questions about brewing techniques, especially about the daily selection of fresh beans. A newer location is in Little Italy (2295 Kettner Blvd.).

Map 7: 5627 La Jolla Blvd., 858/551-1707, www.birdrockcoffee.com; Mon.-Fri. 6am-7pm, Sat.-Sun. 6:30am-7pm

CALIFORNIA

Cusp Dining & Drinks $$

Sitting on the 11th floor of the Hotel La Jolla, a panoramic ocean view might be the only decor Cusp really needs. But inside, a slick contemporary design incorporates organic shapes that contrast the industrial polished steel of its open kitchen. The always-changing menu loosely adopts California and Mediterranean influences, though don't be surprised to find deviations among the pan-seared proteins and house-made pastas. The cocktail list runs even farther afield, with classic drinks and a number of adventurous craft concoctions.

Map 7: 7955 La Jolla Shores Dr., 858/551-3620, www.cusprestaurant.com; Mon.-Thurs. 7am-10:30am and 5pm-9pm, Fri. 7am-10:30am and 5pm-10pm, Sat. 8am-2pm and 5pm-10pm, Sun. 8am-2pm and 5pm-9pm

Nine-Ten $$$

Chef Jason Knibb has earned accolades over the years for the "evolving California cuisine" served at the Grand Colonial Hotel's restaurant. Appetizers may include squid-ink spaghettini with bay scallops in an *uni* emulsion, while entrée options range from a creatively dressed prime steak dish to succulent seafood prepared *sous vide*. Local produce dictates the weekly flavor profiles, and the excellently prepared staff can recommend perfect wine pairings all the way through dessert. Reserve a spot on the sidewalk patio for people-watching along Prospect Street, or request terrace dining for a partial sunset view of the Pacific.

Map 7: 910 Prospect St., 858/964-5400, www.nine-ten.com; Mon. 6:30am-11am, 11:30am-2:30pm, and 3:30pm-9:30pm, Tues.-Sat. 6:30am-11am, 11:30am-2:30pm, and 3:30pm-10pm, Sun. 6:30am-2:30pm and 3:30pm-9:30pm

FARM-TO-TABLE

AR Valentien $$$

Spearheading the farm-to-table movement in San Diego, the restaurant at the Lodge at Torrey Pines crafts delicious charcuterie and simple yet effective dishes, adhering to the principle that quality ingredients results in quality meals. Even something as simple as baked chicken under a brick tastes better when it's done right. The dining room is nice, but it's tough to beat lunch on the gorgeous deck overlooking the 18th hole of the famous Torrey Pines golf course.

Map 7: 11480 N. Torrey Pines Rd., 858/777-6635, www.arvalentien.com; Mon.-Fri. 11:30am-2:30pm and 5:30pm-10pm, Sat.-Sun. 7am-11:30am, noon-2:30pm, and 5:30pm-10pm

★ Whisknladle $$$

The covered patio is where you'll find one of the best dining (and people-watching) experiences in San Diego. Executive chef Chris Powell crafts seasonal dishes prepared from scratch, usually dependent on which organic produce and sustainably sourced meats and seafood are available fresh. The result is out-of-this-world quality; even a routine charcuterie plate stands out, with exceptional house-cured meats, brined-in-house olives, and house-baked breads. You can't go wrong with any pasta entrée, especially a pork sausage *ragù* over tagliatelle that will make you question every Italian restaurant you've ever visited.

Map 7: 1044 Wall St., 858/551-7575, www.whisknladle.com; Mon.-Thurs. 11:30am-9pm, Fri. 11:30am-10pm, Sat. 10am-10pm, Sun. 10am-9pm

MEXICAN
★ Puesto $$

It's tough to do better than this of-the-moment Mexican spot. Mix-and-match tacos include lobster, nopal cactus, or filet mignon served in a house-made corn tortilla with crispy melted cheese, avocado, and pistachio jalapeño salsa. Sample some of the great tequila-based cocktails to wash it down, and if you truly enjoy living, order the flan. A pair of small dining rooms open to a bustling sidewalk. For a larger experience, try the newer Seaport Village location (789 W. Harbor Dr.).

Map 7: 1044 Wall St., 858/454-1260, www.eatpuesto.com; Sun.-Thurs. 11am-9pm, Fri.-Sat.11am-10pm

SEAFOOD
★ El Pescador Fish Market $

Fresh seafood in La Jolla has a long history. This newly expanded local staple dates back to the 70s, and offers a bounty of fresh-catch seafood, served in sandwiches, burritos, or tacos—all very satisfying. High ceilings and picture windows light up a long glass counter filled with local fish, including yellowtail, sea bass, and Mexican white shrimp. To truly embrace the beauty of this spot, grab the sashimi platter of the day.

Map 7: 634 Pearl St., 858/456-2526, www.elpescadorfishmarket.com; Daily 10am-8pm

★ The Marine Room $$$

This high-end restaurant has been a legendary draw since the 1940s, famous for being so close to the ocean that waves splash against the windows during high tide. Diners enjoy a little thrill each time the water splashes only inches away, but ultimately the food lives up to its reputation as well. Globally sourced seafood is supplemented by French gastronomy that includes everything from Maine lobster tail to lamb osso buco.

Map 7: 2000 Spindrift Dr., 866/644-2351, www.marineroom.com; Sun.-Thurs. 4pm-9:30pm, Fri.-Sat. 4pm-10pm

clockwise from top left: a meal at AR Valentien in La Jolla; sea urchin, an example of fresh San Diego seafood; Coronado Brewing Co.

AMERICAN
Coronado Brewing Company ⑤⑤

A local institution, CBC has been serving up pub grub for decades, which goes great with its award-winning beers. Order a tasting flight with appetizers, then settle on a pint to go with your burger, pizza, or taco plate. Aim for lunch or an early dinner to enjoy the shaded dining patio on a sunny day. With the city skyline within view, you can check a few items off your San Diego to-do list all in one place.

Map 8: 170 Orange Ave., 619/437-4452, www.coronadobrewingcompany.com; Sun.-Thurs. 10:30am-9pm, Fri.-Sat. 10:30am-10pm

Delux Dogs ⑤

The quintessential American lunch gets the San Diego treatment at this gourmet hot dog specialist. Serving Vienna Beef sausages and dogs on soft, steamed buns, this minimalist diner offers bacon-wrapped, grass-fed, and cheese-filled options topped by the likes of chili, sauerkraut, and relish with side of regular or sweet potato fries. It goes pretty well with a family beach day.

Map 8: 943 Orange Ave., 619/319-5338, www.deluxdogs.com; Mon.-Sat. 11am-8pm, Sun. 11am-6pm

BREAKFAST
★ The Crown Room ⑤⑤⑤

The Hotel del Coronado's lavish all-you-can-eat brunch includes a truly dizzying number of buffet stations, all served in the Crown Room, one of the city's best architectural examples of jointed wood construction. Eggs are made to order, prime rib roasts are carved, pancakes flipped, and sushi rolled. Even if you go back for thirds, you won't get to it all. You may never even know what you missed by the time you've made it through your second dessert. Reservations are recommended, as the high cost of entry doesn't seem to keep the crowds away.

Map 8: 943 Orange Ave., 619/319-5338, www.hoteldel.com; Mon.-Sat. 11am-8pm, Sun. 11am-6pm

CAFÉS
Coronado Coffee Company ⑤

A scenic location in Coronado's Ferry Landing Marketplace makes this large kiosk a good spot to grab a cup of coffee on the way to or returning from Downtown, especially when they're serving beans from local roaster The West Bean. If you're not taking the ferry, enjoy your cup of joe at the small park just to the left up the coastline.

Map 8: 1201 1st St., Ferry Landing Marketplace, 619/522-0217, www.bluebridgehospitality.com; Mon.-Fri. 7am-8pm, Sat.-Sun. 7am-9pm

RESTAURANTS
CORONADO

Fresh-Catch Seafood Counters

Fish counters have sprung up all around San Diego—wherever you are, you're only a few minutes away from your fill of yellowtail, halibut, sea bass, salmon, or any number of available fillets. Seafood counters are built around the concept that the best way to order fish is to point at it and describe how you'd like it prepared. Meals are typically a grilled fish on a plate with one of a variety of marinades, or built into a sandwich or a couple of tacos.

- **Blue Water Seafood Market & Grill** (3667 India St., 619/497-0914, www.bluewaterseafoodsandiego. com; Mon.-Thurs. 11am-9pm, Fri. 11am-10pm, Sat. 11:30am-10pm, Sun. 11:30am-9pm) in Mission Hills has always attracted a big lunch crowd, mostly repeat visitors who can't get enough of the daily selections cooked with lemon-garlic butter, chipotle, or blackened seasonings.

- **El Pescador Fish Market** (634 Pearl St., 858/456-2526, www. elpescadorfishmarket.com; Daily 10am-8pm) is a personal favorite,

and one of the best lunch values in La Jolla, hands down.

- **Point Loma Seafood** (2805 Emerson St., 619/223-1109, www. pointlomaseafoods.com; Mon.- Sat. 9am-7pm, Sun. 10am-7pm) is a regional classic on Shelter Island, and excuse enough to visit and see all the fishing boats moored in the marina next door.

- If you're in the vicinity of Mission Bay, cap off a fun filled day by stopping in to **Pacific Beach Fish Shop** (1775 Garnet Ave., 858/483-4746, www.thefishshoppb.com; Daily 11am-10pm), which offers great beers in addition to fish.

- Thanks to the recent addition of **Fish 101** (1468 N Coast Highway 101, Leucadia, 760/943-6221, www.fish101restaurant.com, Sun.-Thurs. 11:30am-9pm, Fri.- Sat. 11:30am-10pm) to the Pacific Coast Highway, day-trippers to North County can take a moment to appreciate this Encinitas fish counter that favors healthy cooking techniques.

DESSERTS

MooTime Creamery Ⓢ

A rotating selection of handcrafted ice cream, sorbet, frozen yogurt, and sherbet include unique flavors along the lines of *horchata,* cheesecake, coconut, Girl Scout mint, Irish cream, and Mexican chocolate. Top that with candy bars, marshmallows, gummies, nuts, fruit, or fudge. Then chop, smash, and mix it all together into a waffle cone or bowl, or a waffle cup, or a chocolate-dipped waffle cone. Enjoy.

Map 8: 1025 Orange Ave., 619/435-2422, www.bluebridgehospitality.com; Sun.-Thurs. 11am-9pm, Fri.-Sat. 11am-10pm

FARM-TO-TABLE

Leroy's Kitchen and Lounge $$$

A nearby organic farm supplies this welcoming Coronado eatery with the bulk of its produce, and the chefs respond by crafting the best of whatever's fresh. The menu changes seasonally, but you'll always find deliberately conceived salads, seafood, and meat dishes. Despite their local-source ethos, the restaurant reflects the world-wandering ways of its namesake into its repertoire; eastern and island influences usually pair well with seasonal cocktails or a stellar assortment of local craft beer.

Map 8: 1015 Orange Ave., 619/437-6087, www.leroyskitchenandlounge.com; Mon.-Wed. 11am-10pm, Thurs.-Fri. 11am-midnight, Sat. 10am-midnight, Sun. 10am-10pm

Nightlife

San Diego's Gaslamp is the epicenter for rowdy nightlife in Downtown. Most weeknights—and especially weekends—the bars, clubs, and restaurants bring out large crowds from all over the city.

Businesses cater to this flood of revelers. Most are set up to handle high volume, posting beautiful hostesses and fast-talking pitch men on the sidewalks to lure customers. It's a competitive market, and places open and close all the time, so while it's fine to have a Gaslamp destination, most wind up going somewhere else before, after, or both.

Avoiding Downtown may be the impetus for the growth of North Park's nightlife. The Uptown neighborhood has flourished as a destination for creative and design-savvy types, as well as service industry vets. It's increasingly a hub for craft beer aficionados, with a slew of tap houses and new tasting rooms opening seasonally. The 30th Avenue "restaurant row" entices many to stick around and imbibe craft cocktails as the night wears on.

Nearby Hillcrest caters to the LGBT community, with gleeful dance clubs and pick-up scenes. Guys tend to steer more toward the west side of the neighborhood, while women are more likely to congregate to the east side, from Park Avenue north to University Heights. However, the community is open to everyone, and many nightspots cater to different interests on rotating nights of the week.

When the sun goes down, there's nothing like the beach communities. In Ocean Beach, Newport Avenue brings in a wild mixture of surfers, bohemians, military, bikers, and locals attracted to the laid-back atmosphere and cheap drinks. Nights in OB prove anything but predictable. You might be surprised at the sort of friends you make. Pacific Beach may be a little easier to peg; those cruising the beach and Garnet Avenue are usually out

Previous page top: downtown San Diego at night **bottom:** a flight of beer at Coronado Brewing Co.

Highlights

★ **Best Dance Club:** A little bit of Vegas showed up in San Diego when **Fluxx** opened its doors. The splashy club sets up interesting live shows to balance out the occasional superstar DJ. It's not for the shy or the budget-conscious (page 99).

★ **Best Rock Club:** Every local band covets a slot at **The Casbah**. The small venue has been the go-to destination for in-the-know fans to catch under-the-radar bands, sometimes only a year or two removed from playing giant festivals and arenas (page 102).

★ **Best Wine Bar:** Wine bars with a great selection of reds are easy to come by, but how often does a glamorous location like **Encore Champagne Bar** come along to provide a worthy assortment of bubbly (page 102)?

★ **Best Whiskey Bar:** An extensive menu of bourbons, scotches, and ryes give **Seven Grand** its allure. A tasty take on an old fashioned doesn't hurt; neither does the backroom stage with entertaining jazz acts most nights (page 104).

★ **Best Tap House: Hamilton's Tavern** isn't huge, and everybody knows how great its tap list can be, so there's usually a crowd, sometimes even during the dog-friendly happy hour. I might not even have mentioned it if the secret wasn't already out (page 104).

★ **Best Craft Cocktails: Polite Provisions** bartenders know exactly what they're doing. The lengthy cocktail list will entice whether you like sweet and fruity or prefer quality spirits to shine (page 105).

★ **Best Tequilería:** One of the only legitimate Mexican restaurants in Old Town, **El Agave** doubles as a "Tequila Museum." Thousands of tequila bottles adorn the walls, many of them beautifully wrought, and almost every one special and available for sipping with the house *sangrita* (page 107).

★ **Best Craft Breweries: AleSmith,** with a newly expanded brewery and tasting room, probably has the most awards (page 114); **Stone World Bistro** (page 110) clearly has the widest brand recognition; and relative newcomer **Societe** (page 116) just has delicious IPAs across the board.

to drink and meet members of the opposite sex. It's a casual party area, with a bit of crawling from place to place. Grab a drink, check out the scene, and then settle in with your choice for the night. The best part about partying near the beach is heading over to catch the moon's reflection over the ocean after last call . . . and deciding where to pick up a late-night burrito while you sober up.

Downtown

Map 1

BARS

Barleymash

Open throughout the day to serve food and drink with a party vibe, it's when the Gaslamp nightlife kicks up that Barleymash really comes alive, making room for popular music and heavy flirting that epitomizes San Diego on a Saturday night. Dress to attract the opposite sex at this open-street club, which clears out the dining room at night so people can dance.

Map 1: 600 5th Ave., Gaslamp, 619/255-7373, www.barleymash.com; Mon.-Fri. 11am-2am, Sat.-Sun. 10am-2am

Bootlegger

Whether there's a big game on, it's time to dance, or day drinking is on the agenda, you're likely to find it happening at this classic American bar. Grab a sidewalk table and check out the East Village street life or cozy up in a booth in the back. It's always fun.

Map 1: 804 Market St., East Village, 619/794-2668, www.bootleggersd.com; Mon.-Fri. 3pm-2am, Sat.-Sun. 9am-2pm

Lounge Six

The rooftop lounge at the Salomar Hotel entices with an outdoor bar, poolside cocktails, cabanas, and plenty of lounge chairs from which to lord over East Village from above. Umbrellas shade the daylight, while heat lamps warm up the night, providing everything you need to stay comfortably warm while looking cool.

Map 1: 616 J St., East Village, 619/531-8744, www.hotelsolamar.com; Mon.-Thurs. 11:30am-2:30pm and 3:30pm-11pm, Fri.-Sat. 11:30am-2:30pm and 3:30pm-midnight

Searsucker

Searsucker sets the table for a swanky cocktail hour. A tasty cocktail menu and killer small plates bring in well-dressed young professionals looking to meet and unwind while chill dance music plays. The large bar holds a good number of people; scattered low sofas separate the dining room a few feet away. It doesn't get wild, but it often feels like it could.

Map 1: 611 5th Ave., Gaslamp, 619/233-7327, www.searsucker.com;
Mon.-Thurs. 11:30am-2pm, 5pm-10pm, Fri. 11:30am-2pm, 5pm-11pm, Sat. 10am-2pm, 2:30pm-11pm, Sun. 10am-2pm, 2:30pm-10pm

Star Bar

In case the 6am opening time didn't clue you in, this is a dive—and it doesn't have much more going for it than that. If you start to feel detached from the Gaslamp scene, the stiff-drink, no-pretense baseness of Star Bar will snap you out of it. Cash only.

Map 1: 423 E St., Gaslamp, 619/234-5575; Daily 6am-2am

Tipsy Crow

Tipsy Crow knows it can't please all of the people all of the time, but with three levels and a wide variety of entertainment, it casts an incredibly wide net. The space combines comedy nights, live music, dancing, and chilled lounge vibes, sometimes all on the same night. Expect a mix of people from different walks of life occasionally bonding over drinks at one of the bars.

Map 1: 770 5th Ave., Gaslamp, 619/338-9300, www.thetipsycrow.com;
Mon.-Fri. 3pm-2am, Sat.-Sun. noon-2am

BREWERIES

Ballast Point Brewing

One of the city's most venerable brewers has opened this Little Italy tasting room and restaurant. Plenty of seating, including an outdoor patio, accompanies favorites like Sculpin IPA, Sculpin with habanero, and frequent experimental releases.

Map 1: 2215 India St., Little Italy, 619/255-7213, www.ballastpoint.com;
Mon.-Sat. 11am-11pm, Sun. 11am-9pm

Mission Brewery

Located across the parking lot from Petco Park, this former Wonder Bread factory dates to 1894 and provides a redbrick atmosphere for enjoying a sampling of Mission's brewed-on-site award-winning *hefeweizen* and ales before, after, or during games.

Map 1: 1441 L St., East Village, 858/544-0555, www.missionbrewery.com; Sun.-Thurs. noon-10pm, Fri.-Sat. noon-midnight, opens 2 hours before Padres home games

CLUBS

Float

The rooftop lounge at the Hard Rock Hotel finds any excuse to become a sexy open-air nightclub. During the day, lounge seating and poolside drinks set against the San Diego skyline couldn't feel cooler. Weekend nights and Sunday afternoons in the summer, world-famous DJ's turn the club inside

Legacy of the Stingaree

Between 1860 and 1880, San Diego gained a wharf and a rail connection to the rest of the United States, resulting in exponential population growth by land and sea. The newly formed Downtown expanded rapidly, and the area spreading out from the wharf up to Market Street (between 1st Ave. and 5th Ave.) began to take on a life of its own. Nicknamed the Stingaree, for the stingray-like "sting" a night out in the district provided, the area developed into a bawdy district rife with opium, gambling dens, more than 100 bars, and an estimated 120 brothels. The Stingaree drew comparisons to the San Francisco's Barbary Coast and New York's Bowery. When the 20th century began, it was a hotbed of debauchery, mischief, and crime.

With the completion of the Panama Canal in 1914, San Diego was set to become the first Western port for an onslaught of ships that would bring an even greater number of visitors west; some would attend the Panama-California Exposition at what eventually became Balboa Park. Its location near the wharf meant the Stingaree was the first thing visitors would see when entering San Diego Bay.

In 1912, city officials decided to crack down, raiding gambling houses and opium dens, and giving prostitutes a one-way ticket out of town. They also drafted more stringent health and safety codes, which led to the condemnation and demolition of more than 100 buildings that couldn't

meet the new standards. The Stingaree was flattened in an attempt to rid the nascent harbor town of its bad influences.

Unfortunately for San Diego's **Chinatown,** its borders overlapped with large sections of the Stingaree. Home to many immigrant laborers who came to build the railroads or work on developments in Coronado, the eight-square-block community got caught up both in the Stingaree's nighttime activities and its downfall. Buildings in Chinatown were hit especially hard by the new health codes. The impoverished inhabitants could not afford to rebuild, effectively dismantling the quarter to such a degree that many San Diegans today don't even know a Chinatown ever existed here.

While the Stingaree was gone, its vices were not. In the aftermath of the 1912 raids, drinking and prostitution actually increased, and spread to other parts of the city. The **Gaslamp** remained an unsavory place for decades; businesses were loath to build here because potential customers refused to cross south of Broadway. When the seminal Macy's department store came to San Diego in 1957, it passed up Downtown in favor of on a site in Mission Valley, cementing an urban flight that continued into the mid-1980s, when the revitalization of San Diego's Downtown was finally able to overcome the lasting legacy of its Stingaree.

out, with beautiful young people dancing four stories above the hustling Gaslamp scene. Look your best to get in; some days it can be difficult.

Map 1: 207 5th Ave., Gaslamp, 619/764-6924, www.hardrockhotelsd.com, Daily 11am-2pm

★ **Fluxx**

High concept decor, incredible sounding bands and DJs, bottle service, and go-go dancers are what you can look forward to after standing in line

clockwise from top left: Ballast Point Brewing in Little Italy; the Casbah in Little Italy; the sidewalks of the Gaslamp Quarter

at Fluxx. And most likely a lot of moneyed, beautiful people, dressed like they know it.

Map 1: 207 5th Ave., Gaslamp, 619/764-6924, www.hardrockhotelsd.com; Daily 11am-2am

F6ix

A big sound system gives this basement club some bass, with hip-hop on the decks to keep those bodies moving. A wraparound bar fronts the dance floor, but bottle service is the way to go if you're out to impress *before* showing off your moves.

Map 1: 526 F St., 619/238-0138, www.f6ixsd.com; Fri.-Sat. 9pm-2am

Moonshine Flats

Cheap beer, Jack Daniels, and line dancing: If that's what you look for in a night out, here you are. Jeans are acceptable, but are much better paired with a cowboy hat and a pair of boots. Music takes on a country tone; sometimes the place feels like a large barn with a disco ball.

Map 1: 344 7th Ave., East Village, 619/255-7625, www.moonshineflats.com; Thurs. 6pm-1:30am, Fri.-Sat. 8pm-2am

Sevilla Nightclub

This close to the border, you'd better believe there's a top-flight Latin music club, and *caliente* doesn't begin to describe it. By the time the late-night line has formed out front, you'll wish you had reserved a spot on the guest list.

Map 1: 353 5th Ave., 619/807-4481, www.sevillanightclub.com; Mon.-Thurs. 8pm-2am, Fri. 9:30pm-2am, Sat. 10pm-2am, Sun. 9:30pm-2am

Vin de Syrah

A *Through the Looking Glass* theme makes this basement nightclub a little more fun than the typical wine parlor its name suggests, beginning with a front door that's tricky to find. Be careful while you search for the handle—your image is being beamed via closed circuit to a TV screen inside, much to the amusement of those at the bar. Other head-trips await, along with late-night DJ sessions and plenty of wine, beer, and cocktails.

Map 1: 901 5th Ave., 619/234-4166, www.syrahwineparlor.com; Tues.-Wed. 4pm-midnight, Thurs.-Sat. 4pm-2am, Sun. 4pm-midnight

COCKTAIL LOUNGES

Altitude Sky Lounge

On the 22nd floor of the Marriot Gaslamp, the panoramic views of the city and harbor may almost distract you from the well-dressed clientele of this upscale bar. Not thoroughly impressed? Take your drink to the rooftop and take in one of the highest vantage points in the city.

Map 1: 660 K St., Gaslamp, 619/696-0234, www.sandiegogaslamphotel.com; Daily 5pm-1:30am

10N

NIGHTLIFE DOWNTOWN

El Dorado Cocktail Lounge

The wild nights of the Gaslamp don't appeal to everyone. For those looking to inch away from the Downtown crowds, this cowboy-style bar farther afield in East Village does the trick. Nightly DJs play different grooves—from soul to EDM and hip-hop. It's one of the later last calls in town, making it a worthy last stop any night.

Map 1: 1030 Broadway, East Village, 619/237-0550, www.eldoradobar.com; Fri. 5pm-2am, Sat.-Thurs. 7pm-2am

Prohibition

Speakeasy style keeps this small below-ground bar fashionable, with expertly made drinks you might have found back in the day (order dealer's choice and pay attention to how it's done). Dress appropriately (think dress pants and cocktail dresses; jeans and T-shirts won't fly here) and you should get past the doorman to enjoy the retro vibe and nightly jazz or blues performances.

Map 1: 548 5th Ave., 619/234-4166, www.prohibitionsd.com; Wed.-Thurs. 9pm-2am, Fri.-Sat. 7pm-2am

LIVE MUSIC
★ The Casbah

San Diego's indie rock scene has a clear epicenter, and it's the Casbah, which has brought the nation's best burgeoning talent to its intimate club stage for more than a quarter century. Some of the grayer rockers sipping drinks in the courtyard between sets might reminisce about before-they-were-big shows by Nirvana, No Doubt, or Arcade Fire. Meanwhile, young local and touring bands still know the Little Italy venue to be a vital a stop along the way to making it.

Map 1: 2501 Kettner Blvd., Little Italy, 619/232-4355, http://casbahmusic.com; Daily 8:30pm-2am

WINE BARS
★ Encore Champagne Bar

Whether or not you're feeling celebratory, take a moment to appreciate this pristinely well-designed wine bar that puts the focus on sparkling wine. Decorated like an upscale 1970s vision of how the future might be, it's tough not to feel sexy just walking in the door. Stop in during the two-for-one drink specials (Wed.-Sun. 4pm-7pm), and in a few sips you'll really start to feel high-class.

Map 1: 531 F St., Gaslamp, 619/255-5152, www.encoregaslamp.com; Mon.-Thurs. 4pm-1:30am, Fri.-Sun. 10:30am-1:30am

San Diego Cellars

Producing wines using grapes from Napa Valley, California's central coast, and right here in San Diego County, this Little Italy wine maker may change

Urban Wineries

San Diego's craft beer scene has been well documented, but in the past few years a different sort of craft beverage has been gaining steam. Urban wineries don't grow their own grapes, obviously. Due to geography, San Diego's urban wineries typically truck them in from central and northern California, from terrifically productive regions like Santa Barbara County and Napa Valley, and occasionally local growers. In some ways this can be an advantage: a single urban winemaker may source fruit from multiple vineyards, turning out a more diverse roster of reds and whites. The winemaker ferments and crushes the berries, and barrel-ages them here in town. After a couple of years, they're tapped or bottled for service in local tasting rooms.

The long, slow process may keep the growth of urban wineries in check for a few more years as the processes refines, but a few have been underway long enough to produce some fantastic wines: **San Diego Cellars** (2215 Kettner Blvd., 619/269-9463, www.sdcellars.com; Tues.-Fri. 3pm-10pm, Sat. noon-11-pm, Sun. noon-10pm) in Little Italy; **Blue Door Urban Winery** (4060 Morena Blvd., 858/274-4292, www.thebluedoor-winery.com; Tues.-Fri. 3pm-8pm, Sat. noon-8pm, Sun. noon-4pm) in Clairemont, just off the I-5 freeway; and **Carruth Cellars** (320 S. Cedros Ave., Suite 400) in Solana Beach.

your perception of how good wine is made, with a central urban location, a patio, and occasional music and food-pairing events.

Map 1: 2215 Kettner Blvd., Little Italy, 619/269-9463, www.sdcellars.com; Tues.-Fri. 3pm-10pm, Sat. noon-11-pm, Sun. noon-10pm

Balboa Park   Map 2

LIVE MUSIC

Croce's Park West

Jim Croce's memory lives on thanks to his wife, who owns this restaurant, bar, and music venue. Jazz and singer-songwriters are featured most nights in the restaurant's intimate Expatriate Room.

Map 2: 2760 5th Ave., 619/233-4355, www.crocesparkwest.com; Sun.-Thurs. 11am-10pm, Fri.-Sat. 11am-midnight

The Tin Can

Featuring cocktails and a healthy list of beer sold in cans, this for-musicians by-musicians rock and country club takes up little space at the south end of Banker's Hill, but it makes a big contribution to local music.

Map 2: 1863 5th Ave., 619/955-8525, http://thetincan1.wordpress.com; Mon.-Fri. 11am-2am, Sat. 1pm-2am

BARS

Coin-Op

If given the choice between a well-stocked bar and a well-stocked bar with vintage arcade games, which would you choose? For games, there's only one choice—North Park's Coin-Op. Along with the nostalgic stand-up video game kiosks and pinball machines, there's a legit tap list and cocktails to spare.

Map 3: 3926 30th St., North Park, 619/255-8523, www.coinopsd.com; Mon.-Fri. 4pm-1am, Sat.-Sun. 11:30pm-1am

★ Seven Grand

Somewhere between hunting lodge and jazz club, the main attraction here is whiskey—bourbon, scotch, rye, and Irish. With hunting trophies on walls of plaid wallpaper, the idea that there's a jazz stage in the back seems incongruous, but crowds keep coming back for both the music and the booze. A deep menu features single malts and single casks along with blends, oak barrel-aged, and reserves. Order a favorite right away, because you're going to be reading that menu for a while before deciding on your second.

Map 3: 3054 University Ave., North Park, 619/269-8820, www.sevengrandbars.com; Mon.-Sat. 5pm-2am, Sun. 8pm-2am

BREWERIES

Blind Lady Alehouse

Just sticking to its own label (Automatic Brewing), Blind Lady could sell a decent amount of beer. But most of its 26 taps feature a well-selected variety of international and craft beers. While it's easy enough to say there's something here for everybody, it might be truer to add that there's a beer here to challenge everybody's sense of what kind of beer they like. Order your kids a little pizza to keep them happy while you order a pitcher.

Map 3: 3416 Adams Ave., 619/255-2491, www.blindladyalehouse.com; Daily 11:30am-midnight

★ Hamilton's Tavern

Arguably the best tap house in a town filled with great tap houses, Hamilton's 28 handles and a pair of cask engines bring in pretty much every local craft beer worth drinking, and rotate in top finds from out of town as well. Monthly events feature specific favorites of Hamilton's owners, who also operate a couple of other bars and craft breweries nearby.

Map 3: 1521 30th St., North Park, 619/238-5460, www.hamiltonstavern.com; Mon.-Fri. 3pm-2am, Sat.-Sun. 1pm-2am

Mike Hess Brewing

When in North Park, drop by this large family- and dog-friendly space. There's usually a food truck parked in the loading dock, and a mind-blowing selection of barely remembered vintage board games to play over tasty beers brewed in the large shiny tanks visible downstairs.

Map 3: 3812 Grim Ave., North Park, 619/255-7136, www.mikehessbrewing.com; Sun.-Thurs. noon-10pm, Fri.-Sat. noon-midnight

Modern Times

One of the newer craft breweries to gather a following over the past couple years, Modern Times operates a couple of smartly decorated tasting rooms, including this North Park space, highlighted by a mural of floppy discs and a ceiling made from old lampshades. Style and location wins bonus points, but the tasty beer selection is still the best reason to visit.

Map 3: 1521 30th St., North Park, 619/238-5460, www.moderntimesbeer.com; Mon.-Fri. 3pm-2am, Sat.-Sun. 1pm-2am

Toronado

Toronado is the rare San Diego bar that claims a focus on Belgian ales, but in truth its tap list is just as loaded with San Diego's best. Communal tables and patio seating give patrons the chance to compare and contrast, resulting in one heck of a social place to drink and obsess over everybody's favorite brew.

Map 3: 4026 30th St., North Park, 619/282-0456, www.toronadosd.com; Sun.-Wed. 11:30am-midnight, Thurs.-Sat. 11:30am-2am

COCKTAIL LOUNGES

★ Polite Provisions

Between the skylights and the open windows, this may be the brightest daytime cocktail lounge you'll encounter short of being outdoors, which is another option. The marble and polished brass interior gleams—as does the unique floor layered with shiny nickels. Whatever time of day you visit, the beautiful bar space serves up an extensive list of delicious cocktails to some of the most style-savvy locals.

Map 3: 4696 30th St., 619/677-3784, www.politeprovisions.com; Daily 11:30am-2am

GAY AND LESBIAN

Baja Betty's

From mimosas to margaritas to shots, Betty's has the drinks to match every time of day. This popular gathering spot's impeccable Mexican decor and tequila cocktails make for raucous brunches and happy hours, with build-your-own nacho platters available until the kitchen closes at 11pm, just in case you drank through dinner.

Map 3: 1421 University Ave., 619/269-8510, www.bajabettyssd.com; Mon.-Fri. 11am-1am, Sat.-Sun. 10am-1am

Bourbon Street Bar & Grill

This "never a cover" New Orleans-style piano bar and courtyard hosts theme nights, some dedicated to boys, some to girls, and most for whoever feels like a party. You might find DJs, live music, karaoke, or stand-up comedy, and you'll almost certainly find a lively and engaged crowd.

Map 3: 4612 Park Blvd., 619/291-0173, www.bourbonstreetsd.com; Tues.-Wed. 7pm-2am, Thurs.-Sat. 5pm-2am, Sun. 11am-2am

Brass Rail

If drinking and dancing makes a good formula for a gay bar, consider Brass Rail a rousing success. Theme nights set the mood, with an '80s night on Monday and Latin vibes on Saturday, and everything from hip-hop to a night simply known as "Muscle" in between.

Map 3: 1220 University Ave., 619/298-2233, www.thebrassrailsd.com; Mon. 9am-2am, Thurs.-Sat. 2pm-2am, Sun. 10am-2am

Gossip Grill

The irreverent "home of the two-finger pour," this Hillcrest's women's bar boasts cocktail names among the most poetically bawdy in all of Southern California. It's a lounge and patio space where simply ordering a round of drinks sets the tone.

Map 3: 1220 University Ave., 619/260-8023, www.thegossipgrill.com; Mon.-Fri. 11am-2am, Sat.-Sun. 10am-2am

Hillcrest Brewing Company

Billing itself as "The first gay brewery in the world," this cheeky local brewer serves up suds with names like Banana Hammock scotch ale and an award-winning red ale called Crotch Rocket. Up to 15 guest beers from around San Diego round out the tap list.

Map 3: 1458 University Ave., 619/269-4323, www.hillcrestbrewingcompany.com; Mon.-Fri. 4pm-midnight, Sat. noon-midnight, Sun. 9am-11pm

Lips

Where in San Diego can you find a gender-bending Cher impersonator lip-synching in an outlandish outfit? At Lips, the raunchy and playful drag shows cover any number of celebrity divas, and performers are far from shy about including audience members in their songs. It's a popular spot for bachelorette and birthday parties, with dinner shows most nights as well as a Sunday brunch.

Map 3: 3036 El Cajon Blvd., 619/295-7900, www.lipssd.com; Tues.-Thurs. 7pm-10pm, Fri.-Sat. 6pm-midnight, Sun. 11am-3pm, 7pm-10pm

Urban Mo's

Mo's claims to be the "Best Gay Bar in San Diego," if not the world. The only way to find out for sure is to drop in on its burger-loving patio and find out. Chances are you're going to meet people in the process, drink another couple of rounds, and find yourself declaring something the best of somewhere before the night ends.

Map 3: 308 University Ave., Hillcrest, 619/491-0400, www.urbanmos.com; Daily 9am-1:30am

LIVE MUSIC
Lestat's West

A local stop on the touring singer-songwriter circuit, this intimate venue, affiliated with the 24-hour Lestat's coffeehouse next door, stages mostly acoustic, lyric-driven music, including modest stars of the genre. A long-running open-mike night on Monday gives local troubadours a chance to practice their craft.

Map 3: 3343 Adams Ave., 619/282-0437, www.lestats.com; showtimes vary

WINE BARS
Splash Wine Bar

Anyone who's ever wished they could try a few different wines before deciding on a glass or bottle should like the idea behind this wine bar in North Park. Here a high-tech pouring system allows you to taste and pay for your choice of 72 wines by the ounce. You can try one ounce at a time all night and sample as many as you can handle, or discover one you love and linger with a glass or bottle of your favorite.

Map 3: 3043 University Ave., North Park, 619/296-0714, www.asplashofwine.com; Mon.-Thurs. 4pm-11pm, Fri.-Sat. noon-1am, Sun. noon-10pm

Old Town and Mission Hills Map 4

BARS
★ El Agave

More than 2,000 *blanco, reposado,* and *añejo* bottles line the walls, giving this "Tequila Museum" a decorative leg up. While there's no way you can ever try them all, going with the *catador*'s choice will show you why this agave liquor is meant for sips, not shots. When in doubt, the house brand ain't bad.

Map 4: 2304 San Diego Ave., 619/220-0692, www.elagave.com; Daily 11am-10pm

The Patio on Goldfinch

The beautifully verdant "living wall" decor of this Mission Hills restaurant attracts diners all day long, but anyone who skips the tequila selection is missing out. Alternate between sips of tequila and the fruity, spicy, house *sangrita* and you'll never want to drink it any other way. The open patio restaurant also offers a lengthy list of barrel-aged cocktails worth delving into.

Map 4: 4020 Goldfinch St., Mission Hills, 619/501-5090, www.thepatioongoldfinch.com; Daily 8am-midnight

British pubs are really a global phenomenon. A San Diego favorite is this lower Mission Hills establishment, which serves traditional pub food, classic British ales, and footy on the telly, of course.

Map 4: 3701 India St., Mission Hills, 619/299-0230, www.shakespearepub.com; Mon.-Thurs. 10:30am-midnight, Fri. 10:30am-1am, Sat. 8am-1am, Sun. 8am-midnight

WINE BARS
57 Degrees

This is one of the larger wine bars in town, with high ceilings, an art gallery, a full-service bar, and a view of the skyline . . . and the back side of the airport. Okay, the view's not stellar, but the well-lit airiness of the place makes it a nice spot for drinks after a day at Old Town. And when Downtown lights up at night, the views improve.

Map 4: 1735 Hancock St., 619/234-5757, www.fiftysevendegrees.com; Mon.-Sat. 11am-10pm, Sun. 10am-6pm

Mission Bay and Beaches   Map 5

BARS
Avenue

Avenue offers a range of themed weeknights to attract young men and women who like to party. Karaoke Mondays, University Night Tuesdays, and Trivia Wednesdays end the same way, with DJs spinning popular music to encourage a little bumping and grinding on the dance floor. Lodge decor means wood panels and mounted buffalo heads, but when the flashing lights turn on, the only thing you'll look at is each other.

Map 5: 1060 Garnet Ave., Pacific Beach, 858/263-4514, www.thewoodgroupsd.com; Mon.-Fri. 5pm-2am, Sat. 4pm-2am, Sun. 9am-2am

Pacific Beach Bar & Grill

The de-facto center of PB nightlife, the Pacific Beach Bar & Grill features foosball, shuffleboard, pool tables—and a Breathalyzer test ($2). Sports is on most of the big screens during the day. At night, the huge outdoor space is where people mix and mingle in droves. Music changes nightly, but never strays far from popular tunes known to get booties shaking.

Map 5: 860 Garnet Ave., Pacific Beach, 858/483-9227, www.pbbarandgrill.com; Daily 11am-2pm

BREWERIES
Amplified Ale Works

This brewery, taphouse, and kebab restaurant doesn't stand out from the street or the beach, but when you find it on the second floor of its PB strip mall, you'll be grateful you did. Drink the house beer, eat some döner, or simply grab some sun with an ocean view on the killer west-facing deck, which is alone reason enough to visit.

Map 5: 4150 Mission Blvd. #208, Pacific Beach, 858/270-5222, www.amplifiedales.com; Sun.-Wed. 11am-11pm, Thurs.-Sat. 11am-midnight,

Draft

Since a ban on drinking at city beaches went into effect a few years back, this Mission Beach spot might be the best place to imbibe a craft beer while enjoying the sun, surf, and sand. Located right on the boardwalk, the outdoor seating promotes people-watching while sipping a local brew. When done, simply reapply your sunscreen and head to the beach, only a few steps away.

Map 5: 3105 Ocean Front Walk, Mission Beach, 858/228-9305, www.belmontpark.com; Mon.-Fri. 11am-2am, Sat.-Sun. 9am-2am

SD TapRoom

If you find yourself on Garnet Avenue longing for an education on local beer, drop into the SD TapRoom, which devotes a number of taps to each of San Diego's best and best-loved brewers. A solid rotating roster rounds out the whopping 45 choices on hand daily.

Map 5: 1269 Garnet Ave., Pacific Beach, 858/274-1010, www.sdtaproom.com; Sun.-Thurs. 11am-midnight, Fri.-Sat. 11am-1am

COCKTAIL LOUNGES

JRDN

With all the rowdy beachfront drinking that takes place on the boardwalk, JRDN (pronounced Jordan) proves the clear choice for those seeking a classier Pacific Beach experience. Hotel bar to the swanky boutique hotel Tower 23, you might be inclined to think the place was some sort of Michael Jordan devotional, but the basketball player's name and number is just a coincidence. Marvel at the view and sip something delicious—you'll look great doing so.

Map 5: 723 Felspar St., Pacific Beach, 858/270-5736, www.t23hotel.com; Mon.-Fri. 9am-9pm, Sat.-Sun. 9am-11pm

LIVE MUSIC

Dizzy's

Some of San Diego's top jazz shows happen within spitting distance of Mission Bay, perhaps fittingly in a Jet Ski showroom. As unusual as this sounds, there's nothing frivolous about the performances, which bring in internationally respected talent covering a wide range of styles. Tickets are not available in advance; check the website calendar and choose a show that piques your interest.

Map 5: 4275 Mission Bay Dr., 858/270-7467, www.dizzysjazz.com

Ocean Beach and Point Loma

Map 6

BARS

Sunshine Company

The rooftop deck of the 'Shine hosts the most energetic happy hour in OB, and the vast space downstairs does a good job keeping up with the crowds. On weekend nights, the place fills with locals of every stripe—surfers, military folk, college kids, and anyone with a deep tan to show off.

Map 6: 5028 Newport Ave., Ocean Beach, 619/222-0722, www.sunshinecompanyoceanbeach.com; Mon.-Fri. 11am-2am, Sat.-Sun. 10am-2am

BREWERIES

Pizza Port OB

Part brewing company, tap house, and pizza spot, this local brewpub's proximity to the beach makes it ideal for post-sunset suds. House beers run the gamut from interesting to fantastic, and there are always a number of handles devoted to terrific craft-brewing friends and collaborators.

Map 6: 1956 Bacon St., Ocean Beach, 619/224-4700, www.pizzaport.com; Sun.-Thurs. 11am-10pm, Fri.-Sat. 11am-midnight

★ Stone World Bistro & Gardens Liberty Station

Stone reigns as the biggest and most successful craft brewer in town. This 40,000-square-foot organic, farm-to-table restaurant offers 40 taps of Stone special releases, collaborations, and dozens of handpicked guest beers. Relax on the massive outdoor patio and enjoy a bocce ball game with your beer.

Map 6: 2816 Historic Decatur Rd., Suite 116, Point Loma, 619/269-2100, www.stonelibertystation.com; Mon.-Sat. 11:30am-10pm, Sun. 11am-9pm

COCKTAIL LOUNGES

Pacific Shores

No one seems to remember the last time they went to Pac Shores, but everybody kind of remembers the first. Strong, cheap cocktails are served in a decades-old setting of black-lit mermaid and sea creature carvings that are vintage OB.

Map 6: 4927 Newport Ave., Ocean Beach, 619/223-7549, www.pacshoresob.com; Daily 10am-2am

LIVE MUSIC

Winston's Beach Club

OB's live music mainstay, Winston's caters to the tastes of the neighborhood's laid-back inhabitants, usually offering lineups of reggae, funk, a

Kid-Friendly Places for Beer Lovers

Draft taphouse on Mission Beach

Children don't care that San Diego is a beer mecca, but mom and dad might. Take heart, there are some places the kids can enjoy while mom or dad sneak in a pint.

- **Blind Lady Alehouse** (3416 Adams Ave., 619/255-2491, www.blindladyalehouse.com; Daily 11:30am-midnight): If the kids love pizza, order a simple pie and enjoy the friendly atmosphere and 26 beer on tap.

- **Draft** (3105 Ocean Front Walk, Mission Beach, 858/228-9305, www.belmontpark.com; Mon.-Fri. 11am-2am, Sat.-Sun. 9am-2am): If you're visiting Belmont Park at Mission Beach, grab a seat on or near the patio and order something from the kid's menu while you explore the nearly 70 beers on tap.

- **Mike Hess Brewing** (3812 Grim Ave., 619/255-7136, www.mikehess-brewing.com; Sun.-Thurs. noon-10pm, Fri.-Sat. noon-midnight): North Park locals dig this pet- and child-friendly place, which supplies board games and some refreshing made-on-site suds.

- **Stone World Bistro & Gardens** (2816 Historic Decatur Rd., Suite 116, Point Loma; 1999 Citracado Pkwy., Escondido, 619/269-2100, www.stonelibertystation.com; Mon.-Sat. 11:30am-10pm, Sun. 11am-9pm): You'll find kid-friendly menus and plenty of outdoor space to enjoy at either location.

little bit of crusty rock, and a Grateful Dead cover band Monday nights. Happy hour entertainment often includes comedy, karaoke, and a glimpse of local color bellying up to the bar.

Map 6: 1921 Bacon St., Ocean Beach, 619/222-6822, www.winstonsob.com; Daily 1pm-2am

clockwise from top to bottom: the rainbow flag flies over Hillcrest; Pizza Port in OB; Ocean Beach sunset

WINE BARS
Third Corner

An island of elevated tastes in OB's oasis of grungy charm, this is the sort of wine bar where board shorts go well with a chardonnay. Increasingly higher rents in the neighborhood have gentrified it somewhat, but this place has captured the increased demand for quality drinks with a lovely bottle selection.

Map 6: 2265 Bacon St., Ocean Beach, 619/223-2700, www.the3rdcorner.com; Sun.-Thurs. 11am-10pm, Fri.-Sat. 11am-midnight

La Jolla
Map 7

BARS
Barfly

La Jolla's most central bar attracts a diverse lot—visitors, happy-hour celebrants, and at night, young adults in search of bottle service and dancing as the DJs start up and the club kicks in. Drinking on the patio is definitely the way to go when the weather is right.

Map 7: 909 Prospect St., Suite 100, 858/454-2323, www.barflylajolla.com; Mon.-Fri. 5pm-2am, Sat. 10am-2am, Sun. 10am-9pm

Eddie V's

The upstairs bar of this seafood restaurant offers one of the most scenic drinking venues in town. While nightly jazz performances play, sip drinks overlooking the La Jolla Caves with a view of the shores beyond.

Map 7: 1270 Prospect St., 858/459-5500, www.eddiev.com; Sun.-Thurs. 4pm-11pm, Fri.-Sat. 4pm-midnight

BREWERIES
Karl Strauss Brewing Company

The original San Diego craft brewery has offered beer through its restaurants for more than 25 years. This La Jolla outpost is a great place to slake your thirst with their new pours, seasonal drafts, and signature brews like Red Trolley Ale and Tower 10 IPA. They taste just as good Downtown (1157 Columbia St.).

Map 7: 1044 Wall St., 858/551-2739, www.karlstrauss.com; Daily 11am-10pm

COCKTAIL LOUNGES
Cusp Dining and Drinks

It's all about the sunsets at this 11th floor hotel bar and restaurant. A stellar cocktail list accompanies the view in the slick dining room; the bartender breaks out the champagne to celebrate when pinks, purples, and neon oranges fill the western sky. Enjoy a few drinks at the swank contemporary bar, and seriously consider sticking around for dinner.

Map 7: 7955 La Jolla Shores Dr., 858/551-3620, www.cusprestaurant.com; Sun.-Thurs. 5pm-10pm, Fri.-Sat. 5pm-11pm

Herringbone

Herringbone is a seafood spot offering a great cocktail environment. The greatest reason to drink here is the beautiful interior design: olive trees are planted throughout the high-ceilinged, hangar-like space, softly lit by Edison bulbs. The $1 oyster happy hour doesn't hurt either.

Map 7: 7837 Herschel Ave., 858/459-0221, www.herringboneeats.com; Mon.-Thurs. 11:30am-2pm and 5pm-10pm, Fri. 11:30am-2pm and 5pm-11pm, Sat. 10am-2pm and 5pm-11pm, Sun. 10am-2pm and 5pm-10pm

COMEDY

Comedy Store

Friday and Saturday nights offer an opportunity to see some of the top touring comics pass through La Jolla, with the occasional legend popping up. The rest of the week, watch some of the best local comedians fine-tune their craft on the big stage.

Map 7: 916 Pearl St., 858/454-9176, www.lajolla.thecomedystore.com

Coronado   Map 8

COCKTAIL LOUNGES

Sunset Bar at Hotel del Coronado

San Diego's most famous hotel might be thrilling enough to warrant perusing the cocktail list at the Sunset Bar, but its beachfront locale should not be dismissed. Bottom line: You get to drink at the beach. Cocktail service is provided to those who rent lounge chairs. In winter, an ice-skating rink dominates the view.

Map 8: 1500 Orange Ave., 619/435-6611, www.hoteldel.com; Mon.-Fri. 4pm-11pm, Sat.-Sun. 2pm-11pm

Greater San Diego   Map 9

BREWERIES

★ AleSmith Brewing Company

To many, AleSmith isn't just the best brewery in San Diego—it ranks among the best on the planet. After nearly two decades, the small but prolific company recently expanded its operations, moving into a new building

Best Happy Hours

Olive trees grow near the bar at Herringbone.

You could wait until dark to enjoy a drink at some of San Diego's best bars and restaurants, but why miss out? You'll find great drink and snack specials to go with amazing views and supremely cool atmospheres.

Located within a sculpture garden at Balboa Park, Panama 66 (1549 El Prado, 619/557-9441, www.panama66.blogspot.com; Mon. 11:30am-3pm, Tues.-Thurs. 11:30am-10pm, Fri. 11:30am-11pm, Sat. 11am-11pm, Sun. 11am-10pm) offers the ideal way to wind down from a day of culture seeking.

OB's Wonderland Ocean Pub (5083 Santa Monica Ave., Ocean Beach, 619/255-3358, www.wonderlandob.com; Mon.-Fri. 11am-close, Sat.-Sun. 9am-close) overlooks the beach, serving food and drinks in front of what usually turns out to be a gorgeous sunset.

Sunsets at the swank Cusp Dining and Drinks (7955 La Jolla Shores Dr., 858/551-3620, www.cusprestaurant.com; Mon.-Thurs. 7am-10:30am and 5pm-9pm, Fri. 7am-10:30am and 5pm-10pm, Sat. 8am-2pm and 5pm-10pm, Sun. 8am-2pm and 5pm-9pm) in La Jolla come

with complimentary champagne and an 11th floor picture window to enjoy them by, and on the giant patio of Harbor Island's C Level (880 Harbor Island Dr., 619/298-6802, www.cohnrestaurants.com/islandprime; Daily 11am-close), you'll have a front row seat to see their colors echo off the San Diego Skyline.

If you've seen enough of the ocean, La Jolla's Herringbone serves up top-notch cocktails and a variety of one-dollar happy-hour oysters within their dreamy dining room, while sister restaurant Searsucker (611 5th Ave., Gaslamp, 619/233-7327, www.searsucker.com; Mon.-Thurs. 11:30am-2pm, 5pm-10pm, Fri. 11:30am-2pm, 5pm-11pm, Sat. 10am-2pm, 2:30pm-11pm, Sun. 10am-2pm, 2:30pm-10pm) serves similar drinks with succulent small plates in the Gaslamp.

And if you're really hungry, you can never go wrong with one of the city's best pies at URBN Pizza (3085 University Ave., 619/255-7300, www.urbnnorthpark.com; Sun.-Mon. noon-10pm, Tues.-Thurs. noon-midnight, Fri.-Sat. noon-2am), where happy hour specials include a free large pizza with a pitcher of craft beer.

and vastly increasing brewing capacity, making this a truly exciting time to taste their next potential award winner.

Map 9: 9990 Empire St., Miramar, 858/549-9888, www.alesmith.com; Mon.-Fri. noon-9pm, Sat. 11am-9pm, Sun. 11am-6pm

Green Flash Brewing Company

An indispensable stop on San Diego's craft beer tour, Green Flash's open warehouse space is nice, but its drinking patio is nicer. Though surrounded by industrial park, the sunny patio is bolstered by the presence of daily food trucks and stellar Green Flash beer, as well as occasional kegs from nearby colleagues. Alpine Beer Co. Tours ($5) of the brewery are available daily.

Map 9: 6550 Mira Mesa Blvd., Mira Mesa, 858/622-0085, www.greenflashbrew.com; Tues.-Thurs. 3pm-9pm, Fri. 3pm-10pm, Sat. noon-9pm, Sun. noon-6pm

★ Societe Brewing Company

A couple of California's best up-and-coming craft brewers teamed up and moved to San Diego to join our flourishing beer scene—and just like that our beer scene got even better. Societe's roster of American- and European-style ales runs deep and delicious. This is a must-stop for beer lovers with a long afternoon and an unquenchable thirst who enjoy drinking in the shadow of brewing tanks.

Map 9: 8262 Clairemont Mesa Blvd., Clairemont Mesa, 858/598-5409, www.societebrewing.com; Mon.-Wed. noon-9pm, Thurs-Sat. noon-10pm, Sun. noon-8pm

WINERIES

Blue Door Urban Winery

Procuring premium berries from Santa Barbara County and select local vineyards, this small winery and tasting room barrels a number of different wines each year. The fruits of their labor are starting to show, with tasty reds that can't keep up with demand. Show up on a summer day and watch as they press fermented grapes in the back of their wood-trimmed industrial warehouse space, a truly illuminating experience.

Map 9: 4060 Morena Blvd., 858/274-4292, www.thebluedoorwinery.com; Tues.-Fri. 3pm-8pm, Sat. noon-8pm, Sun. noon-4pm

Arts and Culture

Highlights

★ **Most Underrated Museum:** Most locals even admit they've never been to the **Mingei International Museum,** despite its central Balboa Park location. Its focus on the handmade is captivating (page 124).

★ **Best Place to See a Play:** Pretty much the best place to do anything here is outside, and the outdoor venue at **Old Globe Theatre** stages terrific productions of Shakespeare each summer (page 125).

★ **Best Concert Venue:** You get to see the sunset over a yacht-filled marina followed by a stellar show at **Humphrey's Concerts by the Bay.** It's tough to do better (page 130).

★ **If You Only Go to One Art Gallery:** Proof that you don't need to leave the coastline to find artistic relevance, **Madison Gallery** offers a rich variety of art within view of the beach (page 130).

★ **Best Sculpture Collection:** More than just an excuse to explore the UCSD campus, many of the sculptures in the **Stuart Collection** up the ante on experiential art (page 131).

★ **Most Likely to Spawn a Broadway Run:** A number of successful shows have premiered at **La Jolla Playhouse** before heading to New York—and there will be more (page 131).

★ **Must-See Murals:** A valuable bit of history unfolds with the murals at **Chicano Park,** a rich tapestry of socially relevant artwork presented in a context no museum could match (page 133).

San Diego's well-known image as a sun-drenched surfer's paradise may not merit comparison to major cultural offerings in other cities, but it may surprise you.

The theater scene is not only one of high quality, but it is also one of the most productive in the country, routinely assembling world-class productions and inspiring the curiosity and respect of out-of-towners and local alike.

While endeavors in other artistic areas might not have the same prestige, San Diego is a surprisingly intellectual town once the craft beer bottles and surfboards are put away. There are always a number of interesting things brewing under the surface—outdoor cinemas under the stars, the historical and cultural museums of Balboa Park, and an intense gallery scene in La Jolla. It's tough to balance sunshine, coastline, beer, and culture, yet somehow San Diego manages.

Previous page top: the Junípero Serra Museum **bottom:** Old Globe Theatre

CINEMA

Gaslamp Stadium

With plenty of first- and second-run movies to choose from, this central Gaslamp multiplex has a great location, provided you don't need a parking spot. On rainy days, it's a boon to the neighborhood. Otherwise, its biggest moment comes in October when it hosts screenings for the San Diego Film Festival.

Map 1: 701 5th Ave., Gaslamp, 619/232-0401, www.readingcinemasus.com

GALLERIES

Celebration Fine Art Gallery

Living artists are the focus of this densely packed gallery space located just off the lobby of the U. S. Grant Hotel. At any given time, several distinct styles may be found—from traditionalist to contemporary. Though rarely edgy, these globally sourced paintings prefer a different mode of expression: mastery of technique over flashy subject matter.

Map 1: 326 Broadway, Gaslamp, 619/238-9111, www.celebrationfineart.com;
Mon.-Thurs. noon-7pm, Fri.-Sat. 11am-3pm and 6pm-9pm

Chuck Jones Gallery

A Wile E. Coyote statue greets you at the entrance to this gallery, which celebrates *Looney Tunes* creator Chuck Jones as both an artist and inspiration. A Pepé Le Pew charcoal sketch may not be everyone's idea of fine art, but a number of interesting pieces exhibit Jones's fanciful vision, making for the rare art gallery an entire family may enjoy.

Map 1: 232 5th Ave., Gaslamp, 619/294-9880, www.chuckjones.com;
Mon.-Wed. 10am-7pm, Thurs.-Sat. 10am-8pm, Sun. 11am-6pm

Exclusive Collections

A small but talented group of active West Coast artists are featured within this gallery, which focuses on a strong use of color in pieces alluding to past masters, or channeling unique and fantastic visions. A slow walk through the small space is encouraged.

Map 1: 568 5th Ave., Gaslamp, 619/232-1930, www.ecgallery.com; Mon.-Sat. 10am-9pm, Sun. noon-8pm

Michael J. Wolf Fine Arts

Embracing both contemporary and pop-art movements, many of the pieces in this Gaslamp gallery may border on kitsch. But the range of art on offer doesn't overly rely on conceptual oddities and includes some legitimately stunning pieces by artists with the technical virtuosity to back up their forays into commercial appeal.

MUSEUMS

Gaslamp Museum at the William Heath Davis House

The oldest wooden building Downtown now serves as monument to the efforts of William Heath Davis, who first had the idea to settle San Diego around the bay. While his efforts failed, the idea obviously panned out. Davis's former home was originally shipped from Maine to San Diego in 1850. Walking tours originate from the house to explore the many historic buildings that subsequently sprung up in the Gaslamp—the real perk of a visit here. The **tour** ($15) starts 11am on Saturday and lasts two hours.

Map 1: 410 Island Ave., Gaslamp, 619/233-4692, www.gaslampquarter.org;
Tues.-Sat. 10am-5pm, Sun. noon-4pm; $5 adults, $4 seniors, students, and military

Museum of Contemporary Art San Diego

This Downtown branch of the Museum of Contemporary Art San Diego (MCASD) features rotating exhibitions highlighting engaging artists, groups, and collections. Everything form street art to large installations fills the high ceilings of its two adjoining spaces. Admission includes entrance to the branch in La Jolla (700 Prospect St.).

Map 1: 1100 and 1001 Kettner Blvd., 858/454-3541, www.mcasd.org; Fri.-Tues. 11am-5pm,
Thurs. 11am-7pm; $10 adults, $5 seniors and students over age 26, free for students under
age 26 and military

San Diego Chinese Historical Museum

Housed in a historic 1927 building, this museum preserves and documents Chinese culture and history, particularly local history. The old Chinese Mission building itself is symbolic, as it was saved from demolition in order to establish this museum, and moved several blocks to its current location. Inside are imported Chinese artifacts, like a 19th-century bridal carriage, plus photos and relics documenting the short-lived existence of San Diego's Chinatown. The museum hosts temporary exhibitions of Chinese and Chinese American art at its annex buildings, the **Dr. Sun Yat-Sen Memorial** Extension (328 J St.) and the **Chuang Archive and Learning Center** (541B 2nd St.).

Map 1: 328 J St., 619/338-9888, www.sdchm.org; Tues.-Sat. 10am-4pm, Sun. noon-4pm;
$2 adults

PERFORMING ARTS

Balboa Theatre

This historic 1924 Vaudeville and movie palace sat empty for decades before being faithfully restored and reborn as a state-of-the-art music and comedy venue. Its Southwestern appeal and Gaslamp location provides a great setting for some good shows.

Map 1: 868 4th Ave., Gaslamp, 619/570-1100, www.sandiegotheatres.org

ARTS AND CULTURE
DOWNTOWN

Copley Symphony Hall

Also known as the Jacobs Music Center, this home of the **San Diego Symphony** also brings in touring philharmonics and ballet companies. The 1929 building's exterior may not impress, but walk through the doors and the architectural splendor inside will take your breath away.

Map 1: 1245 7th Ave., 619/235-0800, www.sandiegosymphony.org

Horton Grand Theatre

This intimate 250-seat Gaslamp venue stages entertaining shows with a modest price tag. The red-velvet stage hosts the popular **Lamb's Theatre Company** and features local talent. They say there's not a bad seat in the house.

Map 1: 444 4th Ave., Gaslamp, 619/437-6000, www.lambsplayers.org

Lyceum Theatre

Built as part of Horton Plaza shopping center in the mid-1980s, the Lyceum hosts the **San Diego Repertory Theatre,** whose shows often include social, political, countercultural, and other diverse materials. The two intimate stages include local premieres of edgy sensations and classic plays reimagined in different contexts. Recent shows have included *The Who's Tommy* and the dark comedy *Walter Cronkite Is Dead*.

Map 1: 79 Broadway Circle, Gaslamp, 619/544-1000, www.lyceumevents.org

San Diego Civic Theatre

The largest theater in town, both in terms of capacity and scope, the 3,000-seat Civic Theatre might bring a Broadway touring company or stage a large production of the San Diego Ballet. If it's playing here, it's worth seeing.

Map 1: 1100 3rd Ave., 619/570-1100, www.sandiegotheatres.org

Spreckels Theatre

For more than 100 years this onetime Vaudeville venue has seen every manner of cultural performance, ranging from dance companies and rock bands to the Chinese Circus. The beautifully kept space offers terrific lines of sight and acoustics, with plenty of Gaslamp restaurants and bars nearby to make a night of it.

Map 1: 121 Broadway, Suite 600, Gaslamp, 619/235-9500, www.spreckels.net

clockwise from top left: Spreckels Theatre, Downtown; Marston House Museum & Gardens in Balboa Park; the Spreckels Organ Pavilion in Balboa Park

MUSEUMS

Marston House Museum & Gardens

An excellent example of the arts and crafts movement, the Marston House was built in 1905 and belonged to San Diego's "First Citizen," George Marston. The retailer and philanthropist was integral to the inception of Balboa Park, and his magnificent home overlooks its northwest corner. A tour reveals myriad ingenious details added by architects William Hebbard and Irving Gill, including specialized built-in cabinetry and a turn-of-the-20th-century precursor to an intercom system. Tours of the garden are also available.

Map 2: 3525 7th Ave., 619/297-9327, www.sohosandiego.org; tours hourly Sat.-Sun. 11am-5pm; $10

★ Mingei International Museum

Mingei is a Japanese term (rough translation: "art of all people") used to distinguish traditionally handmade crafts from mass-produced industrial objects. The museum brings together handmade works from around the world, celebrating such diverse artifacts as surfboards and quilts, while its collection of theatrical masks represents cultures spanning the globe. Definitely check out Wednesday's Palace, a unique dollhouse constructed of found objects that include feathers, dried leaves, and seashells.

Map 2: 1439 El Prado, 619/239-0003, www.mingei.org; Tues.-Sun. 10am-5pm; $8 adults, $5 seniors, students, military, and ages 6-17, free under age 6

Museum of Photographic Arts

This small museum offers rotating exhibits focusing on local students and artists, particular regions or movements, or the work of obscure artists with an interesting point of view. A great example of work you can expect to find here is the recent exhibit on the history of Czech photographers.

Map 2: 1649 El Prado, 619/238-7559, www.mopa.org; Labor Day-Memorial Day Tues.-Sun. 10am-5pm, Memorial Day-Labor Day Tues.-Sun. 10am-9pm; $8 adults, $7 seniors, $6 students, $7 military, $1 ages 6-14, free under age 6

San Diego Automotive Museum

Classic car buffs won't want to skip this gearhead Shangri-la. Dozens of fully restored cars line this giant hall, beautifully illustrating changes in design and technology over the years. Highlights include a 1914 Model T, a 1931 Cadillac Roadster, a 1953 Jaguar XK120, and even a DeLorean. Motorcycle enthusiasts will find a 1913 Indian Big Twin with sidecar and a road-worn 1914 Harley Davidson.

Map 2: 2080 Pan American Plaza, 619/231-2886, www.sdautomuseum.org; Daily 10am-5pm; $8.50 adults, $6 seniors and military, $5 students, $4 ages 6-15, free under age 6

San Diego History Center

Permanent exhibits offer an informative timeline of San Diego, beginning with the indigenous Kumeyaay people and continuing on through Spanish colonization, the Mexican revolution, and annexation to the state of California. Seasonal exhibits highlight specific regions, historical figures, or ties to industry that shaped the city for better or worse.

Map 2: 1649 El Prado, Suite 3, 619/232-6203, www.sandiegohistory.org; Daily 10am-5pm; $8 adults, $6 seniors and students, $4 ages 6-17, free under age 6 and military

Veterans Museum and Memorial Center

Commemorating the American service members who lost their lives for their nation, this small museum honors them the way these sacrificing individuals might have preferred, without too much pomp or frill. The stories of pivotal battles are told, along with a reminder of the costs of victory.

Map 2: 2115 Park Blvd., 619/239-2300, www.veteranmuseum.org; Tues.-Sun. 10am-4pm; free

PERFORMING ARTS

Casa Del Prado Theatre

The Casa Del Prado stages kid-friendly theatrical, musical, and dance performances Friday evenings and weekend afternoons. Shows star children working in classes and camps put on by the San Diego Junior Theatre, San Diego Civic Youth Ballet, and Civic Dance Arts Program. It's a nice place for kids to take the spotlight, and some of them have gone on to professional success.

Map 2: 1650 El Prado, 619/239-8355, www.juniortheatre.com

★ Old Globe Theatre

Gathered at the northwest end of El Prado, the Old Globe actually comprises three different theater spaces at the **Conrad Prebys Theatre Center.** The Old Globe Theatre is based on Shakespeare's Old Globe in London and features world-class theatrical talent. The 580-seat venue stages classics as well as new productions year-round.

The 600-seat, open-air **Lowell Davies Festival Theatre** stages some of Shakespeare's finest work during the annual **Summer Shakespeare Festival** (June-Sept.). The outdoor venue is backed by Balboa Park, an excellent option on warm summer evenings (but bring a sweater or light jacket).

The smallest of the three, the **Sheryl and Harvey White Theatre** has a theater-in-the-round design—the audience literally surrounds the stage. None of the 250 seats in this intimate venue are more than five rows back, making an ideal setting for small runs of usually artier fare.

Map 2: 1363 Old Globe Way, 619/234-5623, www.theoldglobe.org; ticket prices vary

Military History

A stealth bomber stands sentry at the San Diego Air & Space Museum.

San Diego culture is closely intertwined with the ongoing presence of the U.S. military. Naval bases pepper the bay and coastline, and the Marine Corps Recruit Depot in the center of town turns young volunteers into USMC privates—in other words, they are sent to boot camp. Fittingly, a number of sights around town reflect the military's presence.

The **USS Midway Museum** (910 N. Harbor Dr., 619/544-9600, www.midway.org; Daily 10am-5pm; $20 adults, $10 children, $17 seniors, $15 students, $10 retired military) isn't so much a museum as a retired aircraft carrier loaded with vintage aircraft. It's an invaluable insight into how life on a ship might be (i.e., not entirely pleasant, as you might guess). It's even more cramped at the **Maritime Museum of San Diego** (1492 N. Harbor Dr., 619/234-9153, www.sdmaritime.org; Daily 9am-8pm; $16 adults, $8 ages 3-12, $13 seniors, $13 ages 13-17, $13 military), which features many vessels, including the USS Dolphin submarine, which is not as claustrophobic as the Soviet-era sub on-site.

For closer look at more aircraft, head to Balboa Park's captivating **San Diego Air and Space Museum** (2001 Pan American Plaza, 619/234-8291, www.sandiegoairandspace.org), which is always a crowd-pleaser. It's a short drive north on I-15 to Miramar and the Marine Corps's **Flying Leathernecks Museum** (T-4203 Anderson Ave., Miramar, 877/359-8762, www.flyingleathernecks.org; Daily 9am-3:30pm; free), a yard filled with recent and retired aircraft, many of which saw some serious action. The retired aviators who volunteer at the museum offer the best insights.

The Marines celebrate their land and sea history at the **Marine Corps Command Museum** (Marine Corps Recruit Depot, 1600 Hochmuth Ave., 619/524-6719, www.corpshistory.org; Mon. 8am-3pm, Tues.-Sat. 8am-4pm), located on the recruit depot—you might see young men and women in training.

And if you needed any more proof of the lengths these marines, sailors, and soldiers will go to and have gone in their service, honor the fallen with visits to the **Veterans Museum and Memorial Center** (2115 Park Blvd., 619/239-2300, www.veteranmuseum.org; Tues.-Sun. 10am-4pm; free) in Balboa Park, and the **Fort Rosecrans National Cemetery** (1800 Cabrillo Memorial Dr., Point Loma, 619/553-2084, www.cem.va.gov; Mon.-Fri. 8am-4:30pm, Sat.-Sun. 9:30am-5pm) in Point Loma.

Spreckels Organ Pavillion
Built in 1914 as a donation to the Panama-California Exposition, this 4,518-pipe beauty is the largest outdoor organ in the western hemisphere. Interesting events pop up seasonally (silent movie screenings accompanied by the pipe organ) and free concerts are offered Sunday at 2pm, rain or shine. In summer, Monday evening concerts (7:30pm-9:30pm) fill the 2,500-seat pavilion.

Map 2: 1549 El Prado, Suite 10, 619/702-8138, www.spreckelsorgan.org, free

Uptown   Map 3

CINEMA
Hillcrest Cinemas
This Uptown art-house theater hosts some of the year's best movies—just not major blockbusters. Indie comedies and intimate dramas are what fill this art deco-inspired Landmark theater, and great conversations can be overheard on the way out. Parking in this neighborhood is tough; validate your ticket for accessible parking in the basement of the building.

Map 3: 3965 5th Ave., Hillcrest, 619/298-2904, www.landmarktheatres.com

PERFORMING ARTS
Diversionary Theatre
With a mission to provide theatrical performance space for LGBT voices, the shows here range from serious, introspective, and soul-baring fare to the hilariously absurd, including the occasional *Big Gay Improv Show*, a fund-raising effort.

Map 3: 4545 Park Blvd., Suite 101, 619/220-0097, www.diversionary.org

The Observatory North Park
Once a venue for theatrical productions, this revamped 1929 theater now hosts concerts by well-known rock and pop music artists. Shows are usually all-ages, but may be age-restricted depending on the nature of the show (such as the recent *An Evening with John Waters*).

Map 3: 2891 University Ave., North Park, 619/239-8836, www.observatorynp.com

Unique Moviegoing Experiences

Not every movie is best experienced in a multiplex. Check out some of these great alternative venues.

- **Cinema Under the Stars** (4040 Goldfinch St., 619/295-4221, www.topspresents.com; Thurs.-Sun. 8pm) in Mission Hills provides a comfortable, open-air venue to experience classic films and cult favorites, with plenty of great restaurants nearby.

- During the summer, The **Spreckels Organ Pavilion** (1549 El Prado, Suite 10, 619/702-8138, www.spreckelsorgan.org, free) at Balboa Park presents silent film screenings, accompanied by live music performed on the venue's enormous pipe organ.

- Forgoing stadium seating in favor of cozy reclining chairs, **Cineopolis** (12905 El Camino Real, Del Mar, 858/794-4045, www.cinepolisusa.com) updates the traditional moviegoing experience with a smaller theater space. Adult beverages are even served at some of the 21-and-over screenings.

- Shelter Island boutique hotel **The Pearl** (1410 Rosecrans St., Point Loma, 619/226-6100, www.the-pearlsd.com) projects classics and pop-culture favorites on a wall over its swimming pool, often attracting crowds and the occasional dangling of feet in the water.

- **Stone World Bistro & Gardens Liberty Station** (2816 Historic Decatur Rd., Suite 116, 619/269-2100, www.stonelibertystation.com; Mon.-Sat. 11:30am-10pm, Sun. 11am-9pm) serves some of the city's best beer and terrific food. It also projects a number of cult and comedy classics onto one of its courtyard walls during the summer.

Old Town and Mission Hills Map 4

CINEMA

Cinema under the Stars

Classic movies and cult films are screened in this comfortable outdoor venue, which has a retractable roof in case those stars come with a chance of showers. Reserve your zero-gravity recliner or cabana seating online or at the box office after 6pm on show night.

Map 4: 4040 Goldfinch St., Mission Hills, 619/295-4221, www.topspresents.com; Thurs.-Sun. 8pm

MUSEUMS

Junípero Serra Museum

Spain established its first permanent presence in San Diego on Presidio Hill in 1769. This small museum perched on its crest tells the stories of the settlers who came here, as well as the indigenous Kumeyaay people who lived in communities scattered throughout the region. Named for the Catholic priest who founded the original mission, the Spanish revival building was not part of the original settlement, which fell into ruin more than a century ago. However, it does house relics of the mission, including an 18th-century olive press and one of the cannons that guarded the walls of the fortified presidio built to protect it.

Map 4: 2727 Presidio Dr., 619/220-5422, www.sandiegohistory.org; Fri.-Sun. 10am-5pm; $6 adults, $4 seniors, students, and retired military, $3 ages 6-17, free under age 6 and active military

Seeley Stable

Stables were still a necessity when Old Town was founded, and this 1851 stagecoach station gives interesting insight into the way things were. The large barnlike space is filled with carriages, period saddles, and other tack from a time when paying a visit to La Jolla (currently a 20-minute drive) could take up to four hours.

Map 4: 2648 Calhoun St., 619/220-5427, www.parks.ca.gov; Daily 10am-5pm; free

PERFORMING ARTS

Old Town Theatre

Home of the **Cygnet Theatre Company,** the Old Town Theatre has staged a number of well-known shows by well-known playwrights, many of which had never been produced on a professional level in San Diego before. The company is responsible for producing high-caliber work, and their musicals and plays tend to be great successes.

Map 4: 4040 Twiggs St., 619/337-1525, www.cygnettheatre.com

Ocean Beach and Point Loma

Map 6

GALLERIES

NTC Promenade

When the Naval Training Center opened up its former barracks buildings to the Liberty Station District, creative and performing arts organizations moved in, resulting in a loose-knit community featuring galleries, performances, and workshops. A collection of galleries are open during the **Friday Night Liberty Art Walks** (first Friday of the month) and you'll often find correlating events such as capoeira performances or the riotous storytelling evening *So Say We All*. On a regular basis, different organizations within the NTC network offer workshops teaching topics in music, dance, jewelry-making, improv, visual arts, and creative writing. Notable groups include the Theatre Arts School of San Diego, San Diego Watercolor Society, San Diego Writers, Ink, and the San Diego Ballet Company.

Map 6: 2640 Historic Decatur Rd., Point Loma, 619/573-9300, www.ntclibertystation. com; hours vary

PERFORMING ARTS

★ Humphrey's Concerts by the Bay

People watch summer shows at this outdoor venue from their boats—kayaks, paddleboats, or one of the yachts moored next door to this Shelter Island venue. It's one of the best places in town to catch a music or comedy show. Most simply buy a ticket for a folding seat inside the outdoor amphitheater or reserve one of the hotel rooms connected to the balcony overlooking the stage; these high-end accommodations offer some of the best seats in the house.

Map 6: 2241 Shelter Island Dr., Shelter Island, 619/224-3577, www.humphreysconcerts. com; May-Oct.

La Jolla

Map 7

CINEMA

Arclight La Jolla

This most recent multiplex to open in the area certainly acts like it, with a couple of 3-D auditoriums and even one outfitted with a sophisticated Atmos surround-sound system. A café serves food and drinks in the lobby, where guests may relax until just before showtime (thanks to assigned seating). Select screenings for adults 21 and over permit bringing beer or wine into the theater.

Map 7: 4425 La Jolla Village Dr., 858/768-7770, www.arclightcinemas.com

GALLERIES

★ Madison Gallery

The largest of La Jolla's galleries, this gorgeous oceanfront space has been named among the best 100 galleries in the nation. It hosts the work of up to 15 artists at a time, usually active and well-established names, with a few notable rising talents producing contemporary work across a variety of media.

Map 7: 1020 Prospect St., Suite 130, 858/459-0836, www.madisongalleries.com; Mon.-Sat.10am-6pm, Sun. 10am-4pm

Quint Gallery

For more than three decades, emerging and established artists from all over the world have exhibited a wide range of contemporary works in this small yet impactful gallery. Exhibitions typically run about six weeks, whether highlighting the work of an individual or curating cohesive group shows.

Map 7: 7547 Girard Ave., 858/454-3409, www.quintgallery.com; Tues.-Sat. 10am-5:30pm; free

Originally based in Acapulco, Jose Tasende's gallery has been showing modern artists in this La Jolla space for more than 35 years. The focus on established mid- to late-career artists means you're likely to encounter some familiar names, both inside and among the array of sculptures in front of the building.

Map 7: 820 Prospect St., 858/454-3691, www.tasendegallery.com; Tues.-Fri. 10am-6pm, Sat. 11am-5pm

MUSEUMS

Museum of Contemporary Art San Diego

This oceanfront museum rotates several installations and borrowed collections at any given time, from classic paintings to modern conceptual pieces set next to picture windows overlooking a rocky little cove. Though small by museum standards, the rotating exhibits keeps the place feeling vital during each visit.

Map 7: 700 Prospect St., 858/454-3541, www.mcasd.org; Thurs.-Tues. 11am-5pm; $10 adults, $5 seniors and students, free students under age 25 and military families

★ Stuart Collection

The vast sculpture garden at UCSD boasts 18 striking, beautiful, and thought-provoking pieces—boulders in the shape of a giant teddy bear, a snake path, and a singing tree. However, the collection's most-discussed work sits on a seventh-floor rooftop, accessible only a few hours a week. Do Ho Suh's *Fallen Star* consists of a tiny blue cottage hanging off a ledge atop Jacobs Hall. While it can be viewed from beneath, it's only upon entering the meticulously constructed little home that you understand its purpose. Be warned, the sense of displacement may stay with you afterward.

Map 7: 9500 Gilman Dr., 858/534-2117, www.stuartcollection.ucsd.edu; Daily 6am-midnight, Fallen Star installation Tues. and Thurs. 11am-2pm; free

PERFORMING ARTS

Athenaeum Music & Arts Library

An unusual and cherished institution, this lovely venue houses a library of books devoted to art and music that contains a small gallery of rotating work. An intimate music space also hosts a culturally rich lineup of mostly jazz or chamber music performances, with the occasional experimental artist. Lectures, art shows, film screenings, children's storytelling hours, and the occasional reception round out the many engagements of this cultural hub.

Map 7: 1008 Wall St., 619/454-5872, www.ljathenaeum.org

★ La Jolla Playhouse

With a reputation as incubator for Broadway productions, this nonprofit theater group located on the UCSD campus stages original productions

Historic Arts and Crafts Homes

Craftsman homes beautify North Park.

Architecturally, San Diego has few showstoppers outside the Hotel del Coronado. A spate of historic buildings in the Gaslamp make for a nice walking tour from the William Heath Davis House Museum, and Old Town's oldest buildings, along with the brightly colored houses of Heritage Park Victorian Village, are fascinating.

The truth is that some of the best architecture in town is found in private residences. The intriguing **Marston House** (3525 7th Ave., 619/297-9327, www.sohosandiego. org; tours hourly Sat.-Sun. 11am-5pm; $10) was a tech-savvy home of the future when it was built in 1905. One of its chief architects, Irving "Jack" Gill, was a pioneer of modern architecture, particularly for the arts and crafts movement; his influence is felt all over town. The **Lodge at Torrey Pines** (11480 N. Torrey Pines Rd., 858/453-4420, www. lodgetorreypines.com) was inspired by his work, and **The Museum of Contemporary Art San Diego** (700 Prospect St., 858/454-3541, www.mcasd.org; Thurs.-Tues. 11am-5pm; $10 adults, $5 seniors and students, free students under age 25 and military families) in La Jolla is a home he originally designed for Ellen Browning Scripps.

The term *Craftsman* refers to homes based on designs from the early-20th-century magazine *The Craftsman*, which relied heavily on arts and crafts practices. These affordable house plans became very popular in the early development of San Diego; many of the neighborhoods surrounding Downtown feature a great number of these homes, which are characterized by wood construction, wide porches, low gables, open beams, built-in cabinetry, stone chimneys, and stained or leaded glass windows. Craftsman homes range from large multiroom wonders to small bungalows. **North Park's Historic Craftsman Neighborhood** (28th St. and Pershing Dr.) provides a great example of these homes, many of which have been lovingly restored by their owners.

with a remarkable success rate. Recent years have seen the world premieres of *Jersey Boys* and *The Who's Tommy*. The group was cofounded by Gregory Peck and manages to stay vital whether producing unknown shows of emerging talents or bringing the very best to local audiences.

Its four spaces include the original **Mandell Weiss Theater**, the lavish

Mandell Weiss Forum, and the smaller **Shank and Potiker** black-box theater. A variety of performances are held year-round, from experimental pieces to those destined for greatness.

Map 7: 2910 La Jolla Village Dr., 858/550-1010, www.lajollaplayhouse.org

Coronado
Map 8

CINEMA

Village Theatres Coronado

Don't be fooled into thinking this simple three-screen theater in the center of Coronado isn't state-of-the-art. A recent remodel brought the 65-year-old venue up to spec, with 4K digital projection technology as well as 3-D and surround sound. Come for first-run blockbusters as well as the occasional indie flick.

Map 8: 820 Orange Ave., 619/437-6161, www.vintagecinemas.com

PERFORMING ARTS

Lamb's Players Theatre

An "intimate" 350-seat venue used by this popular local production company, this auditorium was originally built in 1917 by notable Coronado resident John Spreckels. Lamb's has been in residence for more than 20 years, producing four or five shows annually, often crowd-pleasers. The Horton Grand Theatre in the Gaslamp serves as a second stage.

Map 8: 1142 Orange Ave., 619/437-6000, www.lambsplayers.org

Greater San Diego
Map 9

★ Chicano Park

Tucked under the base of the Coronado Bridge, this small park paints a picture of the suffering and resilience of Mexican-American San Diego. Barrio Logan has been predominantly Latino since refugees fleeing the Mexican Revolution settled here at the end of the 19th century. Back then, the neighborhood extended to the waterfront, but Naval installations built during World War II closed that off. When freeway construction cut the neighborhood in half, the bridge itself closed off part of the sky. In 1970, the city tried to pave this little bit of designated park space to put in a highway patrol parking lot. The Latino residents protested, occupying the park for nearly two weeks and forcing the city to invest in the park's preservation. Artists came to beautify the concrete pillars and walls with murals and sculptures, resulting in one of the city's most singular art collections and landscapes.

Map 9: 568 5th Ave., Barrio Logan, 619/232-1930, www.chicanoparksandiego.com;
Mon.-Sat. 10am-9pm, Sun. noon-8pm

MUSEUMS

Flying Leatherneck Museum

Marine Corps Air Station Miramar is home to some of the world's best jet pilots. Wander through the yard of this museum to watch the jets fly up close, then peruse the retired military planes, helicopters, and ground support vehicles often famous for their service, such as the *Sea Knight* chopper, whose heroic crew proved courageous and indispensable during the evacuation of Saigon. Inside you can get a close look at flight suits and read detailed stories about the heroics of military pilots, including Alfred A. Cunningham, the father of U.S. Marine Corps aviation.

Map 9: T-4203 Anderson Ave., Miramar, 877/359-8762, www.flyingleathernecks.org; Daily 9am-3:30pm; free

Marine Corps Command Museum

The Marine Corps Command Museum tells the history of the Marine Corps and its presence in San Diego with detailed information about the often unsung roles of these devil dogs who shaped modern history. Valid identification is required to gain entry to this military base in the Midway district.

Map 9: Marine Corps Recruit Depot, 1600 Hochmuth Ave., 619/524-6719, www.corpshistory.org; Mon. 8am-3pm, Tues.-Sat. 8am-4pm

PERFORMING ARTS

Open Air Theater

A beautiful outdoor venue on the San Diego State University campus, the outdoor Open Air Theater brings top-level talent on a regular basis, hosting some of the most popular bands in rock and pop music.

Map 9: 5500 Campanile Dr., 619/594-0234, www.as.sdsu.edu

Sleep Train Amphitheatre

The named has changed over the years (many, many times), but no matter who the corporate sponsor is, the suburban setting of this large outdoor stage results in great sound for some of the biggest rock acts on tour.

Map 9: 2050 Entertainment Circle, Chula Vista, 844/854-1450, www.amphitheatrechulavista.com

Sports and Activities

Look for ★ to find
recommended sports and activities

Highlights

★ **Sailing in San Diego Bay:** You don't have to know ropes and knots, but you may learn while going out on a boat with **Seaforth Boat Rental** (page 138).

★ **Cycling around Mission Bay:** You'll spot a lot of Jet Skis, kayakers, and sailboats while riding along **Bayside Walk,** a walking, jogging and cycling path circumnavigating the entire bay (page 143).

★ **Best Spot for a Picnic:** Pick up some picnic items from Bread & Cie or Siesel's and head up to the grassy slopes of **Kate O. Sessions Memorial Park** for a panoramic view of the city, bay, and beaches (page 144).

★ **Best Surfing:** It may not be the top choice for experienced surfers, but for the novice, a mild day at **Tourmaline Surf Park** will feed your stoke (page 146).

★ **Jet Skiing in Mission Bay:** The easiest way to learn how to Jet Ski around the bay is by checking out one of two **Adventure Water Sports** locations (page 147).

★ **Best Beach:** Gorgeous **La Jolla Shores** provides the right mix of access, size, cleanliness, family friendliness, amenities, and approachable surf. Little wonder it's one of the most popular beaches in San Diego (page 153).

★ **Best Golf Swing with a View:** Try your mettle at **Torrey Pines,** the site of the 2021 U.S. Open and one of the most scenic courses around (page 154).

★ **Paragliding at Torrey Pines:** At **Torrey Pines Glider Port** it's tough to call the better thrill—winds lifting you up to greater heights, or the view of the cliffs and the coastline while it happens (page 155).

★ **Best Underwater Encounters:** The protected marine habitats of the **La Jolla Underwater Park** offer a great scuba and snorkel environment (page 155).

Many people come to San Diego to relax on the beach and let all of life's stresses melt away—and that's always a great reason to visit.

But when you get a look at just how many different kinds of thrills you can experience with two large bays and 80 miles of coastline at your disposal, you might want to get off your beach blanket and live a little. There are a lot of fun things to do in San Diego that you simply can't do most other places, and sometimes that's motivation enough for seizing the day by flying, riding, skiing, or diving.

Some come here to surf, but it's not all about action sports. There are so many ways to engage, it's really more about setting your tempo and going with it. Kayak on Mission Bay, sip drinks on a sailboat, swing a club on the greens at Torrey Pines, hold tight to a tow-line while gliding across the water's surface, or practice yoga on a stand-up paddleboard. Some enterprising souls find a way to do it all, even squeezing in a little time to lounge on the sand between activities, and following it up by drinking a couple of the region's celebrated craft beers before enjoying a most satisfying and well-earned night of sleep.

Previous page top: surfers on La Jolla Shore beach **bottom:** bikes in La Jolla

BOATING

Ocean Adventure Sail

Most summer weekends, the Maritime Museum's 1848 cutter replica *The Californian* sets out on a four-hour sail. The tall ship boasts 7,000 square feet of canvas sails as well as four deck guns—it had to be fast to chase down smugglers and tax evaders. Passengers may man the helm, haul some line, and finish the voyage with a cannon salute, the type of sailing adventure few get to embark upon.

Map 1: 1492 N. Harbor Dr., 619/234-9153, www.sdmaritime.org; summer only Sat.-Sun. 11:30am-4pm; $60 adults, $48 under age 13, $57 ages 13-17, seniors, and military

★ Seaforth Boat Rental

If you didn't bring your sailboat or yacht with you, this company has you covered, with charters and rentals available for each. Larger boats head out from Downtown, or other locations in Harbor Island (955 Harbor Island Dr., Suite 130) and Coronado (1715 Strand Way). For smaller craft, look to Mission Bay (1641 Quivera Rd.).

Map 1: 333 West Harbor Dr., Gate 1, 888/834-2628, www.seaforthboatrental.com; Mon.-Fri. 10am-5:30pm, Sat.-Sun. 9am-5:30pm

BOWLING

East Village Tavern + Bowl

With only six lanes, this place gives a little more real estate to the tavern than the bowl, but that shouldn't keep anyone from whiling away a rainy day shooting pool and knocking down pins while drinking better beer than most bowlers in the world.

Map 1: 930 Market St., 619/677-2695, www.tavernbowl.com; Mon.-Fri. 11:30am-2am, Sat.-Sun. 11am-2am

CYCLING

Bayshore Bikeway

The Bayshore Bikeway's 24-mile route begins or ends at the Broadway Pier, depending how you look at it. Your best bet is to take the ferry to Coronado and ride south through Silver Strand and back. Or take a more leisurely course from Marina Park South (1 Marina Park Way) and pedal north along Harbor Drive.

Map 1: 1000 North Harbor Dr., www.keepsandiegomoving.com

The Bike Revolution

The Revolution is the sort of bike shop where the mechanics on staff can set up your rental bike and tune it to your needs. Whether you're just looking to roll over to Little Italy or tackle the Bayshore Bikeway, Revolution has mountain bikes, road bikes, and cruisers for rent and even offers delivery service.

Map 1: 522 6th Ave., Gaslamp, 619/297-5500, www.thebikerevolution.com;

Daily 9am-5pm

PARKS
Embarcadero Marina Park

Marina Parks North and South are two parks built around the embarcadero marina that offer grassy fields, shoreline access, and terrific views of San Diego Harbor. Park South features basketball courts with a view of the Coronado Bridge, while Park North connects to Seaport Village shops and restaurants. They're not a bad place to picnic or fly a kite.

Map 1: 1 Marina Park Way, 619/686-6200, www.portofsandiego.org;

Daily 6am-10:30pm; free

Waterfront Park

Just across Pacific Highway from the Maritime Museum, this county park includes a grassy field, playground equipment, and ankle-deep fountains with lots of water jets to keep you cool in summer—all within view of unfurled sails and the harbor beyond.

Map 1: 1600 Pacific Hwy., 619/232-7275, www.sdcounty.ca.gov/parks;

Daily 6am-10pm; free

SPECTATOR SPORTS
Petco Park

When the home of the **Padres** opened in 2004, local fans rejoiced. Though the Padres still didn't make the postseason, we do love the stadium, which easily boasts the best beer selection in the Major Leagues. An iconic brick Western Metal Works building backs up the left field fence, while an ingenious Park within the Park (open to the public during nongame times) sits behind the center field bullpen, a grassy slope with a partial view into the stadium and a large screen televising any game action hidden from view. Anyone with a ticket can check out this brilliant 7th inning stretch territory, which also happens to be served by favorite local vendors including Stone Brewing, Green Flash, Hodad's, and Phil's BBQ.

Map 1: 100 Park Blvd., 619/795-5000, www.petcoparkevents.com; hours and admission vary

TOURS
Another Side of San Diego Tours

These Segway tours guide you throughout San Diego, with packages designed to tour Downtown, Balboa Park, and the beach areas. You'll ride along with ease, silently mocking pedestrians using their own two feet, and probably being mocked back on occasion.

Map 1: 308 G St., 619/239-2111, www.anothersideofsandiegotours.com; Daily 8am-6pm

DISC GOLF

Morley Field Disc Golf Course

Between the Frisbee and golf influences, this isn't exactly an action sport. But it's a great way to spend a few hours walking around Morley Field, tucked within the tree-lined northeast corner of Balboa Park, one of the city's greenest areas. It's a casual course for a casual game, and everybody seems to enjoy themselves. Frisbees are for sale or rent; if you want to do the course right, you'll need at least a couple of different sizes.

Map 2: 3090 Pershing Dr., 619/692-3607, www.morleyfield.com; Daily sunrise-sunset; $3 weekdays, $4 weekends

GOLF

Balboa Park City Golf Course

Certainly not the best-known city golf course, Balboa Park's 18 holes deserve better notice, if only for the view. One end of the course looks out at the bay and skyline, while another strolls past beautiful the Craftsman homes of the North and South Park neighborhoods. Warm up on one of the 14 station driving ranges, practice on the putting green, or beef up your technique with instruction from one of the PGA-certified golf pros on staff.

Map 2: 2600 Golf Course Dr., 619/239-1660, www.balboagc.com; Daily 7am-4pm

PARKS

Desert Garden

At the eastern end of El Prado, cross the pedestrian bridge over Park Boulevard to find this richly diverse desert garden. Succulents and drought-resistant plants typical of the Mojave and Colorado Deserts are displayed across 2.5 acres. Time your visit from January through March for wild-flower blooms.

Map 2: 2525 Park Blvd., www.balboapark.org

Top to bottom: San Diego Bay; Petco Park, Downtown

PARKS
Presidio Park

The grassy slopes of this Old Town park catch a cool western breeze; on a clear day, you might see out to SeaWorld, Mission Bay, and the ocean. Find shade in the tree-covered arbor in the lower southern section of the park, or enjoy a view of Mission Valley from Inspiration Point in the northern part.

Map 4: 2811 Jackson St., 619/235-5935, www.sandiego.gov; Daily 24 hours

GOLF
Presidio Hills Golf Course

Established in 1932, this small course is the oldest in town, featuring 18 par-3 holes for a cheap, short course central to the city. Pay special attention to the clubhouse, which predates the golf course by more than a century (built in 1820, it would be the oldest residential structure in San Diego, were it not part of the golf course). Weekly clinics and by-appointment lessons are offered for adults and children.

Map 4: 4136 Wallace St., 619/295-9476, www.presidiohillsgolf.com; Daily

TOURS
Old Town Trolley Tours

You'll see the orange and green Old Town Trolley buses all over town, providing hop-on, hop-off tours to visitors. Originating from Old Town every 30 minutes, a tour can be a convenient way to see some of the top city sights, with 11 stops in key locations, including the Maritime Museum, Seaport Village, Horton Plaza, Gaslamp, Marina, Coronado, Balboa Park, and Little Italy. It takes two hours to complete a loop, with guides offering a running narrative along the way.

Map 4: 4010 Twiggs St., 619/298-8687, www.trolleytours.com/san-diego; Daily 9am-6pm

Mission Bay and Beaches   Map 5

BEACHES
Crown Point Park

A large inner bayside beach with grassy areas and picnic tables, Crown Point sees a lot of grilling and light watercraft activities. A popular place for birthday parties or just a friendly gathering for a game of horseshoes or Frisbee, the beach also has a boat ramp where you can launch kayaks, motorboats, catamarans, and Jet Skis. Parking is plentiful.

Map 5: 1759-1799 Moorland Dr., Mission Bay, 619/525-8213, www.sandiego.gov

Mission Beach

You can cruise about two miles along Mission Beach Boardwalk and still not run out of beach or boardwalk. At its northern point it becomes Pacific Beach, while the southern point is dominated by Belmont Park. While the huge parking lot in south Mission Beach offers easy access, it also means crowds. Meanwhile, PB to the north usually means rowdy singles. That long stretch in the middle? *That's* Mission Beach, where you finally just settle on an empty spot and enjoy, provided you can find street parking.

Map 5: Ocean Front Walk, between Pacific Beach Dr. and N. Jetty Rd.

Pacific Beach

Pacific Beach offers a beach experience with a party atmosphere, with people (mostly young adults, including lots of singles) partying at the edge of the sand. They used to party *on* the sand until a city beach alcohol ban was put into effect, but a number of beachfront bars and restaurants ensure that the good times continue, especially south of Crystal Pier. North of the pier tends to be a little quieter, with swimming, surfing, and beach volleyball just a few of the popular activities. A dearth of parking can make street parking hit or miss, especially in the summer.

Map 5: Ocean Front Walk, between Pacific Beach Dr. and Law St.

Beach Rentals
Beach House Bikes & Rentals

This specialized rental service delivers beach equipment to you at your vacation home or hotel, whether it's bikes, body boards, beach chairs, jogging strollers, beach cabanas, coolers, or beach games.

Map 5: 619/752-4534, www.beachhousebikes.com

CYCLING
★ Bayside Walk

A biking, walking, and jogging path hugs almost the entire inner circumference of Mission Bay, offering 27 miles to explore. You can pretty much pick your starting point: a block east of Mission Boulevard in Mission Beach, or a block south of Pacific Beach Drive at Fanuel Street Park. You can also pick up the trail as it cuts through Crown Point Park. Wherever you are in Mission Bay, look for the narrow paved path running alongside the water's edge.

Map 5: W. Mission Bay Dr. at Gleason Rd., 4000 Fanuel St., 2688 E. Mission Bay Dr., www.sandiego.org

Ray's Rentals

All sorts of bikes, Rollerblades, and skateboards can be rented at this spot that clearly caters to the boardwalk cruising lifestyle. Choose from tandem bikes, beach cruisers, and BMX wheels, or rent a towable cruiser for those too young to ride.

Map 5: 3221 Mission Blvd., Mission Beach, 866/488-7297, www.rays-rentals.com; Daily 9am-7pm

KITEBOARDING
Manta Wind & Water Sports

A variety of kiteboarding packages aim to get you into the air and out on the sea, with pricing designed to benefit groups. Rental boards and harnesses are available for those traveling to the area with their own kite.

Map 5: 2203 Denver St., 858/610-6000, www.mantawatersports.com; Daily 10am-4pm

FISHING
Seaforth Sportfishing

Heading out into deep waters to troll for big fish is what this outfit is all about. They'll take you as far as coastal Mexican waters on half-day or overnight trips in search of active spots. Choose from large boats with dozens of people, or smaller private charters.

Map 5: 1717 Quivira Rd., 619/224-3383, www.seaforthlanding.com; Daily 5am-6pm

GOLF
Mission Bay Golf Course and Practice Center

This small and aging city course has a couple of things going for it: location and lights. Located at the northeast corner of Mission Bay, it's easy to get to whether you're staying in Mission Beach or Pacific Beach. The 18-hole, mostly par-3 course is the only lighted one in town, making it the best bet for a late round on a quick, inexpensive course.

Map 5: 2702 N. Mission Bay Dr., 858/581-7880, www.sandiego.gov; Daily 6:30am-10pm

PARKS
★ Kate O. Sessions Memorial Park

One of the best parks in San Diego for a picnic, this grassy hillside space is named for the celebrated horticulturist and so-called "Mother of Balboa Park." While it may not have quite as many nonnative plants as Sessions would have liked, she would admire the view, which extends from the Downtown skyline through Mission Bay north into Pacific Beach. There's a small playground, picnic tables, and restrooms, but mostly just green slopes and a smattering of relaxed people enjoying the gorgeous scenery.

Map 5: 5115 Soledad Rd.; Daily 24 hours

Mission Bay Park

Mission Bay Park covers the entirety of Mission Bay, including the water, where so many action and water sports happen. However, the grass and sand landforms along the east coast of the bay also include contiguous small areas—De Anza Cove, Leisure Lagoon, Playa Pacifica Park, and Tecolote Shores—that offer waveless beaches and picnic tables for landlubbers.

Map 5: 2688 E. Mission Bay Dr., 619/525-8213, www.sandiego.gov; Daily 4am-midnight

clockwise from top left: Mission Bay; Kate O. Sessions Memorial Park; the boardwalk at Mission Beach

SURFING

Surf Spots

★ Tourmaline Surf Park

A dedicated surf park in every sense of the word, Tourmaline's charm begins in the parking lot, where crusty old surfers congregate over longboards and listen to classic rock anthems on the stereo of someone's VW bus. The waves breaking along the beach often favor longboards, but the way waves spread out across the length of the beach make it possible for different levels of surfers to coexist. This is one of the top beaches for beginner surfers to learn, though watch out for kelp beds floating in to the beach (the ropey seaweed can wrap around your arms, legs, and surfboard leash). Whenever the surf forecast is below four feet, the free parking, lifeguards, restrooms, showers, ease of access, and gentle surf make Tourmaline a great spot to be among surfers.

Map 5: Tourmaline St., west of La Jolla Blvd.

Surf Shops and Schools

Cheap Rentals

Rent surfboards, bikes, kayaks, paddleboards, wetsuits, snorkeling gear, beach umbrellas, and chairs from this, as they say, cheap spot. Other items for rent include a GoPro camera to attach to the front of your surfboard to capture the highs and lows of your wave session. The main shop sits on Mission Boulevard, a short walk from the beach or bay.

Map 5: 3689 Mission Blvd., Mission Beach, 858/488-9070, www.cheap-rentals.com; Daily 9am-7pm

Surfari

If you don't learn to surf during your first lesson, your second is free. Such is the guarantee from this North Mission Beach rental shop and surf school. Lessons head out at 9am, 11am, 1pm, and 3pm, each lasting an hour and a half plus an extra hour with the board for practice. Class sizes run 3-5 people per instructor, with prices favoring groups signing up together. Stand-up paddleboarding classes and rentals are also available.

Map 5: 3740 Mission Blvd., 858/337-3287, www.surfarisurfschool.com; Daily 9am-5pm

Lessons and Rentals

La Jolla Water Sports

These guys will take you to look at sharks, dive for lobster, or teach you how to spear fish. Or simply motor along the water's surface with a water scooter, goggles down, watching the underwater life unfold as you explore La Jolla Cove and caves.

Map 5: 1551 Grand Ave., Pacific Beach, 619/788-6416, www.lajollawatersports.com; Daily 9am-5pm

Beginner's Surf Spots

There's a lot of beach in San Diego, but there are only a few surf spots appropriate for beginners—and even then, only on days when the waves don't go much higher than your kneecaps.

Stick to these breaks on calm, easy days and remember—there are probably other surfers trying to catch the same waves as you. (The person closest to the middle of the wave has the right of way, so look over your shoulder and make sure there isn't someone else riding in behind you.)

- **Tourmaline Surf Park** (Tourmaline St., west of La Jolla Blvd.): This wide beach offers a number of different areas; better surfers tend to stick to the north end. Beginners can't compete for waves against experiences riders, so stick to the smaller waves while you learn.

- **La Jolla Shores** (8200 Camino Del Oro): There are several designated surf zones along the La Jolla Shores. As you move south, the breaks are safe bets for beginners. Just keep an eye out for swimmers who veer into a surf zone by mistake.

- **Coronado Beach** (Ocean Blvd. from Hotel del Coronado to North Island Naval Air Station): Coronado isn't known as a great surf destination, which makes it a good option for learners. Provided there are small breaking waves, the lack of experienced surfers will give beginners a chance to catch a few waves, which is really the only way to learn.

WATER SPORTS

★ Adventure Water Sports

Mission Bay is a watery playground, and this place has all the toys and equipment you need to join in the fun. Rent a powerboat and cruise the bay, go wakeboarding or waterskiing, ride Jet Skis, or take it slow with pedal boats, aqua cycles, and stand-up paddleboards. All their gear offers direct access to the south portion of the bay; there's a second location on the north end at Campland on the Bay (2211 Pacific Beach Dr., 858/581-9300).

Map 5: 1710 W. Mission Bay Dr., Mission Beach, 619/226-8611, www.adventurewatersports.com; Daily 8am-5pm

Jetpack America

Jetpack America uses water jets to aerially propel (or "jetpack") you over water. While it may not be the fiery flight of science fiction, it can be a lot of exhilarating fun. Packages include classroom instruction, with options for a video of your efforts set to the music of your choice.

Map 5: 1010 Santa Clara Pl., Mission Beach, 888/553-6471, www.jetpackamerica.com; Daily 9am-6pm

Mission Bay Aquatic Center
A lot of Mission Bay watersports take a little instruction the first time. This large instructional facility offers lessons to help you get your sea legs. Windsurfing, wakeboarding, stand-up paddleboarding, kayaking, sailing: just listing all the classes this place offers is enough to wipe you out. It's certainly the kind of coursework that can make for a memorable vacation.

Map 5: 1001 Santa Clara Pl., Mission Beach, 858/488-1000, www.mbaquaticcenter.com; Daily 8am-6pm

Mission Bay Sports Center
Watersports rentals abound at this large Mission Bay facility, which covers tow sports, paddle sports, wave and wind sports—basically a little bit of everything you might want to do in San Diego. Rentals don't require any pre-instruction or certification, so you can enter your small catamaran on the bay right there and see how well your instincts handle turning a small sail into the wind. If you want to rent a powerboat and add a couple of wakeboards or Jet Skis, this is your spot.

Map 5: 1010 Santa Clara Pl., 858/488-1004, www.missionbaysportcenter.com; summer: Mon.-Fri. 10am-6pm, Sat.-Sun. 9am-7pm; winter: Daily 10am-5pm

San Diego Jet Ski
If you already know how to Jet Ski and would like to keep your rental for a while, visit this shop. It's not on Mission Bay, but it does offer tow equipment so that you can take the rental wherever you'd like to go. Your best bet is the Ski Beach launch located at Crown Point (1799 Moorland Dr.).

Map 5: 4275 Mission Bay Dr., 858/272-6161, www.sdjetski.com; Daily 9am-6pm

WHALE-WATCHING
San Diego Whale Watch
San Diego's ocean is teeming with life, and it's ironic that the largest creatures out there may be the toughest to spot. These three-hour whale-watching tours help seek them out, hopefully on days they're willing to breach. The boat departs from this bayside facility; snacks and drinks are available during the tour and there are some activities for kids. Bring a jacket, as it's usually cooler out on the ocean than it is on land.

Map 5: 1717 Quivira Rd., 619/839-0128, www.sdwhalewatch.com; Fri.-Tues. 10am-1pm and 1:30pm-4:30pm, Wed.-Thurs. 10am-1pm

BEACHES

Ocean Beach

This 0.5-mile stretch of sand runs from the OB Pier in the south to the shallow San Diego River bordering the beach's northern edge. Around the pier are surfers and some saltier souls that earn the place comparisons to Venice Beach. Move north to find a welcoming stretch of sand with beach volleyball courts, restrooms, and areas designated for swimming and body boarding. Beach bonfires (within designated fire rings) are popular summer nights, and there's an off-leash dog beach at the park's northernmost section. Parking lots are at the end of Voltaire Street and Santa Monica Avenue.

Map 6: west of Abbott St., between Newport Ave. and Voltaire St., 619/221-8899; lifeguards on duty daily 9am-dusk; free.

BOATING

California Cruisin

Want to sleep on a yacht? You can—and that's only one of the choices offered by this charter boat service, which includes private dinner cruises, sailing charters, and houseboat rentals on San Diego Bay.

Map 6: 1450 Harbor Island Dr., Harbor Island, 619/296-8000, www.californiacruisin.com; Daily 8:30am-5:30pm

San Diego Bay Adventures

Mission Bay doesn't get to have all the fun. Jet Ski and stand-up paddleboard rentals and tours from this outfit puts you out in the big bay, within view of skyscrapers, clipper ships, and actual active naval vessels.

Map 6: 1880 Harbor Island Dr., Harbor Island, 619/889-4294, www.sdbayadventures.com; Daily 9am-5pm

San Diego Sailing Tours

These guys offer shared sailing packages to individuals and small groups, taking up to six people at a time for two- to four-hour tours of San Diego Bay. You can help work the boat, or sit back and enjoy complimentary drinks and snacks. Reasonable private packages are also available.

Map 6: 1450 Harbor Island Dr., Harbor Island, 619/786-0173, www.sandiegosailingtours.com; Daily 9am-7pm

Dog-Friendly San Diego

dogs frolic at Ocean Beach Dog Beach

Dogs have it pretty good here. Plenty of parks around town are designated off-leash (at least part of the time) and entire chunks of beach are given over to rollicking pooches eager to swim (some even learn to surf).

- **Fiesta Island** (1590 E. Mission Bay Dr., 619/235-1169, www.sandiego. gov; Daily 6am-10pm): Shallow water and endless shoreline make this massive bayside beach the park of choice for dogs who feel the urge to cover some ground. It's mostly sand and scrub, but to a dog, the myriad smells and long runs are the hallmarks of a favorite destination.

- **Grape Street Dog Park** (Grape St. and 28th St., www.balboapark. org; Mon.-Fri. 7:30am-9pm, Sat.-Sun. 9am-9pm): This sprawling, grassy, five-acre off-leash dog park is surrounded by eucalyptus and edges a canyon off the Balboa Park city golf course. The park is not fully fenced in, so it might not be suitable for runners. Most of the dogs are pampered and friendly, and tend to run in packs. There are restrooms on-site and water fountains for the dogs.

- **South Bark Dog Wash** (2037 30th St., 619/232-7387, www. southbark.com; Daily 10am-7pm): Just around the corner from Grape Street Dog Park, this little shop has a dedicated furry clientele, often in need of a wash in one of the raised basins or just a little post-run treat.

- **Ocean Beach Dog Beach** (western end of Voltaire St.): A wide and very deep patch of beach at the north end of OB has been given over to the dogs. Pups range in size from small to large, and most are deliriously happy to splash and fetch in the shallow waves and sand bars that form along the beach. Visits to the city's only 24-hour off-leash beach are usually during daylight hours. Animal temperament is the responsibility of the owners, so stay vigilant of your pets and clean up after them with the plastic bags provided.

- **OB Dog Wash** (4933 Voltaire St., 619/523-1700, www.dogwash.com; Daily 10am-9pm): If you're doing it right, a visit to OB Dog Beach leaves you with a dirty pup. This shop offers raised tubs and gentle sprays ideal for getting the sand out, with options like hypoallergenic shampoo and blow-dryers available.

O.B.Ebikes

Whether you want to hit the river bike path or just cruise around OB proper, you'll find the right bike for the job here—maybe even a scooter or an electric bike.

Map 6: 4967 Newport Ave., Suite 10, Ocean Beach, 619/764-1804, www.elektrocycle. com; Daily 9:30am-7pm, Tues. call for hours

San Diego River Bike Path

This bike path will eventually extend from the ocean to the mountains. For now, it's a somewhat manageable five or six miles from OB Dog Beach, heading east through parts of Mission Valley and almost entirely removed from car traffic. This trail also connects to the Mission Bay Trail just north, for a longer day of beach riding.

Map 6: end of Voltaire St., west of W. Point Loma Blvd., 619/645-3183, www.sdrc.ca.gov

FISHING

OB Pier

The simplest way to fish in San Diego is at the end of a pier, where you don't need a license or a boat. As you head toward the end of the pier, the bites get fewer but the fish get bigger—anything from mackerel and halibut to white sea bass and the rare yellowtail. Bait and tackle (and tacos) are available in a café set in the middle of the pier.

Map 6: 5091 Niagara Ave., Ocean Beach

Point Loma Sportfishing

With regularly scheduled half-day day trips, long-range excursions, and charters, this sportfishing outfit offers a chance to hit the open sea and chase down some yellowtail. In addition to a small fleet of fishing boats, the shop sells equipment rentals, fishing licenses, and secures permits for trips to the well-populated waters off Mexico. Earn your dinner by bringing home some fresh catch.

Map 6: 1403 Scott St., Point Loma, 619/223-1627, www.pointlomasportfishing.com; Daily from 6am; from $45

PARKS

Cabrillo National Monument

A series of trails crisscross the monument grounds, including the 2.5-mile **Bayside Trail.** From the Old Point Loma Lighthouse, this scenic trek looks east across the bay while traversing rare coastal sage scrub habitat. On the west side of the monument, the 0.5-mile **Coastal Tidepool Trail** winds past a series of protected tide pools. The trail can be found off the parking lot beside the New Point Loma Lighthouse on Cabrillo Road; it continues north to connect to a second parking lot farther up Cabrillo Road.

Map 6: 1800 Cabrillo Memorial Dr., Point Loma, 619/557-5450, www.nps.gov; Daily 9am-5pm; $5 per vehicle, $3 per walk-in

Perhaps the greatest feature of this harbor-side park is its location just across the street from the airport. It's a pretty nice spot to kill time if you're waiting for a flight, are early to catch your flight, or simply want to relax or have a picnic before returning the rental car.

Map 6: 3900 N. Harbor Dr., Harbor Island, 619/686-6200, www.portofsandiego.org

SKATEBOARDING
Robb Field Skate Park

Roll past the grassy fields of Robb Field and you'll come upon this specialized 40,000-square-foot concrete playground, designed street-style, with a series of bowls, ledges, and rails for skateboarders to ply their techniques. Children under 12 should be accompanied by an adult.

Map 6: 2525 Bacon St., Ocean Beach, 619/531-1563, www.sandiego.gov;
Daily 10am-sunset

SURFING
Surf Spots
Ocean Beach Pier

The waters adjacent to the OB Pier are reserved for surfers at all times; anyone wishing to swim or body board must move north of a yellow-checkered flag posted in front of the lifeguard tower. Surfers should respect this delineation, or the lifeguards will let you hear about it. During modest two- to four-foot conditions, this can be a decent beginner's beach—but try to sneak any waves away from well-established locals and they will also let you hear about it. Waves typically break left off the pier on any western swell; newbies are better off trying some fun left and right beach break farther down the line. Once these waves begin to surpass the six-foot range, leave it to the pros and watch from the pier for an amazing close-up look.

Map 6: Newport Ave. and Abbot St., Ocean Beach

Surf Schools and Rentals
Ocean Beach Surf Lessons

Barneys, kooks, grommets, and beginners of all ages can sign up for group or private surf lessons, including stand-up paddleboard instruction and children's day camps during the summer. Equipment is provided and classes are taught by experienced local surfers, delivering a combination of detailed on-beach instruction and in-water guidance, with the hope of getting you up your first time out.

Map 6: 4940 Newport Ave., Ocean Beach, 858/964-3760, oceanbeachsurflessons.com;
Daily hours vary; Group lessons $55, private $85

South Coast Surf Shop

Local board shapers and riders have made this shop an OB surfer hub for 40 years, buying wetsuits, board shorts, bikinis, and surf wax on the reg. Even if you're not a surfer, there's still plenty of gear to help you look the part, as well as surfboard rentals should conditions favor the pier a block away. Women can seek out a better-suited selection at **Wahines** (5037 Newport Ave., 619/223-8808), the South Coast's sister shop a few doors down.

Map 6: 5023 Newport Ave., 619/223-7017, www.southcoast.com; Daily 10am-7pm

TENNIS

Barnes Tennis Center

Low rates and two dozen courts keep this family-friendly tennis center popular. Most options are hard courts, but you might find one of the four clay surfaces available. Turn on the lights to keep your match going.

Map 6: 4490 W. Point Loma Blvd., Point Loma, 619/221-9000, www.barnestenniscenter.com; Mon.-Thurs. 8am-9pm, Fri.-Sun. 8am-7pm

WHALE-WATCHING

Adventure R.I.B. Rides

Once you hear what a R.I.B. is, you'll think this whale-watching trip is a lot cooler. Rigid inflatable boats (R.I.B.) were built for Navy Seal missions. A maximum of six passengers per trip head out in search of whales and dolphins, moving fast enough to find and follow. This badass outfit also conducts scuba charters and offers "Adventure Picnics."

Map 6: 1380 Harbor Island Dr., Harbor Island, 619/808-2822, www.adventureribrides.com; Daily 8am-6pm

La Jolla   Map 7

BEACHES

La Jolla Caves

At the northern end of La Jolla cove, seven sea caves cut into the coastline (some were used by smugglers during prohibition). To explore the caves, sign up for a kayak tour with **La Jolla Kayak** (2199 Avenida de la Playa, 858/459-1114, www.lajollakayak.com; daily 8am-6pm) or enter through **Sunny Jim Cave** (see p. 56). The journey is a blast and the breathtaking sight of the caves is something you can't see from land.

Map 7: 1100 Coast Blvd., 858/459-0746, www.cavestore.com; Daily 10am-5:30pm; $5 adults, $3 under age 16

★ La Jolla Shores

One of the most popular beaches in town, La Jolla Shores offers a nearly 1.5 miles of sand where beach-lovers can swim, surf, body board, play volleyball, scuba dive, and launch small watercraft. A beachside park and playground round out the family friendliness of the place. It's extremely crowded in summer, when small waves and warm water are the norm.

Map 7: 8200 Camino Del Oro, 619/221-8899, www.sandiego.gov; Daily 24 hours

Sandstone cliffs add a little scenic oomph at this state beach between La Jolla and Del Mar. The long, wide stretch of sand offers plenty for swimmers and body boarders, as well as surfers toward the north end. Limited parking is available in a lot beside the beach; if that's full, just loop around to park on Carmel Valley Road. It's just a short walk to the sand via the McGonagle Road underpass.

Map 7: 12600 North Torrey Pines Rd., 858/755-2063, www.parks.ca.gov; Daily 7:15am-sunset

Windansea

A small beach by any standards, this picturesque neighborhood spot amounts to a small sandy cove surrounded by rocky outcroppings. It's not a great place to swim; however, some locals just enjoy the sand here, as it's away from the larger beach crowds farther up the coast. Skilled surfers grab speedy, sculpted waves at a popular reef offshore, but localism runs high. Unless you're an excellent surfer with a great deal of patience and etiquette, stick to spectating, then head to Tourmaline Surf Beach a couple of miles south to grab some mellower rides.

Map 7: 6800 Neptune Pl., 619/221-8899, www.sandiego.gov; Daily 9am-sunset

CYCLING
San Diego Fly Rides

Specializing in electric bikes, this shop offers both rentals and tours, along with some pretty cool cruisers for purchase. The so-called electric assist can really be a boon to riders trying to navigate the canyons and mesas that define San Diego, but you'll still get your pedal on in the flats.

Map 7: 1237 Prospect St., Suite X, 619/888-3878, www.sandiegoflyrides.com; Thurs.-Mon. 10am-5pm

GOLF
★ Torrey Pines

Believe it or not, this home of the 2021 U.S. Open is a city golf course, which means that it's open to the public. It can be tough to get a tee time on the most famous course in town, particularly for nonresidents. Reservations are accepted up to 90 days out, with short-term allotments available via a lottery system. The rewards are playing at one of two world-class William P. Bell-designed 18-hole courses atop bluffs overlooking the Pacific—either the north course or the challenging legendary south course.

Map 7: 11480 Torrey Pines Park Rd., 858/581-7171, www.sandiego.gov; Daily 7am-4pm

KAYAKING
Bike & Kayak Tours

Specializing in bicycle, kayak, and snorkel excursions—with an increasing emphasis on stand-up paddleboards—these guys help you make the most of La Jolla outdoors, providing guidance and gear to show you exactly what you came to see.

Map 7: 2158 Avenida de la Playa, 858/454-1010, www.bikeandkayaktours.com; Daily 8am-8pm

La Jolla Kayak

This popular outfit offers kayak tours of La Jolla's seven sea caves—*and* a snorkeling tour as part of the kayak tour. It's a nice all-in-one way to explore local coastal life. If you want to get a land-based view from the seat of a bicycle, they offer tours for that, too.

Map 7: 2199 Avenida de la Playa, 858/459-1114, www.lajollakayak.com; Daily 8am-6pm

PARAGLIDING

★ Torrey Pines Glider Port

The ocean cliffs of Torrey Pines provide the scenic backdrop for tourism of the high-flying variety. Hang gliding and paragliding excursions are available, and surprisingly little experience or ability are required. An experienced glider rides tandem with you, offering some sense of safety as you float high above the trees and the beach.

Map 7: 2800 Torrey Pines Scenic Dr., 858/452-9858, www.sandiegofreeflight.com; Daily 9am-5pm; paragliding $175, hang gliding $225

PARKS

Ellen Browning Scripps Park

From this grassy park next to La Jolla Cove, picnickers, sunbathers, and frolicking children are privy to a great view of the ocean and the cliffs of Torrey Pines. Though the shops and restaurants and busy sidewalks of Prospect Street are merely a couple blocks away, this spot feels like it's in the middle of a summer vacation.

Map 7: 1133 Coast Blvd., 619/236-5555, www.sandiego.gov; Daily 4am-8pm; free

Torrey Pines State Natural Reserve

The Torrey Pine is San Diego's only native five-needled pine, but that's not what really brings people here for a series of short hikes. That would be the ocean air, and the scenic cliffs overlooking an unspoiled beach. Eight trails weave through the pines, yucca, and chaparral, either to the beach or looping back around through more vistas.

Map 7: 12600 N. Torrey Pines Rd., 858/755-2063, www.torreypine.org; Daily 7:15am-sunset; free

SCUBA AND SNORKELING

★ La Jolla Underwater Park

Two underwater canyons, a couple of reefs, and a kelp forest are some of the highlights of San Diego's deepest water park, which spans the equivalent of 6,000 acres off the coast between La Jolla Cove and La Jolla Shores. Plentiful marine life may be seen for those willing to snorkel or scuba—look for

clockwise from top left: a paraglider at Torrey Pines near La Jolla; the golf course at Torrey Pines; Torrey Pines State Natural Reserve

several nonthreatening species of shark, dolphins, sea lions, starfish, anemones, and hundreds of colorful fish and flora. Several shops offer kayak and snorkeling tours, or rent your own to access the south end of the shores.

Map 7: 2000 block of Avenida de la Playa, 619/221-8824, www.sandiegocoastlife.com

Lessons and Rentals
Snorkel and Scuba

Snorkel and Scuba offers regular dives for scuba-certified clients (including night dives), as well as guided tours below the surface of La Jolla. Newbies can sign up for the beginner's tour or select options from a snorkeling menu.

Map 7: 1133-1188 Coast Blvd., 858/539-0054, www.snorkelsandiegoscuba.com; tours daily 9am, noon, 3pm, 6pm, and sunset

SURFING
Surf Spots
Black's Beach

This underwater canyon off the coast lines up some of the best waves in town, and difficult access never prevents surfers from hitting this beach when the waves are breaking. Getting to the sand from the cliffs above requires a hike, whether down a path from the Torrey Pines Glider Port or walking down a gated, steep, and winding driveway hundreds of yards from La Jolla Farms Road. Between the waves, crowds, and nudists (users consider the beach clothing-optional), it's definitely not for families or beginners.

Map 7: 9601 La Jolla Farms Rd.

La Jolla Shores and Scripps Pier

Most days the smaller waves and shallow water leave conditions hospitable enough for beginners, but when the swell picks up, the breaks at La Jolla Shores are quick and powerful. More experienced riders opt for slightly larger, better-structured waves farther north at Scripps Pier.

Map 7: 8200 Camino del Oro, 619/221-8899, www.sandiego.gov; Daily 24 hours

Surf Schools and Rentals
Surf Diva

Every family member can benefit from the surf lessons, clinics, and camps offered by this female-friendly shop. Kids camps in the summer get boys and girls out in the water and up on their boards. Multiday clinics offer women a chance to get into the swing of it, while men may opt for coed group or private lessons.

Map 7: 2160 Avenida de la Playa, 858/454-8273, www.surfdiva.com; Mon-Thurs. 8:30am-7:30pm, Fri.-Sun. 8:30am-8pm

TENNIS

La Jolla Tennis Club

With nine courts open to the public, you stand a good chance getting court time, though calling ahead to reserve is a good idea. The facility also hosts leagues and tournaments, and offers private lessons by their staff of tennis pros should you need help with your backhand.

Map 7: 7632 Draper Ave., 858/454-4434, www.ljtc.org; Daily dawn-9pm

Coronado

Map 8

BEACHES

Coronado Beach

Routinely listed among the best beaches in the United States, Coronado Beach is what makes this place a dreamy summer destination. Even during fall and winter months, the beach is protected from both large surf and the atmosphere's marine layer; so while beaches to the north may be overcast and full of rip currents, Coronado should be just about right. Bear in mind, when big waves do hit this beach, it ceases to be an ideal place for less-experienced swimmers. There are several access points from Ocean Boulevard along the mile-long beach.

Map 8: Ocean Blvd. from Hotel del Coronado to North Island Naval Air Station, 619/522-7346, www.coronado.ca.us

Silver Strand State Beach

Thanks to its somewhat remote location, this 2.5-mile-long state beach tends to be among the least trafficked in the county. It's the sort of unspoiled beach experience that can be hard to come by. Even the waves are relatively uncrowded (mostly because they're not that great), but that just means more practice for the novice and plenty of opportunity to body board or bodysurf. Campfires and bonfires within designated fire rings help warm summer nights.

Map 8: 5000 Hwy. 75, 619/435-5184, www.parks.ca.gov; Daily 8am-7pm; $10 parking

BOATING

Seaforth Boater Education

Learning to sail doesn't happen in an afternoon, but San Diego's protected bays offer a perfect environment to get started. Offering lessons here, as well as at other locations in Harbor Island (955 Harbor Island Dr., Suite 130) and Mission Bay (1641 Quivira Rd.), Seaforth will teach you how to skipper a 22-foot sloop in moderate conditions. Return for more advanced classes later.

Map 8: 1715 Strand Way, 888/834-2628, www.seaforthboatrental.com; Mon.-Fri. 9am until 30 minutes before sunset, Sat.-Sun. 8am until 30 minutes before sunset

CYCLING

Bayshore Bikeway

The Bayshore Bikeway's 24-mile route begins and ends at the Coronado Ferry Landing. You can ride the whole circuit (which requires taking the ferry and passing south through Chula Vista, then back up through Imperial Beach), or just stick to the Coronado peninsula, arguably the best part of the route.

Map 8: 1201 1st St., www.keepsandiegomoving.com

Cruiser King

Coronado is pretty well fixed for bicycles even without this place, but having it nearby helps. It has some pretty good cruisers and hybrids for getting around the island or hopping the ferry Downtown.

Map 8: 957 Orange Ave., 619/522-6967, www.kruiserking.com; Mon.-Sat. 9am-7pm, Sun. 10am-5pm

GOLF

Coronado Golf Course

This 6,500-yard, par-72 course looks up at the Coronado Bridge and across the south bay. For more than 50 years, it has been considered among the top public courses in town (probably because it requires a collared shirt and prohibits flip-flops).

Map 8: 2000 Visalia Row, 619/435-3121, www.golfcoronado.com; Daily 5:30am-8pm

KITEBOARDING

AZ Kiteboarding

Gaining skill at kiteboarding doesn't happen overnight, but take a few lessons from the experienced instructor at AZ and you might get the hang of it after a few days. At a reasonable $150 per two-hour lesson, it's worth booking to find out if you've got the mettle. Set an appointment and meet your instructor at Silver Strand State Beach for your lesson.

Map 8: 5000 Hwy. 75, 918/740-2894, www.kiteboardcoronado.com; by appointment only

STAND-UP PADDLEBOARDING

SUP Coronado

Coronado is a great place for learning stand-up paddleboarding. Between the Pacific Ocean and San Diego Bay, the island offers ideal water conditions and scenery; most of the time it's going to be mellow. SUP Coronado offers lessons, tours, and even some SUP yoga sessions.

Map 8: 2000 Mullinex Dr., 619/888-7686, www.supcoronado.com; by appointment only

PARKS

Mission Trails Regional Park

These 5,800 acres of open-space preserve will give you a little idea what San Diego's natural landscape is truly like. Popular hikes include trails up to the 1,500-foot Cowles Mountain and the 6.5-mile hike to the scenic Lake Murray.

Map 9: 1 Father Junípero Serra Trail, Santee, 619/668-3281, www.mtrp.org; Daily 9am-5pm

SPECTATOR SPORTS

Qualcomm Stadium

Formerly known as Jack Murphy Stadium, this Mission Valley stadium plays home field to both the National Football League's **San Diego Chargers** and the Aztecs of San Diego State University. It also comes alive every so often hosting international club soccer matches.

Map 9: 9449 Friars Rd., Mission Valley, 619/641-3100, www.sandiego.gov/qualcomm

TOURS

Brew Hop Brewery Tours

A wise solution to the problem of getting from brewery to brewery without a designated driver, these customized beer tours tote you to several of your preferred destinations, and will be happy to offer guidance to ensure you hit the right places at the right times as well as picking you up and dropping you off.

Map 9: 2330 1st Ave., Suite 411, 858/361-8457, www.brewhop.com

San Diego Sky Tours

I'm assuming every city offers aerial tours from the open cockpit of a biplane? It's an adventurous way to see the city, and only slightly less so to book a small party in a small, enclosed plane instead.

Map 9: 3717 John J Montgomery Dr., 619/757-6419, www.sandiegoskytours.com

Shops

Highlights

★ **Best Home and Design:** Little Italy has grown into one of the hippest neighborhoods in town, mostly due to the high levels of taste found in the **Kettner Art & Design District.** Ingenious designers and impeccably curated shops will make you want to hang around here too (page 164).

★ **Best Farmers Market:** The **Saturday Mercato** in Little Italy is so popular and well-run that farmers, artisans, and purveyors clamor to sell here. You'll find delicious organic produce to sample, fresh fish to taste, and more good flavors than your appetite can handle (page 165).

★ **Best Children's Shop:** If you seek young children's toys and gifts, slip into **So Childish.** Many of the handpicked assortment of baby and toddler clothes, plushies, toys, musical instruments, and books manage to steer clear of commercial influence (page 166).

★ **Best Gift Shop:** Finding something for anyone is a tall order, even in the best gift shops. But **Pigment** has got something for drinkers, gardeners, pop culture buffs, design hounds, sentimentalists, children, and health nuts (page 169).

★ **Best Bottle Shop:** Spend a few days in San Diego and you'll want to fill your suitcase with beer. When the time comes, hit **Bottlecraft** to load up on the best of local craft, by the bottle or the can, mixed and matched as you see fit (page 169).

★ **Most Authentic Souvenirs:** To take something home that feels like San Diego, head to the **Bazaar del Mundo** in Old Town, which has Spanish and Mexican influences (page 174).

★ **Best Antiques:** OB's Newport Avenue may be the preferred home of beach rats, but just a few blocks from the beach, **Ocean Beach Antique District** turns out some stellar vintage shopping (page 177).

★ **Best Fashions:** Whether you seek high-end designer fashions or the latest looks from nationally known labels, the boutiques on **Girard Avenue** in La Jolla have your shopping day pegged (page 180).

★ **Best Window Shopping:** Window-shopping on **Orange Avenue** ranges from beachy to kitsch. It starts around 8th Street and continues all the way to the Hotel Del (page 183).

★ **Best Surf Shop:** There's only one **Bird's Surf Shed**—it's part museum, part epic surf story waiting to happen. Nose around for a glorious new or vintage board, or just hang out and let the locals sing tales of their SoCal adventures (page 185).

San Diego may be many things, but a world-class shopping destination is not one of them. While it may boast better-than-average surf shops and more swimsuits than most cities, rare is the person who plans a trip just to push the limit of his or her credit card.

Aside from surf and beachwear, San Diego's proximity to the Mexican border means access to a great deal of Mexican crafts, folk art, and decor, including pottery, textiles, and (sometimes kitschy) religious artifacts.

While many individual shops may not warrant recommending on their own merits, like-minded shops have the good sense to cluster together on a single street or district, so shoppers may pop in and browse each in turn in search of what they're looking for. This holds especially true for clothes and accessories, as San Diego fashionistas tend to have very different ideas about what's in vogue at any given time.

Previous page top: hand-painted clay pots at El Centro Artesano **bottom:** peppers at Little Italy's Saturday Mercato

ANTIQUES AND VINTAGE

Antiques on Kettner

With about 9,000 square feet of space dedicated to estate sales, antiques, and collectibles, this central stop in the Kettner Art & Design District can keep you browsing for hours, whether you're looking for furnishings, decorative art, curios, or cabinets for your curios.

Map 1: 2400 Kettner Blvd., Little Italy, 619/234-3332, www.antiquesonkettner.com; Daily 10am-6pm

Architectural Salvage

When old and antiquated buildings are torn down or refurbished, the original construction materials have to go somewhere. The good stuff goes here. Stained-glass windows, vintage drawers and cabinet hardware, wooden doors, and iron gates are merely some of the fascinating items you'll uncover. Much of it can't even be categorized, and it's rarely things you'd expect. Homeowners will be thrilled, while dreamers and design enthusiasts will be inspired.

Map 1: 2401 Kettner Blvd., Little Italy, 619/696-1313, www.architecturalsalvagesd.com; Sun.-Mon. 11am-5pm, Tues.-Sat. 10am-6pm

Casa Artelexia

Mexican folk art inspires many of the crafts, jewelry, and decorative wares at this shop, whether it's Roman Catholic mysticism, *papel picado,* or the skull-heavy styling of Día de Muertos (Day of the Dead). It's unique, often kitschy, and usually enriching—you won't find the likes of it elsewhere.

Map 1: 2400 Kettner Blvd., Suite 102, Little Italy, 619/544-1011, www.artelexia.com; Tues.-Sat. 11am-6pm, Sun. 11am-4pm

★ Kettner Art & Design District

This loose cluster of furniture shops, art galleries, and design boutiques operates out of the north end of Little Italy. Some shops are temporary, some are well known, and some are obscure, but all hold potential. Interior and landscape design buffs should loop through the neighborhood, stopping at **Mixture** (2210 Kettner Blvd.), with occasional forays up side streets to check out places like **Love and Aesthetics** (621 W. Fir St.). Keep your eyes open—any little door could lead to something amazing.

Map 1: Kettner Blvd. and India St., between Laurel St. and Hawthorn St., Little Italy

GOURMET TREATS

Best Damn Beer Shop at Krisp

In a city teeming with great beer, this bottle shop found within the Krisp grocery store consistently offers one of the best selections in town. Nearly every local brew, as well as top craft bottles from around the country and international ales, are sold. The shop also hosts specialty beer events, like the Best Damn Sour Fest.

Map 1: 1036 7th Ave., Gaslamp, 619/232-6367, www.bestdamnbeershop.com; Mon.-Sat. 9am-5:30pm, Sun. noon-4pm

★ Saturday Mercato

The city's best farmers market convenes every Saturday to sell produce, local seafood, and a few craft goods to happy throngs of locals who make a date of it week in and week out. Copious California sunshine helps regional farmers grow year-round, so there's always something in season, and usually more than enough for a great meal. Walk away with some fresh avocados, or order breakfast or lunch to go at any number of booths.

Map 1: Cedar St. from Kettner Blvd. to Front St., Little Italy, Sat. 8am-2pm

SHOPPING MALLS

Horton PLaza

Horton Plaza opened in 1985 in an effort to revitalize Downtown after rough times through the 1970s. Anchored by Macy's, Nordstrom's, and Jimbo's (a natural grocery store), the colorful open-air mall fills about six square blocks with typical mall stores. There's an eight-screen movie theater, a playhouse and music venue, and an outdoor ice rink that opens in the winter. Stores validate up to three hours of parking in a vast parking garage, giving you enough time to shop, see a movie, and maybe catch a drink or a meal in the Gaslamp.

Map 1: 324 Horton Plaza, Gaslamp, 619/239-8180, www.westfield.com/hortonplaza

Seaport Village

Perched on the waterfront just off **Marina Park,** Seaport Village feels more like a collection of shops next to a beach park (along with a few uninspired restaurants). Scenery aside, most shops are focused on San Diego-themed souvenirs, sunglasses, and beach styles. The exceptions are **Upstart Crow** (619/232-4855, daily 9am-9pm), a bookstore and gift shop, and the always fun, occasionally functional **Village Hat Shop** (619/233-7236, daily 10am-9pm). It's worth a visit for the walk along the waterfront and for the hand-carved carousel that's been in operation since 1895.

A neighboring Headquarters extension opened to create more retail space and to provide a venue for some decent restaurants, including **Puesto** (619/233-8880, daily 11am-10pm) and **Pizzeria Mozza** (619/376-4353, daily noon-midnight). Formerly the old police headquarters, you can also check out the old jail cell. Shops include **Geppetto's Toys** (619/615-0005) and the made-in-San Diego marketplace **Simply Local** (Mon.-Sat. 10am-9pm, Sun. 10am-8pm).

Map 1: 849 W. Harbor Dr. and 789 W. Harbor Dr., 619/235-4014, www.seaportvillage.com; Mon.-Sat. 10am-9pm, Sun. 10am-9pm

GIFTS AND HOME
Make Good

This one-of-a-kind South Park boutique sources more than 100 local and handmade products from artisans in San Diego and Tijuana for its stock of clothing, jewelry, home goods, toys, stationery, and gifts. Brimming with creativity, this spot feels like a brick-and-mortar Etsy shop. Talented local craftspeople provide intriguing objects that represent the city, including hand-knit baby gifts, locally designed skirts and dresses, and glassware made from recycled local craft beer bottles.

Map 2: 2207 Fern St., 619/563-4600, www.themakegood.com; Tues.-Thurs. noon-7pm, Fri. noon-8pm, Sat. 10am-8pm, Sun. 11am-6pm

Progress

Design-savvy housewares, mid-century furniture, and locally made stationery and gifts populate this eclectic local favorite, which features items that tend to be as clever or kitschy as they are innovative or functional. From hanging planters to cookbooks and from handmade greeting cards to skateboarding army figures, there may be, as the shop promises, "something for everyone."

Map 2: 2225 30th St., 619/280-5501, www.progresssouthpark.com; Mon.-Thurs. 10am-7pm, Fri.-Sat. 10am-8pm, Sun. noon-5pm

KIDS AND PETS
★ **So Childish**

This children's boutique can only be characterized as "delightful," providing South Park locals with the perfect place to pick up a baby shower or kid's birthday gift. Ranging from adorable necessity to cherished keepsake, the curated selection makes big-box kid shops seem plastic and hollow.

Map 2: 1947 30th St., 619/238-0800, www.sochildish.com; Tues.-Sat. 10am-5pm, Sun. 10am-4pm

Uptown
Map 3

ANTIQUES AND VINTAGE
Adams Avenue Antique Row

San Diego's largest cluster of antique and vintage furniture shops may be found along Adams Avenue, at the northern end of North Park. Anywhere from six to a dozen stores offer rare finds and consignments, and the serious browser will find something cool in nearly all of them. Most, like **Antique Cottage** (2873 Adams Ave.) and **Zac's Attic** (2922 Adams Ave.), are found west of 30th Street, though occasional outliers such as **Revivals**

clockwise from top left: Architectural Salvage, Downtown; Horton Plaza, Downtown; heirloom tomatoes at Little Italy's Saturday Mercato

(3220 Adams Ave.) are east along the same street going into the next-door neighborhood of Normal Heights.

Map 3: Adams Ave. between Hamilton St. and 30th Ave., North Park

ART AND DESIGN
Ray Street Arts District

North Park's arts community peppers the neighborhood with ad hoc galleries within hair salons, coffee shops, wine bars, and restaurants. But the epicenter of the local visual arts scene is this little block of Ray Street, just off the happening corner of 30th Street and University Avenue. While the studios and galleries vary, classes, workshops and exhibitions are kept alive by the **San Diego Art Department** (3830 Ray St.). Every second Saturday, during the **Ray at Night** art walk, artists display their creations, often accompanied by live music, food, and wine.

Map 3: Ray St. between University Ave. and North Park Way, North Park

Visual

Other than the occasional sketchbook, what you'll find at this North Park art store is paints, pens, and pencils—but they're great quality paints, pens, and pencils. Local visual artists may be here browsing color palettes or checking out the artwork displayed on its walls.

Map 3: 3776 30th St., North Park, 619/501-5585, www.visualshopsd.com; Mon.-Fri. noon-7pm, Sat.-Sun. noon-5pm

CLOTHING AND ACCESSORIES
Mint Footwear

Shoe fetishists and sneaker fiends should browse this local center of foot fashions. The store packs a lot of hip, fun, and funky shoes for men and women into a relatively small space. Popular sneaker brands like Asics, Puma, and Adidas get plenty of play, as do boots and heels. Styles range from sandals to oxfords, from standard Chucks to Sperry Topsiders. The shop stays current, carrying of-the-moment brands and blink-and-you'll-miss-it trends, and is proudly locally owned and operated.

Map 3: 525 University Ave., Hillcrest, 619/291-6468, www.mintshoes.com, Sun.-Fri. 10am-8pm, Sat. 10am-9pm

Village Hat Shop

Let's be honest: there are few more entertaining things to shop for than hats. At this local hat shop, you'll try on Stetsons and Kangols, fedoras, pageboys and top hats, women's hats with floral or feather adornments, cowboy hats and Panama hats. They often play '80s music so that you can do your own montage. Ultimately you'll walk away with the perfectly styled hat for your head. Look for the smaller sister shop at Seaport Village (853 W. Harbor Dr.).

Map 3: 3821 4th Ave., Hillcrest, 619/683-5533, www.villagehatshop.com; Mon.-Thurs. 10am-6pm, Fri.-Sat. 10am-8pm, Sun. 11am-6pm

A lot of fashionable folks live in the Hillcrest neighborhood, so it's not surprising to find this little pocket of vintage shops on 5th Avenue. Top among them is the funky foraging of **Flashbacks Recycled Fashion** (3849 5th Ave., 619/291-4200). While you're sifting through the vintage racks on this short block, check out **Lost and Found** (3840 5th Ave., 619/291-4200), **Luigi Vera** (3823 5th Ave., 619/683-2199, www.luigivera.com), and **Buffalo Exchange** (3862 5th Ave., 619/298-4411, www.buffaloexchange.com).

Map 3: 5th Ave. between Robinson Ave. and University Ave., Hillcrest

GIFT AND HOME
Babette Schwartz

Like any good neighborhood, Hillcrest appreciates good kitsch, and this "babulous gift emporium" provides plenty of it. Rubber duckies, pinup-themed barware, and Buddha pens are just a small sample of the delightfully frivolous but (usually) functional items packing the colorful retail space, and that's saying nothing about the exquisitely expressive stationery.

Map 3: 421 University Ave., Hillcrest, 619/220-7048, www.babette.com, Mon.-Thurs. 11am-7pm, Fri.-Sat. 11am-9pm, Sun. 11am-5pm

★ Pigment

San Diego's best home and gift shop, Pigment became popular for its selection of air plants, plus a gorgeous variety of wall and ceiling planters, but there are dozens of great gifts and conversation starters here, from a make-your-own gin kit to USB hubs crafted from polished wood. This North Park mainstay recently expanded into a larger space to offer more cleverly conceived decorative items. It's the kind of place where browsing is its own reward.

Map 3: 3801 30th St., North Park, 619/501-6318, www.shoppigment.com; Mon.-Sat. 10am-7pm, Sun. 10am-5pm

GOURMET TREATS
★ Bottlecraft

San Diego's favorite beverage receives special treatment in this boutique bottle shop featuring the best of local brands plus rotating selections from the world's top craft brewers. Bottle shelves are arranged by geographic origin, while coolers split cold bottles and cans by style, with entire sections dedicated to IPAs, stouts, lagers, and seasonal releases. Buy by the bottle, make your own five-, six-, or seven-pack to go, or drink on-site at the Little Italy location (2161 India St.).

Map 3: 3007 University Ave., 619/487-9493, www.bottlecraftbeer.com, Mon.-Fri. noon-10pm, Sat.-Sun. 11am-10pm

SHOPS
UPTOWN

ANTIQUES AND VINTAGE
Sea Junk
You can't find nautical antiques just anywhere. This Maidhof Brothers shop, near the border of Mission Hills and Old Town, sells gorgeous wood stateroom furniture and oil lanterns, plus ridiculously cool items like spyglasses, sextants, portholes, ship's telegraphs, and inclinometers.
Map 4: 1891 San Diego Ave., 800/732-5865, www.seajunk.com, Mon.-Fri. 10am-5pm, Sat. 11am-5pm

CLOTHING AND ACCESSORIES
Johnson House Haberdashery
Where else are you going to go to find proper saloon garb? This small entertaining shop features vintage clothing, custom hats, and unique accessories, whether you're into steampunk or just enjoy the fineries of ye olde times.
Map 4: 2706 Calhoun St., 619/291-5170, Daily 10am-6pm

Miner's Gems & Minerals
While greater San Diego did experience a small and short-lived gold rush, this gem, rock, and fossil retailer does not technically match the historical accuracy of Old Town. Nevertheless, it offers a unique and interesting assortment of geodes, old bones, and precious stone jewelry.
Map 4: 2616 San Diego Ave., 619/688-1178, www.minersgemsandminerals.com, Sun.-Thurs. 10am-6pm, Fri.-Sat. 10am-7pm

Toler's Leather Depot
Presumably, the residents of 19th-century Old Town wore a lot of leather—at least that's the conceit of this leather specialist. Plenty of belts, buckles, bolo ties, cowboy hats, and moccasins are on hand to help complete your Western outfit.
Map 4: 2625 Calhoun St., 619/295-7511; Daily 10am-6pm

GIFT AND HOME
Captain Fitch's Mercantile
Old Town teems with souvenir and gift shops; those searching for better offerings might appreciate this shop, which embraces both the cowboy and sailor sides of the city's history. Vintage compasses, Marshall's stars, and model ships, in addition to quite a few children's books and assorted San Diego-themed trinkets, offer a more interesting variety to choose from.
Map 4: 2627 San Diego Ave., 619/298-3944, Mon.-Fri. 10am-6pm, Sat.-Sun. 10am-8pm

El Centro Artesano
Made-in-Mexico planters and wind chimes are the reasons to visit this pottery lot, which is both colorful and well stocked. It's also a great spot to

clockwise from top left: Pigment in North Park; Prospect Street in La Jolla; North Park's Bottlecraft

Mexican Folk Arts and Crafts

The *Santa Muerte* culture involves a lot of skull motifs.

Mexico isn't just geographically close to San Diego—it's been less than 200 years since San Diego *was* Mexico. The city is steeped in Mexican culture, including food, architecture, and local crafts. Some of the best Made in San Diego products have Mexican origins and make for great shopping opportunities and souvenirs.

- *Papel Picado.* A precise and detailed paper-cutting craft (it translates to "perforated paper"), *Papel Picado* most often depicts floral patterns or sun and skull imagery. The brightly colored paper is often strung like Tibetan prayer flags. You'll find great examples at **Casa Artelexia** (2400 Kettner Blvd., Suite 102, 619/544-1011, www.artelexia.com; Tues.-Sat. 11am-6pm, Sun. 11am-4pm) or in the booths of **Old Town Market** (4010 Twiggs St., 619/278-0955, www.oldtownmarketsandiego.com; Daily 10am-9pm).

get acquainted with the *chimenea;* many a local backyard uses this outdoor fireplace to keep warm on cool nights.

Map 4: 2637 San Diego Ave., 619/297-2931, Mon.-Thurs. 9:30am-6pm, Fri.-Sun. 9:30am-9pm

Four Winds Trading Company

Featuring Native American and Mexican folk arts, crafts, and jewelry, this small shop doesn't focus strictly on artifacts from the region, but it does pride itself on the authenticity of its wares. It's a fine place to browse for the serious or casual collector.

Map 4: 2448 San Diego Ave., 619/692-0466, www.4windsarts.com, Daily 10am-5pm

Racine and Laramie Tobacconist

San Diego's first cigar store dates back to 1868 and still sells stogies as well as pipes and other tobacco products. It also doubles as a museum of sorts, with a few vintage pipes, lighters, and matchbooks on display, making it the rare smoke shop of some interest to nonsmokers.

- **Pottery.** Head over to **El Centro Artesano** (2637 San Diego Ave., 619/297-2931, Mon.-Thurs. 9:30am-6pm, Fri.-Sun. 9:30am-9pm) to peruse the red terra-cotta and hand-painted clay work, ranging from simple and decorative planters to wind chimes and *chimeneas* (small wood-burning fireplaces).

- **Religious Artifacts.** Mexican culture is predominantly Roman Catholic, but some of its indigenous folklore remains, infused into Roman Catholic mysticism that manifests in a fascination with death. Hence you'll find skull iconography depicting Santa Muerte (Our Lady of the Holy Death) and the celebration of Día de los Muertos (Day of the Dead). Skulls adorn jewelry, bride and groom figurines, and colorful shrines. **Casa Artelexia** (2400 Kettner Blvd., Suite 102, 619/544-1011, www.artelexia.com; Tues.-Sat. 11am-6pm, Sun. 11am-4pm), in Little Italy, offers a fascinating sampling of this cult phenomenon.

- **Talavera Tile.** These ornate, hand-painted tiles look great on their own, but together they become beautiful walls, floors, decorative trim, or garden decor. A whole shop is dedicated to them within **Fiesta de Reyes** (2754 Calhoun St., 619/220-5040, www.fiestadereyes.com; Daily 10am-9pm).

- **Textiles.** You'll find plenty of Mexican-influenced clothes, blankets, rugs, and table settings at **Bazaar del Mundo** (4133 Taylor St., 619/296-3161, www.bazaardelmundo.com; Daily 10am-6pm), just at the edge of Old Town. Based either on the brightly colored stripe and diamond patterns of the serape shawl (or poncho), or the airy, white, embroidered tunic called a *huipil*, these designs have evolved through colonial sewing and weaving methods from their indigenous inceptions.

Map 4: 2737 San Diego Ave., 619/291-7833, www.racineandlaramie.com; Mon.-Sat. 10am-8pm, Sun. 10:30am-6pm

GOURMET TREATS

Venissimo Cheese

If "All the best cheese from all over the world" sounds like something you want to experience, stop by San Diego's top dedicated cheese shop. Sample anything you see within the small shop's glass cases; you only have to ask the friendly and helpful staff. Color-coded labels identify which cheese were made from cow's milk, goat, sheep, or buffalo. If you get hungry while nibbling away, order a cheese board or fresh-made salami or *soppressata* sandwich. Other locations include The Headquarters (789 W. Harbor Dr.), in the Marina District, and Bottlecraft (3007 University Ave.) in North Park.

Map 4: 754 W. Washington St., Mission Hills, 619/491-0708, www.venissimo.com; Mon.-Sat. 10am-6pm, Sun. 11am-4pm

MARKETS

★ **Bazaar del Mundo**

Just around the corner from Old Town State Historic Park, this little complex of shops steps up the Mexican cultural experience by offering a better brand of wares in a less hectic environment. While there's still plenty of kitschy fun, there's also some seriously tasteful and colorful merchandise—from hand-painted textiles and clothing to Native American jewelry and Mata Ortiz pottery. You can accomplish some serious shopping here.

Map 4: 4133 Taylor St., 619/296-3161, www.bazaardelmundo.com; Daily 10am-6pm

Fiesta de Reyes

Tucked into the northern corner of Old Town State Historic Park, this courtyard complex holds three Mexican restaurants and has a small stage for traditional music and dance performances. You'll also find a number of specialty shops devoted to Mexican Talavera tiles, olive oil, silver jewelry, beef jerky, and souvenirs galore. It's clearly designed to please visitors and occasionally succeeds.

Map 4: 2754 Calhoun St., 619/220-5040, www.fiestadereyes.com; Daily 10am-9pm

Old Town Market

A bazaar of more than 40 small shops, this enclosed open-air shopping center on the southern edge of Old Town State Historic Park offers a colorful collection of rustic and Mexican clothing, accessories, and decorative items, including Talavera tiles, *papel picado*, woven blankets, ornaments, and folk art.

Map 4: 4010 Twiggs St., 619/278-0955, www.oldtownmarketsandiego.com;
Daily 10am-9pm

MUSIC

M-Theory Music

Not a lot of independent music stores operate in San Diego anymore, but this favorite is still at it, serving up vinyl and CDs instead of downloads. It also stocks a fair number of local recordings, and the clerks will gladly turn you onto some of the best homegrown music.

Map 4: 915 W. Washington St., 619/220-0485, www.mtheorymusic.com;
Mon.-Sat. 10am-8pm, Sun. 11am-7pm

BOOKS

Pennywise

Pacific Beach may seem an unlikely place for a great used bookstore, but what better time to grab an old paperback than on your way to relax on the sand? If it gets a little wet, no big deal; it only cost a few bucks. This used and trade books shop stocks sci-fi, fantasy, romance, suspense, westerns, and all manner of nonfiction, most of it small enough for a big pocket. Just don't get so wrapped up in the plot that you forget to reapply sunscreen.

Map 5: 1331 Garnet Ave., Pacific Beach, 858/270-1640, www.pennywisebooks.info; Tues.-Sat. 10am-5:30pm

CLOTHING AND ACCESSORIES

Garnet Avenue

Three blocks east of the beach on Garnet Avenue is where San Diego women's beach fashions live. Boutiques pepper the blocks with summer dresses, sandals, swimwear, cover-ups, short shorts, and tube tops—all the accoutrements of the sun-lovin' gal. Keep an eye out for **Madison** (1031 Garnet Ave., 858/270-2222), **Closet** (875 Garnet Ave., 858/270-1293), **Pink Zone** (931 Garnet Ave., 858/273-8809), and **The Fabulous Rag** (829 Garnet Ave., 858/270-1993), but plenty of others offer different ways to dress for summer.

Map 5: Garnet Ave. between Mission Blvd. and Dawes St., Pacific Beach

South Coast Wahines

A shop "for girls who surf or just want to look like they do," this local beach outpost dedicated to *wahines* (Hawaiian for "females") sells both functional and fashionable surf clothing, including beach gear with a feminine touch.

Map 5: 4500 Ocean Blvd., 858/273-7600, www.southcoast.com; Mon.-Sat. 10am-6:30pm, Sun. 10am-5pm

Sun Diego

Surfer style takes front and center at this spot, which also sells some surf and skate gear with plenty of stuff for women. But it's dudes who'll benefit the most from the jeans, T-shirts, flannels, shorts, and hoodies that make up the pre- and post-surf uniforms favored by local wave riders.

Map 5: 3126 Mission Blvd., 858/866-0108, www.sundiego.com; Daily 10am-8pm

Sun Splash Swimwear

Forgot to pack a swimsuit? No problem; just stop into this locals' favorite bikini source. The selection of beach-friendly wear ranges from maxi dresses to tankinis, but don't be surprised if the weather and tides direct most options in a skimpier direction.

Map 5: 979 Garnet Ave., Pacific Beach, 858/581-3400, www.sunsplashswimwear.com; Mon.-Fri. 10am-8pm, Sat. 10am-7pm, Sun. 10am-6pm

San Diego Style

San Diego offers a looser definition of what's considered a good look, and a few signature looks never go away—especially the closer you get to the beach.

Guys

Board shorts are popular. These loose-fitting, knee-length shorts are paired with flip-flops or sandals—and that's pretty much year-round. Jeans and sneakers show up when it gets cold or relatives come to visit. A T-shirt, or even a loose collar, and a short-sleeved, button-down top complete the ensemble. In fall and winter months, guys can express themselves with plaid flannels, knit beanies, and choice hoodies. The rigid, striped Baja (or gaucho-style) hoodie still makes an appearance, but even to us dudes that can feel a little too *Fast Times at Ridgemont High*. Dress down at the local surf shops, or at **Sun Diego** (3126 Mission Blvd., 858/866-0108, www.sundiego.com; Daily 10am-8pm) in Mission Beach.

Gals

Women show a lot more variety, and sometimes a lot more skin. Cut-off denim shorts and bikini tops work just as well for cruising the beach as they do for shopping. Athletic clothes, such as yoga pants, have become more common, but when a local gal really wants to turn it up, she finds the perfect summer dress, whether a strapless maxi or something short and flirty. Take a stroll around Pacific Beach, then hit the boutiques along **Garnet Avenue** (Garnet Ave. between Mission Blvd. and Dawes St., Pacific Beach) to find your own.

GIFT AND HOME

Great News!

Voted "Best Kitchenware Retailer in the USA," you can tell that the people working here love to cook. The shop is outfitted with fantastic cookware and kitchen gadgets like mandolin slicers and smoking guns. There are even regular cooking classes that will teach you how to use some of this stuff. It's unlike most of the vacation-friendly shops found in Pacific Beach, but too good for the serious gourmet foodie to miss.

Map 5: 1788 Garnet Ave., Pacific Beach, 858/270-1582, www.great-news.com; Daily 9:30am-6pm

OUTDOOR GEAR

Play It Again Sports

If you're looking for some fun and games to play with at the beach, drop by this shop selling new and used gear, including bikes, body boards, and other kid-size stuff as well as some possible bargains.

Map 5: 1401 Garnet Ave., Pacific Beach, 858/490-0222, www.playitagainsportssd.com; Mon.-Fri. 10am-8pm, Sat. 9am-7pm, Sun. 10:30am-6pm

SURF SHOPS

Mission Surf Shop

For more than 20 years, surfers have been trying out boards from this full-service surf shop, conveniently located near the pier at Pacific Beach. Pick up fresh wax and a surf report in the morning, and maybe some new threads in the afternoon after returning one of many rental options.

Map 5: 4320 Mission Blvd., Pacific Beach, 858/483-8837, www.missionsurf.com; Daily 10am-7pm

Ocean Beach and Point Loma

Map 6

ANTIQUES AND VINTAGE

★ Ocean Beach Antique District

Just a couple of blocks from the beach, Ocean Beach's main drag suddenly becomes an antique-lover's dream. A half dozen well-stocked shops offer unique assortments of vintage furniture and decorative treasures. Some are connected to local history and culture, accumulated over 100 years of San Diego's importance as a shipping gateway to points international. Check out **Vignettes** (4828 Newport Ave., 619/222-9422) or **Newport Avenue Antiques** (4836 Newport Ave., 619/224-1994) for starters.

Map 6: Newport Ave. between Cable St. and Sunset Cliffs Blvd., Ocean Beach

BOOKS

Bookstar

While technically a Barnes & Noble, you won't know it from the sign out front, which is built into the neon-emblazoned marquee of the Loma Theater. The single-screen art deco theater was built in 1944 and became a bookstore about 20 years ago. The large full-service store still feels like a vintage theater, with paisley rugs, swirls, and patterns painted on the ceiling, some original art deco fixtures, and even the old movie screen. It makes browsing books feel adventurous.

Map 6: 3150 Rosecrans Pl., 619/225-0465, www.barnesandnoble.com; Mon.-Sat. 10am-9pm, Sun. 10am-9pm

Galactic Comics

Every funky beachside community needs a comic book store. Galactic jibes pretty well with OB's out-there mentality; it's just a couple of laid-back guys, into graphic arts and storytelling, offering comics, video games, and rental DVDs to a dedicated clientele.

Map 6: 4981 Newport Ave., Ocean Beach, 619/226-6543, www.galacticcomics.com; Daily 11am-9pm

CLOTHING AND ACCESSORIES

Pride Surf & Skate

This shop's so relaxed you could walk by a couple times without catching on. But locals know it as a great hassle-free spot for a small but quality assortment of gear and fashions, kids included.

Map 6: 5035 Newport Ave., Ocean Beach, 619/222-1575; Mon.-Sat. 10am-7:30pm, Sun. 10am-6pm

GIFT AND HOME

The Black

A whiff of incense hits you the moment you walk through the doors of this OB mainstay that's been selling countercultural goods more than four decades. Locals come here for everything from replacement guitar strings and harmonicas to beaded jewelry and smoking implements.

Map 6: 5017 Newport Ave., Ocean Beach, 619/222-5498, www.theblackoceanbeach. com; Mon.-Sat. 10am-8pm, Sun. 10am-7pm

La Jolla
Map 7

ART AND DESIGN

La Jolla Design District

Close to the ocean, fashionable Girard Avenue caters to apparel, but past Kline Street it turns into a top notch home and design district, with antiques, designer interiors, high-end furniture, and architectural boutiques. Visit **Design Studio West** (7422 Girard Ave., 858/454-9133) for big ideas or **La Jolla Fiber Arts** (7644 Girard Ave., 858/454-6732) for exciting textiles. These shops thrive here for a reason—each ranges from interesting to outstanding, offering an amazing resource for decorators and dreamers.

Map 7: Girard Ave. between Kline St. and Genter St.

Prospect Street Arts and Crafts

Decorative art shoppers will find plenty to browse with a short stroll on the north end of Prospect Street, which might be entirely devoted to artisanal goods were it not for the occasional restaurant. Specialty shops like **Africa and Beyond** (1250 Prospect St., 858/454-9983) and **Arte de Origen** (1264 Prospect St., 858/456-2200) feature African and Central American craft objects, while other shops focus on photography, fine-art prints, or digital creations.

Map 7: Prospect St. between Herschel Ave. and Cave St.

BOOKS

DG Wills Book Shop

Exactly the sort of dusty old bookshop that bibliophiles fear will become extinct, DG Wills is stacked to the ceiling with a mixture of old, new,

top to bottom: Ocean Beach's Antique Row on Newport Avenue; Bird's Surf Shed, Morena

and collectible volumes crammed together on wooden shelves. The store hosts readings with venerable authors and is home to the La Jolla Cultural Society.

Map 7: 7461 Girard Ave., 858/456-1800, www.dgwillsbooks.com; Mon.-Sat. 10am-7pm, Sun. 11am-5pm

Warwick's

The Warwick's family has been selling books, stationery, and gifts since 1896. Four generations have run this place, which moved to its La Jolla location more than 75 years ago. It's a book-tour stop for many best-selling authors and a great way to supplement your vacation reading list.

Map 7: 7812 Girard Ave., 858/454-0347, www.warwicks.com; Mon.-Sat. 9am-6pm, Sun. 10am-5:30pm

CLOTHING AND ACCESSORIES

Ascot Shop

Any man who wants his wardrobe to be absolutely on point should step inside this independently owned shop that has provided top fashions from this location since 1950. Aside from a turn-of-the-20th-century redesign by the architect of the Coronado Bay Bridge, this upscale destination operates as it has for decades, outfitting men with the finest selection of dress and casual threads in town.

Map 7: 7750 Girard Ave., 858/454-4222, www.ascotshop.com; Mon.-Sat. 10am-6pm

Bowers Jewelers

A beautifully presented shop by anyone's standards, this family-owned jewelry and gift boutique has served La Jolla for nearly 70 years. Polished wood display cases display both affordable and lavish settings, with gorgeous jewels that make for fine romantic gestures. Decorative *objets* throughout the store qualify as great and unique gift ideas.

Map 7: 7860 Girard Ave., 858/459-3678; Mon.-Sat. 9:30am-5:30pm, Sun. 11am-4pm

Echoes Too

After perusing the designer apparel lining the sidewalks of Girard Avenue, step a couple of blocks over to check out the discounted wares of this small consignment boutique. Any designer jeans in your size are bound to be a score, and there'll surely be enough dresses, blouses, and accessories to stoke the imagination.

Map 7: 7705 Fay Ave., 858/459-6588; Mon.-Fri. 11am-5pm, Sat. 10am-5pm

★ Girard Avenue

Fashion boutiques come and go, and vary by season or taste. What remains constant is that Girard Avenue (east from Prospect St.) plays home to a wealth of trendy and designer women's clothing and accessories boutiques.

This is a window shopper's dream, with internationally known retailers along the lines of **Ralph Lauren** (7830 Girard Ave., 858/459-0554) and **Kate Spade** (7931 Girard Ave., 858/454-2548), exquisitely curated local boutiques like **Kerut** (7944 Girard Ave., 858/456-0800) and **La Donna** (937 Silverado St., 585/459-3410), and national retailers like **Chico's** (7855 Girard Ave., 858/456-6273) and **White House Black Market** (7925 Girard Ave., 858/459-2565).

Map 7: Girard Ave. between Prospect St. and Kline St.

Jewels by the Sea

With estate, vintage, and fashion jewelry—including those of several local designers—the selection at this independently owned shop differs from most jewelry retailers, which is part of the charm. Pieces range greatly in price; walk away with a fashionably affordable scarf or an exotic gemstone gift.

Map 7: 1237 Prospect St., 858/459-5166, www.jewelsbythesea.biz; Mon. noon-6pm, Wed.-Sat. noon-6pm, Sun. 1pm-6pm

Le Chauvinist

"There exists a substantial difference between being in style and having style," states the owner of this men's clothing and accessories shop, which offers a mix of new and consignment fashions. Prepared to outfit a guy for a business meeting, a rock concert, or opening day at the Del Mar racetrack, their selection ranges from socks and cufflinks to seersucker suits and Panama hats.

Map 7: 7709 Fay Ave., 858/456-0117, www.lechauvinist.com; Mon.-Fri. 10am-5pm, Sat. 11am-4pm, Sun. 9am-2pm

Take 2 Ladies Consignment Boutique

South of La Jolla Village, near Windansea Beach and away from the heavy foot traffic of Girard Avenue and Prospect Street, this designer boutique carries the rarely worn attire of local fashionistas who need to make room for next season's looks. It's an excellent place to find attire bearing the instantly recognizable names of the world's best-known designers, without the world's biggest price tags. Clothes this fine rarely go out of fashion; they merely stop being new.

Map 7: 6786 La Jolla Blvd., 858/459-0095, www.take2ladiesconsignor.com; Mon.-Fri. 11am-6:30pm, Sat. 11am-5pm, Sun. 11am-4pm

KIDS AND PETS

Geppetto's

Consider this as much a warning to young parents as a recommendation: This fabulous local shop looks amazing and will lure your children from the sidewalk. You'll follow, too, because its unique toy selection is tough to beat. The prices aren't, however, so be prepared to dash your child's dreams or break out your wallet.

Map 7: 7850 Girard Ave., 858/456-4441, www.geppettostoys.com; summer Mon.-Thurs. 9am-7pm, Fri.-Sat. 9am-9pm, Sun. 10am-6pm, fall-spring Mon.-Thurs. 9am-7pm, Fri.-Sat. 9am-7pm, Sun. 10am-6pm

Muttropolis

This small Southern California chain has a full-service online shop, so you can get a pretty good idea what type of pampering pet products it offers for dogs and cats. But shopping is always more fun in person. This colorful, organized space presents tasteful leashes and collars, designer pet carriers, and food dishes representative of the La Jolla lifestyle.

Map 7: 7755 Girard Ave., 858/459-9663, www.muttropolis.com; Mon.-Fri. 10am-7pm, Sat. 10am-6pm, Sun. 10am-5pm

Spoiled Rotten Boutique

How do the upscale tots dress in a ritzy town like La Jolla? Find the answer in this children's boutique, which sells dapper duds and designer items of impossible cuteness. Show up at a baby shower with something from this shop and you win.

Map 7: 7556 Fay Ave., Suite C, 858/459-1904, www.spoiledrottensd.com; Mon.-Sat. 10am-5pm

SHOPPING MALLS
Westfield UTC

Possibly the best mall in town, UTC (aka University Towne Centre) includes the new ArcLight theater, the best local food chain (Tender Greens), and all the relevant department stores (Macy's, Nordstrom) and mall franchises you'd expect, plus a number of stores you might have thought too high brow to be seen within reach of a food court.

Map 7: 4545 La Jolla Village Dr., 858/546-8858, www.westfield.com/utc; Mon.-Sat. 10am-9pm, Sun. 11am-7pm

SURF SHOPS
Mitch's Surf Shop

La Jolla's go-to surf shop since the late 1960s, Mitch's sells great longboards, short boards, paddleboards, wetsuits, and other beach gear for those inspired by the azure waters off the coast. Think of it as an important first stop in the pursuit of an endless summer.

Map 7: 631 Pearl St., 858/459-5933, www.mitchssurfshop.com; Mon.-Sat. 10am-7pm, Sun. 10am-5pm

BOOKS

Bay Books

Independently owned on Orange Avenue for nearly a quarter century, this well-stocked local favorite carries current titles and magazines, as well as a deep inventory of must-read books. Various staff and regular customers have placed hand-written recommendations around the shop, calling attention to titles they've discovered and enjoyed through the years.

Map 8: 1029 Orange Ave., 619/435-0070, www.baybookscoronado.com; Mon.-Sat. 9am-8pm, Sun. 9am-6pm

SHOPPING MALLS

Ferry Landing Marketplace

Where the ferry lands in Coronado, a small circle of shops and restaurants have developed, including gift shops like the Paris-inspired **French Room** (619/437-4325) and foodie **Regali Gourmet & Gifts** (619/522-0288). Most interesting may be the **Stephen Clayton Galleries** (619/435-1319), home to many Dr. Seuss prints. Seuss lived in nearby La Jolla for many years, and while many prints resemble his story illustrations, he also created grander, more fully realized imagery.

Map 8: 1201 1st St., 619/435-8895, www.coronadoferrylandingshops.com; Daily 10am-9pm

★ Orange Avenue

Orange Avenue serves as Coronado's main drag. In the southwest corner of the island, near the Hotel del Coronado, it's home to a bevy of restaurants, gift shops, and boutiques. Most shops sell swimwear, housewares, funny T-shirts, or kitschy beach-themed souvenirs. There are few you'd go out of your way to visit, but Orange Avenue is a nice stroll.

Map 8: Orange Ave. between 8th St. and Dana Pl.

Shops at the Del

A left turn from the lobby leads down to small mall of shops within the Hotel del Coronado. Offerings include resort boutiques, travel goods, bath and body items, photography services, and designer sunglasses. You'll also find a branch of MooTime Creamery serving cones of the favorite local ice cream.

Map 8: 1500 Orange Ave., 619/435-6611, www.hoteldel.com; Daily 8am-9pm, individual shop hours vary

BOOKS
Adams Avenue Bookstore
Dating back to 1965, this independently run bookstore features a deep collection of used and rare books, plus a couple of cats who consider the stacks their turf. The two-story shop gets so packed to the gills with hardcovers and paperbacks that the stairwell is lined with bookshelves. Upstairs, cookbooks appropriately stock what used to be somebody's kitchen, and downstairs in back, a kid's play area occupies a room full of children's titles.
Map 9: 3502 Adams Ave., 619/281-3330, www.adamsavebooks.com;
Mon.-Tues. 10am-6pm, Wed. 10am-8pm, Thurs.-Sat. 10am-6pm, Sun. noon-5pm

GOURMET TREATS
Catalina Offshore Products
San Diego has enough fresh seafood restaurants in town that going out of the way to pick up your own fish hardly seems worthwhile. And yet people do—this fish market is that good. Shop for local oysters, fillets of the best fish in season, and wild-caught Mexican shrimp, or crack open a sea urchin for some fresh *uni* and taste the ocean.
Map 9: 5202 Lovelock St., Morena, 619/297-9797, www.catalinaop.com;
Mon.-Fri. 8am-3pm, Sat. 8am-2pm

Seisel's Old Fashioned Meats
To pick up a fine cut of meat, make this gourmet market your only stop. Prime and choice cuts are available at the butcher's counter (take a number), along with some of the best sausages in town. They always have a few surprises in stock, whether the exquisitely marbled *wagyu* beef or pheasant. A freezer near the back wall contains an unheard-of variety of game meats, and the deli counter is nearly as good.
Map 9: 4131 Ashton St., Morena, 619/275-1234, www.iowameatfarms.com;
Mon.-Sat. 9am-7pm, Sun. 10am-6pm

OUTDOOR GEAR
Adventure 16
Hiking, camping, rock climbing—when San Diegans need outdoor gear, they stop by this local retail alternative to REI. Staffed by outdoors enthusiasts, they'll be able to guide you to some great trails and secret spots if you ask.
Map 9: 4620 Alvarado Canyon Rd., Alvarado Canyon, 619/283-2374,
www.adventure16.com; Mon.-Fri. 10am-8pm, Sat. 10am-6pm, Sun. 11am-5pm

SHOPPING MALLS

Fashion Valley

Not terribly far from Mission Valley is this similar though slightly higher-end mall with a movie theater, food court, shops, and the Nordstrom, Neiman Marcus, and Bloomingdale's department stores. Fashion Valley tends to be a little more high-concept and trending, and therefore more likely to be crowded. It's also accessible on the trolley line.

Map 9: 7007 Friars Rd., Fashion Valley, 619/688-9113, www.shopfashionvalley.com; Mon.-Sat. 10am-9pm, Sun. 11am-7pm

Mission Valley Mall

Westfield Mission Valley is conveniently located, with loads of parking, a movie theater, and department stores such as Macy's and Target as well as a number of places for cheap eats.

Map 9: 1640 Camino Del Rio N., Mission Valley, 619/296-6375, www.westfield.com/missionvalley; Mon.-Sat. 10am-9pm, Sun. 11am-6pm

SURF SHOPS

★ Bird's Surf Shed

The only true must-visit surf shop in town isn't found in a beach neighborhood. The Shed (really a Quonset hut) is a bit of a local legend, and often the site of celebrity surfer clinics, movie premieres, and the epic recounting of burly sessions after big swells hit. The huge selection of boards includes vintage models and custom rarities, and a devout wave rider can get lost for hours just soaking it all in.

Map 9: 1091 W. Morena Blvd., Morena, 619/276-2473, www.birdssurfshed.com; Mon.-Sat. 11am-6pm, Sun. noon-5pm

SHOPS
GREATER SAN DIEGO

Hotels

PRICE KEY

$ Less than $100 per night

$$ $100–200 per night

$$$ More than $200 per night

San Diego is a sprawling city, with a mix of neighborhoods and attractions. Hotels spring up mostly around the areas where people visit most—Downtown and the beach neighborhoods—with the exception of Balboa Park and Old Town, which would have to sacrifice charm for lodging.

Most hotels are pretty standard, with virtually every national chain represented, along with a number of motels and budget inns. There are a few resorts around the beach areas, plus some hip boutique hotels and backpacker's hostels. Mission Valley is home to most of the larger chain hotels, with rates more affordable than those downtown, but you'll need a car to see anything other than the I-8 freeway.

Picking a hotel for its location always makes some sense, but in truth this is the kind of city where you may have breakfast in one neighborhood, lie on the beach in another, visit a museum across town, and then get dinner in the opposite direction before returning to your home base for drinks. In other words, where you stay may have more to do with where you want to be when you call it a night, or what you want to see when you wake up in the morning.

CHOOSING A HOTEL

There is no shortage of hotel rooms in San Diego—unless the unbelievably popular Comic Con is taking place, in which case rooms fill up well in advance and rates triple. But aside from that one long weekend in July, you should have your pick of locations to lay your head at night. Deciding where is all about where you want to go and how you want to get around.

Previous page top: boats moored next to Humphrey's Half Moon Inn & Suites
bottom: cabanas at Bahia Bay Resort

Highlights

★ **Best Value:** Little Italy's **La Pensione** offers good clean rooms on the cheap, some with harbor views. The neighborhood is within walking distance of the Gaslamp, great restaurants, the bay, and the trolley (page 191).

★ **Best Apartment-Style Hotel:** Beautiful Craftsman-style rooms with private kitchens and updated amenities make **Mudville Flats** in the East Village a satisfying place to return to at night (page 191).

★ **Best Hotel in a Nontouristy Area:** A stay at Uptown's well-appointed **Lafayette** allows a little respite from the heavily trafficked tourist areas that can wear you down during the day, but is still close to some great evening entertainment (page 194).

★ **Best Beach Hotel for Adults:** A boutique hotel on the beach in a lively area with a hip restaurant and bar, Pacific Beach's **Tower 23 Hotel** is convenient to Mission Bay, Mission Beach, and the seemingly endless nightlife of Garnet Avenue (page 197).

★ **Best Golf Resort:** The **Lodge at Torrey Pines** is hallowed ground—overlooking the ocean and close to the sights and shopping of La Jolla. Plus your stay earns you preferred tee times (page 201).

★ **Best Hotel You Never Need to Leave:** If you're just looking to unpack your bags and enjoy going nowhere for a few days, head to the legendary **Hotel del Coronado,** where you can eat, drink, shop, play by the pool, and enjoy a perfect beach in an idyllic setting. It's like vacationing in another era (page 202).

If you've got a car, quick freeway access will be easy, but parking will not. Hotels in the Downtown area typically charge $15-35 per night for parking on top of their room rates, and you won't be able to get around that by finding street parking unless you get really lucky, repeatedly. That said, if you plan to spend a lot of time around Downtown—going to a ballgame in East Village, nightclubs in the Gaslamp, and harbor-front museums in the Marina District—having hotel parking can be a real plus, as you may explore other areas where spaces are easier to come by, yet always have a spot waiting for you back at your place. Little Italy may be a few steps removed from these neighborhoods, but it's easy to get in and out, and rates are still low considering how hip the neighborhood has become and how great the restaurants are.

Decent walking neighborhoods like North Park, Hillcrest, and Mission Hills offer little choice of accommodations. In Mission Valley, a short freeway drive from these areas, there's a street called Hotel Circle, which features more than a dozen hotels alongside the east-west I-8. The easy freeway access of these establishments is undisputable, but other than a few sprawling malls, there's little to see and do within walking distance, and with few exceptions, these rooms are the kind you leave early in the morning and return to only to sleep at night.

Of course, everybody at some point wants to stay by the beach, and most of the beach communities can accommodate, in many cases right on the sand—although you'll find better values going even a block or two inland. If you score a Mission Bay-front hotel, you may even benefit from watersports lessons and rentals right outside your door. While it's easy to spend entire sunny days on foot in the right beach area and never once regret it, none of them are really that easy to get to without a vehicle.

Downtown

Map 1

500 West Hotel $

Conveniently situated near the Santa Fe Depot, this hostel's location earns it a second look for those traveling by train. A short walk from harbor attractions, it's only about 10 minutes on foot to the Gaslamp or Little Italy. Trolley and Coaster trains offer quick access to Old Town and North County beaches. The bare-bones private and shared rooms may not be homey, but they are clean. Guests have free access to the basement YMCA, plus TV and games in common lounges.

Map 1: 500 W. Broadway, 619/234-5252, www.500westhotelsd.com

Gaslamp Plaza Suites $$

Occupying San Diego's first skyscraper, this tidy, friendly hotel and time-share offers 64 rooms, each named for a famous author. While a stay in the Dr. Seuss room might sound special, the decor is fairly standard throughout. The building's 1913 charm shines through at every turn, whether in marble, brass, mosaic, or carved wood. A comfortable 11th-floor roof deck offers a view of San Diego only a high-rise could provide.

Map 1: 520 E St., Gaslamp, 619/232-9500, www.gaslampplaza.com

Horton Grand Hotel $$$

Originally built as two separate hotels during the 1880s, the architecture of this beautifully appointed boutique hotel leaves a fine impression. The two buildings connect to form a graceful, shady courtyard. No two rooms are alike, though a number do offer a lovely courtyard balcony.

Map 1: 311 Island Ave., Gaslamp, 619/544-1886, www.hortongrand.com

Hostelling International San Diego, Downtown $

Classed up by a recent remodel, this central Gaslamp hostel offers 60 dorm beds, 38 private rooms, and a fully equipped shared kitchen, providing clean accommodations at bargain prices. A no-alcohol policy keeps the place quiet, and reading and TV lounges offer a nice respite from exploring the dozens of bars, clubs, and restaurants within a five-block radius.

Map 1: 521 Market St., Gaslamp, 619/525-1531, www.sandiegohostels.org

Hotel Indigo $$

Overlooking Petco Park, this pet-friendly, LEED-certified hotel isn't just an environmentally friendly place to bring your dog and catch a ballgame. It's also centrally located to explore Downtown, or just relax on the rooftop lounge. Prices vary with a range of sleeping and view options, including rooms with a clear view of the Padres at work.

Map 1: 509 9th Ave., East Village, 619/371-5756, www.hotelinsd.com

Hotel Solamar $$$

Situated just between the Gaslamp and the East Village, this stylish, modern hotel sits right in the middle of the action, whether you're going to a game at Petco Park, attending an event at the convention center, or hitting the local nightlife. The hotel has a comfortable and hip rooftop pool and lounge, and an excellent farm-to-table restaurant, J Six. The hotel hosts a complimentary happy hour (daily 5pm-6pm), serving local wine and beer. Pet-friendly and allergy-free rooms are also available.

Map 1: 435 6th Ave., Gaslamp, 619/819-9500, www.hotelsolamar.com

Hotel Vyvant $$

Clean, independently decorated rooms give this Little Italy boutique hotel a fair amount of charm. Quick access to the freeway and airport also make it a decent launch pad for exploring the city. The only drawback is the lack of parking, but given the nice rooms at a low rate, it could be the key to a stress-free visit—no getting lost, no designated drivers. Plus, plenty of the city's best restaurants happen to be in the neighborhood.

Map 1: 505 W. Grape St., Little Italy, 619/230-1600, www.hotelvyvant.com

The Keating Hotel 💲💲

An urban boutique hotel in every sense of the word, this place doesn't try to dazzle with a lot of on-site amenities. Instead it puts everything into its four-star rooms, which include espresso machines, goose-down duvets, and tech-friendly entertainment systems. Styled somewhere between Italian sophistication and New York sensibility, the Keating provides a fitting return home after a night out in the surrounding Gaslamp and East Village.

Map 1: 432 F St., Gaslamp, 619/814-5700, www.thekeating.com

★ La Pensione Hotel 💲💲

A central Little Italy location gives this clean and simple hotel a leg up, whether or not you opt for a room with a harbor view. A trolley stop is a couple of blocks away, and a short walk gets you to the Midway and Maritime Museums, not to mention all the great restaurants in the neighborhood, starting with a pizza place and café in the shared courtyard. Biggest drawback? Limited daily parking on a first-come basis.

Map 1: 606 W. Date St., Little Italy, 619/236-8000, www.lapensionehotel.com

Manchester Grand Hyatt 💲💲💲

Steps from the Marina, Seaport Village, Convention Center, and USS *Midway* Museum, the dual high-rises of this bay-front hotel overlook Downtown. The large rooftop pool and cabanas are a favorite of the celebrities working Comic Con each July, and the luster seems to hold most of the year. Other rooftops feature tennis, basketball, and volleyball courts, and a separate lap pool. The business-friendly place has an excellent hotel bar, the penthouse Top of the Hyatt, known for panoramic views and a mostly sophisticated clientele.

Map 1: 1 Market Pl., 619/232-1234, www.manchestergrand.hyatt.com

HOTELS
DOWNTOWN

★ Mudville Flats 💲💲

Experience the quaint appeal of San Diego's gorgeous Craftsman homes by renting one of the fully furnished apartments of this 1905 boutique hotel. Rooms feature built-in shelves and wood detailing that make Craftsmans so appealing, plus private kitchens and one amenity few of those cottages can claim: air-conditioning.

Map 1: 747 10th Ave., East Village, 619/232-4045, www.mudvilleflats.com

Omni San Diego Hotel 💲💲💲

Best known for having a sky bridge granting direct access to Petco Park, this luxury high-rise hotel has some rooms that actually overlook the field along the third base line, so having a ticket to the game or concert may not even be necessary. A spacious rooftop terrace and pool offer views of the Coronado Bridge and the convention center across the street. The lively Gaslamp is out the front door, the edgier East Village is nearby, and a trolley stop is even closer than home plate.

Map 1: 675 L St., East Village, 619/231-6664, www.omnihotels.com

clockwise from top left: the Cosmopolitan Hotel in Old Town Historic Park; the Lafayette hotel in North Park; the Downtown Horton Grand Hotel

Porto Vista Hotel ⑤⑤

This urban boutique hotel with a rooftop deck offers a variety of options at reasonable rates. The on-site restaurant has a nice a view of the harbor, which some rooms also share. Located in a great neighborhood with quick trolley and freeway access.

Map 1: 1835 Columbia St., Little Italy 619/544-0164, www.portovistasd.com

Urban Boutique Hotel ⑤⑤

This renovated and independently owned boutique lodging doesn't stand out or thrill, but neither does it disappoint. Affordability, location, and a dog-friendly first floor warrant consideration for those looking to stay within Little Italy and who don't mind parking in a nearby pay lot. It's a quick walk to a trolley stop, the Maritime Museum, and Waterfront Park, in a neighborhood with great walking streets, bars, and restaurants.

Map 1: 1654 Columbia St., Little Italy, 619/232-3400, www.urbanboutiquehotel.com

U. S. Grant Hotel ⑤⑤

Built by the family of the 18th president and named in his honor, the U. S. Grant opened in 1910 with much pomp. This classic century-old hotel offers a grand entrance: An elegant lobby presents marble floors and silk carpets with high ceilings furnished with crystal chandeliers. A 2006 restoration renewed glamor to the place, with 47 luxurious suites. Standard rooms go for reasonable rates, considering the style and location, though pricey parking ($40 per day) can eat into that.

Map 1: 326 Broadway, 619/232-3121, www.usgrant.net

Westgate Hotel ⑤⑤

Old European elegance is on display at this central Gaslamp hotel. The lobby features vintage furniture, a curved staircase, and a grand piano; on weekends a high tea comes complete with a harpist. A third-floor roof deck adds an outdoor lounge, a swimming pool, and even a small running track—all benefit from the views of Downtown and the harbor. Good-size comfortable rooms figure nicely into the continental motif, and many share a private foyer with the room next door, great for groups booking rooms together.

Map 1: 1055 2nd Ave., Gaslamp, 619/238-1818, www.westgatehotel.com

Balboa Park

Map 2

Inn at the Park $$

Across the street from Balboa Park, and within walking distance of Hillcrest restaurants and nightlife, this all-suite 1926 historic hotel property in Banker's Hill offers 82 suites ranging from studios to two bedrooms. With high ceilings, Sealy Posturepedic mattresses, and fully stocked kitchens, the spacious, classically tasteful rooms feel like home, even while adhering to the vintage building's original apartment-building layout.

Map 2: 525 Spruce St., Banker's Hill, 619/291-0999,

www.shellhospitality.com/Inn-at-the-Park

Keating House $$

With only nine rooms within this 19th-century Victorian mansion, each has its own peculiar charm—and private bath. The romantic and affordable bed-and-breakfast stands a mere four blocks from the western edge of Balboa Park in a quiet part of Banker's Hill. Aside from a little gold-leafing, the home's colorfully painted exterior and interiors adhere to its original 1888 palette. A full breakfast is made from scratch each morning, using mostly natural and organic ingredients. Room prices remain constant year-round.

Map 2: 2331 2nd Ave., Banker's Hill, 619/239-8585, www.keatinghouse.com

Uptown

Map 3

★ Lafayette $$

North Park has emerged as one of San Diego's hippest neighborhoods, but the Lafayette was here long before it was cool. When it first opened 70 years ago, it was a popular destination for celebrities and jet-setters. Amid the recent resurgence, this historic hotel has been redesigned to bring its amenities up to par with its vintage charm. Contemporary decor and comfortable beds make all the bungalows and suites desirable—but especially those sitting poolside. Today, the Lafayette can be quite the scene, hosting pool parties in the summer with occasional live music events during holiday weekends. Within a few blocks are North Park, Hillcrest, and University Heights restaurants and bars.

Map 3: 2223 El Cajon Blvd., North Park, 619/296-2101, www.lafayettehotelsd.com

Cosmopolitan Hotel ❸❺

To get into the spirit of Old Town, reserve one of the 10 guest rooms in this 19th-century hotel located within the historic park. Rooms are outfitted with furnishings from the era, such as claw-foot tubs, with views of San Diego's original city center. Guests should pose for a photograph in the hotel's vintage saloon.

Map 4: 2660 Calhoun St., 619/297-1874, www.oldtowncosmopolitan.com

Mission Bay and Beaches Map 5

Bahia Resort Hotel ❸❺

Just a short distance from Belmont Park, the Bahia fronts Mission Bay, offering a laid-back bit of beachfront in contrast to the lively boardwalk and amusement park scene. Both the price point and the calm waters of the bay suit families with young children, and the resort offers some mellow activities, including a steamboat ride to the Catamaran, its sister resort across the bay.

Map 5: 998 W. Mission Bay Dr., Mission Bay, 858/488-0551, www.bahiahotel.com

Banana Bungalow ❺

Located in the center of the action with a community patio overlooking the rowdy PB boardwalk, Banana Bungalow offers coed dorms or private rooms, each with a bath, plus beach rentals and 24-hour access. Nobody ever recommends a youth hostel based on its rooms, but if you're going the low-budget backpacker route, you'll never get closer to the sand than this.

Map 5: 707 Reed Ave., Pacific Beach, 858/273-3060, www.bananabungalowsandiego.com

Catamaran Resort ❸❸❺

Inspired by a trip to Hawaii, the Catamaran captures a tropical resort atmosphere with leafy plants, colorful birds, and twice-weekly luaus along its bayside beach. Water activities are available on the placid bay, and a short walk across Mission Boulevard takes you to the Pacific side of the peninsula.

Map 5: 3999 Mission Blvd., Pacific Beach, 858/488-1081, www.catamaranresort.com

Crystal Pier Hotel ❸❺

How central to Pacific Beach do you want to be? Crystal Pier juts right out from the center of PB, and these historic, moderately appointed guest cottages sit right on top of the pier itself. Cottages feature kitchenettes and decks, with prime views of the surfers and beach life below.

Map 5: 4500 Ocean Blvd., Pacific Beach, 858/483-6983, www.crystalpier.com

Choosing the Right Beach Neighborhood

San Diego's beaches have different personalities, so choosing a beach hotel begins with finding the personality that suits you.

- **Pacific Beach (PB):** Attracts lots of athletic students and young adults who like to party and who usually try to find ways to impress other singles with their fit bodies or acts of incomprehensible stupidity. Great beaches for surfing and quick access to Mission Bay.

- **Mission Beach:** Stretching two miles south and north, the north end bleeds into PB, while father south the mood becomes decidedly less rowdy. The southern stretch passes through quiet residential areas and comfortable vacation rentals, eventually reaching Belmont Park, with its rides, games, and souvenir shops. Hotels around Mission Beach give you the option of visiting beaches on either side of its narrow peninsula: the oceanfront, with its waves and sunsets, or the bay side, with sandy coastline on calm waters that feel safer for young children.

- **Ocean Beach (OB):** OB whoops it up, though the atmosphere is decidedly more laid-back than PB (at least during the day). At night a unique blend of hippies, surfers, military folk, and misfits take to the bars, which skew a little wider in age range and have a slightly less meat-market feel. These are also great beaches for surfing, with easy access to Mission Bay.

- **La Jolla:** La Jolla Shores is one of the better family beaches in town. While the long strip of sand is served by only a handful of hotels and a tiny two-block commercial district, it's the stuff beach getaways are made of. It's also remarkably crowded in summer with youngsters splashing around in the waves. The Village of La Jolla, just up the road, is entirely different—an upscale pocket of glamor with a few tiny beach coves and parks running parallel to its shops, galleries, and restaurants. Plenty of fine hotels juggle urban and beach amenities.

- **Coronado:** Across the bay from Downtown, Coronado offers quality relaxation. Families tend to thrive here, though something about being across that bridge seems to cap the crowds just bit. Orange Avenue, Coronado's main drag, is only a few blocks inland and offers convenient restaurants and shopping. The legendary Hotel del Coronado sits at the south end of the beach, always worth a visit if only for a beachfront cocktail.

Pacific Terrace Hotel $$$

The 73 rooms at this beachfront hotel aim for a "Tommy Bahama" vibe, which suits the vacation feel offered by playful surrounding Pacific Beach. The hotel lies on the northern, quieter end of the beach, and most of the rooms have at least a partial view of the beach. A light breakfast is served around the small pool each morning. The many bars and restaurants within walking distance provide nourishment and entertainment.

Map 5: 610 Diamond St., Pacific Beach, 858/581-3500, www.pacificterrace.com

Paradise Point Resort & Spa ⑤⑤⑤

Many of the comfortable rooms in this bay-front resort look right out at Mission Bay. Guests can rent equipment from the on-site water-sports company, or take advantage of the miniature golf, basketball, tennis, croquet, boccie, and Ping-Pong on offer. The spacious property is peppered with myriad water features, including ponds, fountains, and a number of swimming pools. Calm, shallow beaches surround most of the hotel, with bonfire pits for relaxing evenings.

Map 5: 1404 Vacation Rd., Mission Bay, 858/274-4630, www.paradisepoint.com

Surfer Beach Hotel ⑤⑤

It's tough to find fault with this moderately priced, pet-friendly boutique hotel right on the boardwalk at Pacific Beach. Standard rooms feature king or double beds, some with balconies. Amenities include on-site parking ($15) and a heated pool. Access to the surf is almost immediate, and the nightlife of PB is a just a few minutes' walk.

Map 5: 711 Pacific Beach Dr., Pacific Beach, 858/483-7070, www.surferbeachhotel.com

★ Tower 23 Hotel ⑤⑤⑤

A Tempur-Pedic mattress in every room ensures this designer boutique hotel remains the most comfortable place to sleep in Pacific Beach. Its location fronting the boardwalk gives you plenty to do and see to earn that sleep. Guests may enjoy the view from their balconies or the shared rooftop deck, or step onto the beach from the hotel's well-appointed JRDN restaurant and bar. With surf lockers available, and beach and bike rentals on-site, it's a chic home-base for a beachy stay in this lively part of town.

Map 5: 723 Felspar St., Pacific Beach, 858/270-2323, www.t23hotel.com

Ocean Beach and Point Loma

Map 6

Humphrey's Half Moon Inn ⑤⑤⑤

This tropical, bay-front hotel offers a unique set of views. In the distance is the San Diego skyline; look a little closer to admire the San Diego Yacht Club boats moored just outside. But the real views are of the city's best summer concert venue. The intimate outdoor stage sits right on the water and attracts some of the world's most celebrated musicians and comedians. Room packages may be paired with front-and-center seating, and some suites open up to a balcony with the best view in the house. Regardless of whether there's a show scheduled, this is one of the most enjoyable hotels in the city.

Map 6: 2303 Shelter Island Dr., Shelter Island, 619/224-3411, www.halfmooninn.com

The Inn at Sunset Cliffs $$$

If you like the idea of chillin' poolside on a cliff overlooking the Pacific, check out this cozy mid-century gem. It's almost impossible to sleep closer to the ocean than this, whether you opt for a simple individual room or a decked-out hot-tub suite. The soothing sound of breaking waves more than makes up for the hotel's only flaw—it's a good 10-minute drive from the nearest freeway, but an optimal choice if you plan to relax in the area.

Map 6: 1370 Sunset Cliffs Blvd., 619/222-7901, www.innatsunsetcliffs.com

Ocean Beach Hotel $$

Mixed reviews about the condition of some of the rooms occasionally tarnish this hotel's reputation, but as far as OB is concerned, that's part of the zeitgeist. Its location cannot be beat—smack on the corner of action-packed Newport Avenue right where it hits the sand. Affordable rooms, sweet ocean views, and close proximity to the lively world of Ocean Beach will keep you living like a local: up late, rowdy, and never wanting to leave the neighborhood.

Map 6: 5080 Newport Ave., Ocean Beach, 619/223-7191, www.obhotel.com

Ocean Beach International Hostel $

Backpackers and world travelers are just as woven into the fabric of OB as surfers and Volkswagen buses blasting "Hotel California" from their cassette players. This place is like a Hostel California, where a constant flow of curious young people gather, regardless of language, to sleep in bunk beds and embrace the countercultural SoCal beach lifestyle. Adventurers tend to find an engaging temporary home here.

Map 6: 4961 Newport Ave., Ocean Beach, 800/339-7263, www.californiahostel.com

The Pearl $$

Believe it or not, there's a hip place to stay in Point Loma that doesn't command a harbor view. The Pearl is central to Shelter Island, but makes its mark through stylish decorating at modest rates and the sort of local-friendly hotel scene that makes dinner in the courtyard worth dressing for. In summer, the hotel hosts movie screenings, projecting cult and comedy classics on a blank wall over the swimming pool. It's a surprisingly fun way to watch a movie, and smiling crowds of savvy locals attending couldn't agree more.

Map 6: 1410 Rosecrans St., Point Loma, 619/226-6100, www.thepearlsd.com

clockwise from top left: hotels and beaches in Pacific Beach; Crystal Pier Cottages, Pacific Beach; The Lodge at Torrey Pines and its famous golf course, near La Jolla

The Bed & Breakfast Inn at La Jolla $$

To feel at home in La Jolla, stay in one of the 13 distinctive rooms or two suites of this gourmet and wonderfully situated bed-and-breakfast. A host of amenities adds a sense of warmth: Laptop desks and down pillows are available, and there's complimentary wine and cheese at sunset. The quiet location just steps from the beach and village center will seem ideal after a day in the middle of the action.

Map 7: 7753 Draper Ave., 858/456-2066, www.innlajolla.com

Hotel La Jolla $$

This high-rise hotel sits a 10-minute walk from the beach at La Jolla Shores, and a short drive down the hill from La Jolla Village. While this doesn't make it incredibly convenient to either location, it does make it a much easier process for getting in and out of the La Jolla area and back to the freeway. You can sense the design in the comfortable, contemporary decor of the rooms and public areas of the hotel, including the great **Cusp Dining & Drinks** restaurant and bar, which, like many rooms on the upper floors, commands a terrific ocean view.

Map 7: 7955 La Jolla Shores Dr., 858/459-0261, www.hotellajolla.com

La Jolla Beach and Tennis Club $$$

Instant beach access—and of course tennis courts—make this gated La Jolla Shores resort a pretty cushy vacation destination. It's the kind of place that comps beach chairs and umbrellas, lets you upgrade to a cabana, and even go so far as to outfit and cater a beach barbecue (for a fee). Plenty of kids' activities allow more time for mom and dad to play or relax or catch an elegant meal at one of the highly rated hotel restaurants, including the vaunted **Marine Room.** To make the most of the property's private beach, aim for a beachfront deluxe suite or cottage.

Map 7: 2000 Spindrift Dr., 858/412-2036, www.ljbtc.com

La Jolla Cove Suites $$

Specializing in ocean-view suites, this resort hotel offers some reasonable rates considering the rooftop deck, heated swimming pool, and other amenities. Grab one of the few single rooms without a view for a really good deal, but you might be cranky when you realize what you're missing: a chance for balcony views of Scripps Park and the ocean off La Jolla Cove.

Map 7: 1155 Coast Blvd., 858/459-2621, www.lajollacove.com

La Jolla Riviera Inn $$

A few blocks from the beach at La Jolla Shores, this small apartment building-turned-suite hotel offers a reasonable option for families looking to keep costs down. Homey dwellings include full kitchens, dining areas, and living rooms with foldout couches, plus access to a small heated pool.

La Jolla Shores Hotel $$

The best thing about this hotel is its location—right on La Jolla Shores, one of the best family beaches in San Diego. Guest rooms come with patios or balconies and an on-site restaurant hosts a Sunday brunch buffet. With a pool, Ping-Pong tables, and plenty of beach activities on hand, there's little chance of getting bored. A courtesy shuttle can whisk you into downtown La Jolla when you're ready to shop or dine.

Map 7: 8110 Camino Del Oro, 858/459-8271, www.ljshoreshotel.com

La Jolla Village Lodge $$

A lot changes if you move a few blocks east of La Jolla Cove—at least the hotel rates do. This spot won't win any design awards; it doesn't have a pool, and there are no luxury suites. However, complimentary parking and affordable rates make it feel like a steal this close to the action.

Map 7: 1141 Silverado St., 858/551-2001, www.lajollavillagelodge.com

La Valencia Hotel $$$

With a central a location in downtown La Jolla, this high-end hotel overlooks the lovely Scripps seaside park on one side and the many shops, galleries, and restaurants of Prospect Street on the other. The Spanish Colonial beauty was built in 1926, but recent updates ensure its guests experience contemporary comforts, whether from an ocean or garden view room. A terraced layout keeps the entire property open to sunlight and ocean air, lending a Mediterranean feel that's tough to improve upon.

Map 7: 1132 Prospect St., 858/454-0771, www.lavalencia.com

★ Lodge at Torrey Pines $$$

Sitting on the 18th hole of the famous Torrey Pines golf course atop cliffs overlooking the Pacific, this beautifully designed arts and crafts hotel offers a wealth of amenities, including spa services, access to hiking trails in Torrey Pines Nature Reserve, and a shuttle to La Jolla's nearby village or idyllic shores. It also boasts one of the city's most highly regarded restaurants, **AR Valentien,** and a more casual restaurant, **The Grill.** It's rare to encapsulate so much of the San Diego experience in so luxurious a package, though none will appreciate it more than the golfers in your party. One of the hotel's greatest perks is its preferred tee times for guests at the always booked-solid Torrey Pines golf course.

Map 7: 11480 N. Torrey Pines Rd., 858/453-4420, www.lodgetorreypines.com

Pantai Inn $$$

Combine the exoticism of Bali with the oceanfront appeal of La Jolla and you'll get this boutique hotel with a bevy of well-appointed ocean-view rooms and suites. The Southeast Asian furnishings stand out among high-end properties in the area, and while the hotel may lack a pool or restaurant,

HOTELS
LA JOLLA

the quality of the rooms speaks for itself. Suites feature sun porches and kitchens, and with a cozy little beach out front and all of La Jolla in back, you may decide you've found a second home.

Map 7: 1003 Coast Blvd., 858/224-7600, www.pantaiinn.com

Coronado
Map 8

Cherokee Lodge $$

No two rooms are alike in this 1896 "bed and board" just a block off Orange Avenue and a short walk from Coronado beach. The 12-bedroom property doesn't serve breakfast, instead sending guests a few doors down for a complimentary meal at Panera Bread. There's also no designated parking, though plenty of charm—and some of the more affordable rooms in the area—make up for it.

Map 8: 964 D Ave., 619/437-1967, www.cherokeelodge.com

Glorietta Bay Inn $$

The one-time mansion and residence of John Spreckels, one of the wealthiest and most influential men in San Diego history, the Glorietta Bay Inn may not seem so grandiose sitting in the shadow of the Hotel del Coronado across the street. However, opt for one of the 11 mansion rooms and you'll experience a taste of what life may have been like for the real-estate magnate. A spate of modern accommodations offer the same bayside location at more affordable rates, but all guests enjoy the splendor of the mansion's sitting room, where you can take your coffee with a little Old World opulence.

Map 8: 1630 Glorietta Blvd., 800/283-9383, www.gloriettabayinn.com

★ Hotel del Coronado $$$

Historically one of San Diego's finest resorts, the Hotel Del doesn't come cheap, but it delivers a great number of amenities and charm in addition to its incredible beachfront location. Accommodations fall into a few distinct categories. While most people may gravitate toward the rooms filling the 19th-century halls of the original all-wood Victorian structure, these may not be the best choice for everyone. Those travelling with families might prefer the poolside California Cabanas, which offer more space, easier access, and more modern comfort. The modern architecture of the Ocean Towers may seem less appealing, but with the best ocean views and an adults-only pool, couples may prefer this to the main building. The gated Victorian Village is an exclusive little neighborhood of high-end villas featuring its own restaurant, parking lot, pools, and jetted tubs. Wherever you stay, you'll have access to the hotel's restaurants and shops, beach rentals, and spa services. The hotel is ideally situated to enjoy Coronado village and Downtown San Diego just across the bay, but many visitors seem

Best Family Hotels

Traveling with children presents a different set of requirements for a good hotel. Most San Diego hotels accommodate children, however, some do so a bit better or more conveniently than the others.

- **Bahia Resort Hotel** (998 W. Mission Bay Dr., Mission Bay, 858/488-0551, www.bahiahotel.com). Sitting on the calm bay side of the Mission Beach peninsula, you can still walk over to the Pacific Ocean, which happens to sit next to the amusements of Belmont Park. The resort beach sees zero waves; a small strip of sand runs along the gentle waters, offering all the fun of sandcastle building without the fickle currents.

- **Catamaran Resort** (3999 Mission Blvd., 858/488-1081, www.catamaranresort.com). This might be a better option for older kids. The bayside hotel offers some water activities on its beach, and north

Mission Beach can be reached by crossing Mission Boulevard.

- **La Jolla Shores Hotel** (8110 Camino Del Oro, 858/459-8271, www.ljshoreshotel.com). Set right on top of La Jolla Shores, this hotel has easy access to the family friendly beach, surf schools, kayaking and snorkeling rentals, and a pretty great playground.

- **Hotel del Coronado** (1500 Orange Ave., 619/435-6611, www.hoteldel.com). The beach resort caters to kids and families, with a nice pool, beach toys at the ready, and an ice cream shop on-site.

- **Handlery Hotel** (950 Hotel Circle N., Mission Valley, 619/298-0511, www.sd.handlery.com). Every family doesn't have to stay at the beach. The Handlery sits a short freeway hop inland and offers good budget accommodations with a bit of greenery and a generous pool.

content to spend their entire trip within the memorable landscape of the Del's 28 acres, just as so many of Hollywood's elite have done during the resort's 125-year history.

Map 8: 1500 Orange Ave., 619/435-6611, www.hoteldel.com

1906 Lodge $$$

Named for the year it was built, this century-old lodge was actually refurbished in 2009, including additional suites and a basement garage. Designed by noted local architect Irving Gill, the arts and crafts beauty features abundant structural charm—be sure to note the unique leaded glass window built into the middle of the chimney. Each distinctive room has been decorated with early-20th-century period furniture and vintage photographs pertaining to Coronado history. Orange Avenue is just a couple of blocks away, or make use of complementary bikes and golf carts to get around.

Map 8: 1060 Adella Ave., 619/437-1900, www.1906lodge.com

Villa Capri by the Sea $$

A small boutique motel with a big neon sign, the instantly recognizable Villa Capri boasts a luxury hotel location with budget accommodations prices and not too many frills. Given the area, the parking alone is practically worth the price of a standard room. Suites and weekly rates may make you consider longer stays at this well-maintained inn.

Map 8: 1417 Orange Ave., 619/435-4137, www.villacapribythesea.com

Greater San Diego   Map 9

Handlery Hotel $$

One of San Diego's better budget options is this hotel tucked between I-8 and the Riverwalk Golf Course. With 217 rooms, a large pool, on-site dining, and occasional entertainment, it's a decent place to relax even if its greatest asset is easy access to other San Diego attractions with a quick hop on the freeway.

Map 9: 950 Hotel Circle N., Mission Valley, 619/298-0511, www.sd.handlery.com

Excursions
from San Diego

Highlights

★ **Best Place to Lose a Bet:** Horses running in circles shouldn't be this fun, but the ocean breeze and the thunderous hooves of the racetrack at the **Del Mar Fairgrounds** seem to pair well (page 210).

★ **Best Walk in the Moonlight:** As gorgeous a beach as you'll ever find close to civilization, **Moonlight Beach** is the San Diego ideal (page 215).

★ **Best of the Missions: Mission San Luis Rey de Francia** is the king of the missions and it shows (page 222).

★ **Best Place to Run Wild: San Diego Zoo Safari Park** gives animals what we all want for them—more room to run (page 225).

★ **Best Brew with a View:** Everybody comes to **Stone World Bistro & Gardens** for the same reason: They love to drink great beer—and talk about drinking great beer—surrounded by a beautiful park-like setting (page 225).

As San Diego's metropolitan sprawl stretches north, a series of independent beach communities—Del Mar, Encinitas, Carlsbad, and Oceanside—pepper the coast.

These beautiful little towns, with breathtaking beaches interspersed among estuaries, lagoons, state parks, and campgrounds, are desirable day-trips, even among locals.

Still, not everybody lives at the beach. As North County stretches inland, the terrain starts to change from windswept beaches and rugged cliffs to chaparral-covered mountains, verdant pine forests, and even desert. A few communities, like Escondido and Julian, have spring up closer to nature, either basking in the extra 10 degrees of warmth away from the coast or providing snowy winter wonderlands.

These places may not be integral to the typical San Diego vacation, but an hour or more on the road may offer a different perspective worth considering, whether exploring suburban beaches, historic locations, or the top beer destination in town.

PLANNING YOUR TIME

North County beach towns appear one after another as you drive north on I-5. It's possible to make a full day of stopping at all the North County beaches (hop on U.S. 101 at Via de la Valle and enjoy the coastal route), or drive straight to Oceanside in the morning and keep the Pacific on your right as you retrace your way south to Del Mar. But I recommend picking one general area and soaking it in. None of these trips require an overnight stay, though it's certainly an option, and especially warranted if you plan to enjoy a couple of beach-filled days on the coast.

Previous page top: Cardiff by the Sea; **bottom:** Oceanside

Choosing Excursions

- **Del Mar:** Bet on your horse at this seaside track and feel the thrill as they come galloping down the stretch so hard you feel it in your chest. Stick around for a free concert after the last race, Friday afternoons at 5pm.

- **Encinitas:** The beautiful cliff-side beaches of Encinitas represent the ideal backdrop for Southern California life. The city is within reach, but nobody can think of a reason they'd need to go there.

- **Carlsbad:** Cast your eyes on the gold coastline of Carlsbad, then look the other direction for the startlingly vivid Flower Fields, which bloom each summer.

- **Oceanside:** Mission San Luis Rey de Francia is a turn-of-the-19th-century California mission in whitewashed glory, a commingling of Spanish colonial architectural styles and an active friary.

- **Escondido:** The San Diego Safari Park is the zoo blown up to a grand scale, recreating global habitats where animals may run and raise families, including tigers, rhinos, and gorillas.

- **Julian:** Come for the cider, stay for the pie. This apple-growing small town sprung up during a short-lived gold rush, and it's old-timey downtown is filled with sweet thrills of the fruit and baked goods variety.

Del Mar appears first, just 30 minutes from Downtown, with another beach town every 5-10 minutes farther north. There are enough beaches, restaurants, and shopping that Del Mar and **Solana Beach** can fill a day on their own, perhaps more if there's an event at the track or the fairgrounds.

Encinitas and **Cardiff** may possess the best stretch of coastline in the county, with clean beaches braced against sandstone cliffs. Encinitas makes an idyllic vacation destination for those looking for a relaxing couple of days away from urban life. Both towns are a 40-minute drive from Downtown San Diego.

Carlsbad and **Oceanside** occupy the coastline, with much of Carlsbad given over to camping, RVs, and state beaches. Beaches in Oceanside tend to spread out and are relatively uncrowded, although there are few amenities other than the pier. Legoland and Mission San Luis Rey de Francia are the draws here. Carlsbad could make a nice two-night beach getaway if you pace yourself. Expect a 45-minute drive from Downtown San Diego to either city.

San Onofre qualifies as a surf trip; head straight for waves in the morning, and stop at one of the beach towns for lunch on the way back. From Downtown San Diego, count on at least 50 minutes to get here, or longer with traffic.

Visiting Inland North County means driving west via either Highway 78 from Oceanside, or north on I-15 from Downtown. The best reason to visit **Escondido** is San Diego Safari Park. Plan to visit Stone Brewery and

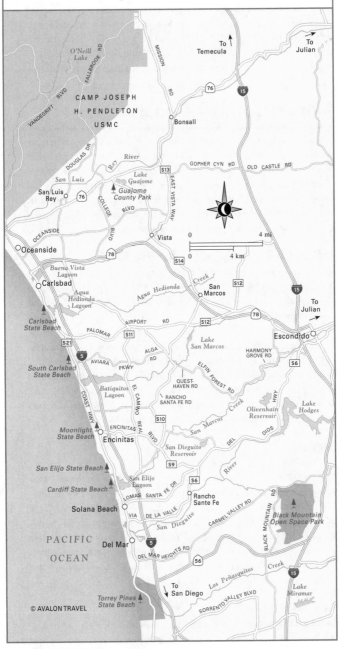

North County

© AVALON TRAVEL

stop over neighboring San Marcos for a pint at Lost Abbey. Plan on 35 to 45 minutes of driving, or more if you encounter rush-hour traffic.

Julian is a gold-mining town turned apple producer, and offers a good reason to visit the mountains east of San Diego. While you'll encounter delicious apple pie and cider, a little on-foot exploration of the 19th-century town offers a glimpse into frontier life. From Downtown San Diego, expect a little over an hour's drive in good conditions. Stay a night or two.

North County Beaches

Anything north of La Jolla is considered North County; still part of the city sprawl, but far enough to adopt a suburban lifestyle. North County beach towns and their pristine beaches make the region an enviable place to live. The Southern California lifestyle flourishes here, with many stereotypical blond surfers and sunbathers building their lives around the sun and sand. Spend a little summertime living as the locals do, and you'll find yourself caring less about the problems of the outside world too.

DEL MAR AND SOLANA BEACH

Del Mar is an upscale residential community nestled between the cliffs of Torrey Pines and the San Dieguito Lagoon. A Tudor-style village spreads out from the central beach, with a smattering of high-priced shops and restaurants. The town is best known for its namesake fairgrounds and racetrack.

Less than three miles north is Solana Beach, a small town independent of Del Mar, though their proximity makes them feel more like adjoining neighborhoods. Solana Beach is best known for shopping in the Cedros Avenue Design District, which offers furniture, designer antiques, and a smattering of high-end stores for the home decorator. Solana Beach anchors the North County music scene at its Belly Up nightclub.

Sights

★ Del Mar Fairgrounds

The San Diego County Fair takes place each June at the Del Mar Fairgrounds (2260 Jimmy Durante Blvd., 858/755-1161, www.delmarfairgrounds.com), culminating in a big Fourth of July celebration. Along with the typical fair fare—attractions, rides, farm animals, and fried food—the fair hosts concurrent events such as The San Diego International Beer Festival as well as concerts headlined by internationally known artists. The fairgrounds share an address with the racetrack, often featuring horse shows and competitions.

Restaurants

Del Mar's known to have a lot of upscale restaurants, but none do fine dining as well as the five-star, five-diamond Addison (5200 Grand Del Mar

Del Mar and Solana Beach

LOMAS SANTA FE DR
S8

Tide Park

PIZZA PORT

To Encinitas

Fletcher Cove

STEVENS AVE

CEDROS AVE

HWY 101

Solana Beach

BELLY UP

Seascape Surf

CUCINA ENOTECA

VIA DE LA VALLE
S6

S21

DEL MAR RACETRACK

DEL MAR FAIRGROUNDS

JIM DURANTE BLVD

Del Mar City Beach

PACIFIC OCEAN

Del Mar

CAMINO DEL MAR

SEE DETAIL

Powerhouse Park

Seagrove Park

HOTEL INDIGO

0   0.5 mi

0   0.5 km

STRATFORD CT

DEL MAR HEIGHTS RD

Torrey Pines State Reserve

EL CAMINO REAL

I 5

To Grand Del Mar

S56

CARMEL VALLEY RD

To La Jolla

NORTH TORREY PINES RD

S21

SORRENTO VALLEY RD

Torrey Pines State Reserve

DETAIL:

Del Mar City Beach

18TH ST

CAMINO

JAKE'S DEL MAR

Powerhouse Park

L'AUBERGE DEL MAR

POST OFFICE

COAST BLVD

STRATFORD ST

15TH ST

14TH ST

LUNEZA DR

DEL MAR ST

MAIDEN LN

Torrey Pines State Beach

Seagrove Park

BOARD & BREW

13TH ST

12TH ST

© AVALON TRAVEL

Way, 858/314-1900, www.addisondelmar.com, Tues.-Thurs. 6pm-9pm, Fri.-Sat. 5:30pm-9:30pm, $98-125). The refined tastes and disciplined kitchen of renowned chef William Bradley send seasonally designed dishes to a dining room sitting above the 18th green of the exclusive golf course of the Grand Del Mar resort, complete with a Mediterranean-style patio to enjoy the sommelier's best picks.

Not far from the racetrack, **Cucina Enoteca** (2730 Via De La Valle, 858/704-4500, www.urbankitchengroup.com, Mon. 5pm-9pm, Tues.-Sat. 11:30am-10pm, Sun. 11:30am-9pm, $15-30) offers its own brilliant wine selection, served with exceptional, creative Italian dishes at a more reasonable price—a terrific post-race option. If you prefer your meals coastal, **Jake's Del Mar** (1660 Coast Blvd., 858/755-2002, www.jakesdelmar.com, Mon. 4pm-9pm, Tues.-Thurs. 11:30am-9pm, Fri.-Sat. 11:30am-9:30pm, Sun. 10am-9pm, $20-36) is famous among locals for its Sunday brunch directly overlooking the beach at Del Mar's Powerhouse Park, but it actually has the same view all day long, serving California cuisine mixed with a few Hawaiian dishes.

For a quick, cheap bite, the beachy sandwich shop **Board & Brew** (1212 Camino Del Mar, 858/481-1021, www.boardandbrew.com, daily 10am-6pm, $5-10) has kept its loyal customers well fed for more than 35 years, and still gets a line out the door come lunchtime. To enjoy a few beers with your meal, grab some local craft and pizza at the **Pizza Port** (135 N. U.S. 101, Solana Beach, 858/481-7332, www.pizzaport.com, Sun.-Thurs. 11am-10pm, Fri.-Sat. 11am-midnight, $20-25).

Arts and Culture

Catching a movie in Del Mar may be worthwhile just to check out **Cineopolis** (12905 El Camino Real, 858/794-4045, www.cinepolisusa.com). The luxury cinema chain offers cushioned, reclining seats in small, uncrowded theaters, showing first run films with table service, including cocktails if you attend a dedicated 21-and-over screening.

Nightlife

You'll find a little evening action on Cedros Avenue. One of the county's best rock venues, **The Belly Up** (143 S. Cedros Ave., Solana Beach, 858/481-8140, www.bellyup.com) offers nightly shows ranging from tribute bands to indie rockers to music legends that fill the intimate venue with devoted fans.

Across the street from Belly Up, check out the urban winery **Carruth Cellars** (320 S Cedros Ave., Suite 400, Solana Beach, 858/847-9463, http://carruthcellars.com, daily noon-9pm), which brings grapes from up north to make wine right here amid the ocean-scented breeze.

Sports and Activities

"Where the surf meets the turf," the **Del Mar Racetrack** (2260 Jimmy Durante Blvd., 858/755-1161, www.delmarfairgrounds.com) comes alive

top to bottom: the Del Mar Racetrack; Cedros Avenue in Solana Beach

during the summer racing season (mid-July-Labor Day) and again for the Bing Crosby Season (Nov.). Basic admission grants access to the charming coastal facility. Upgrades allow entrance to the clubhouse, with options for reserved seating or dining tables with a view of the action. The track hosts free concerts after Friday races, including some internationally known talent. On Saturdays a mix of concerts, beer, and food festivals take place. A day at the track can be rousing fun even for those who don't gamble, and it offers women the rare opportunity to wear elaborate hats.

Del Mar Beach (http://www.delmar.ca.us) runs the length of town, and is accessible at the town center via grassy **Powerhouse Park** (1658 Coast Blvd.). The two-mile stretch of beach is popular among local surfers and casual beachgoers, and many like to walk along cliffs rising to the south during low tide. A small section north of the San Dieguito Lagoon offers volleyball courts and an off-leash dog area outside the summer months.

While beaches get a fair amount of use, many visitors come to bike the **Coast Highway** (U.S. 101), which picks up just south of San Dieguito Lagoon and extends north about 20 miles to the Marine Corps Base Camp Pendleton. Great scenery and cool ocean breezes make this one of the county's most popular cycling routes; it's particularly well-trafficked on weekends.

For a leisurely exploration, book a tour with **Skysurfer Balloon Company** (858/481-6800, www.sandiegohotairballoons.com, 1 hour before sunset, $210 pp, $350 per couple). Its late sunset hot-air balloon tours head inland then back toward the coast, serving champagne and soft drinks as the sun sets over the Pacific.

Hotels

Those wishing to stay near the beach in Del Mar may opt for the **Hotel Indigo** (710 Camino Del Mar, 858/755-1501, www.hotelindigosddelmar.com, $150-250), which offers ocean views, spa services, and comfortable accommodations from the cliffs on the south side of town. Closer to sea level is the highly rated luxury resort, **L'Auberge Del Mar** (1540 Camino Del Mar, 858/259-1515, www.laubergedelmar.com, from $250), nestled between the village and the beach.

For unmatched opulence, nothing compares to the **Grand Del Mar** (5300 Grand Del Mar Ct., 866/305-1528, www.thegranddelmar.com, from $250). The extravagantly built resort overlooks the 4,000-acre Peñasquitos Canyon Preserve, giving the whole place the feel of a country estate. Marble columns and parquet floors set off breathtaking rooms filled with beautiful yet comfortable furniture. It's the kind of place where the Presidential Suite has hosted actual presidents.

Practicalities

Del Mar lies about 20 miles north of Downtown San Diego. The easiest way to get here is by car; take I-5 north for about 20 miles and exit at Villa de la Valle, about a 30-minute drive.

For public transit options, you can take the **Amtrak** *Pacific Surfliner* (www.amtrak.com) route from the Downtown Santa Fe Depot (1050 Kettner Blvd.) or Old Town Transit Center (4009 Taylor St.) in Old Town. Much cheaper is the **Coaster** (760/966-6500, www.gonctd.com/coaster, $4-12) service offered by the North County Transit District. The nearest Coaster stop is Solana Beach Station (105 North Cedros Ave., Solana Beach). From there, buses travel regularly to the Del Mar racetrack and fairgrounds and Del Mar Village. The Coaster generally takes 10 to 15 minutes longer than driving.

ENCINITAS AND CARDIFF BY THE SEA

The idyllic coastal village of Encinitas sprawls between a couple of lagoons north of Solana Beach. One of these communities, Cardiff by the Sea, features a beautiful state beach, a popular destination for campers that possesses an epic reef break favored by longboarders. Encinitas features artsy shops that run parallel to breathtaking cliff-side beaches, including the area's top surf spot—Swami's. Spend a couple of hours anywhere along this stretch and you'll start plotting ways to uproot your life and move here.

Sights

★ Moonlight Beach

Moonlight Beach (end of D St., Encinitas) is a sight to behold, with turquoise waters and light-sand beaches backed by sandstone cliffs—you won't really *get* Encinitas until you've seen its beach. Visit during the day, although it also happens to be pretty nice when the moon is out.

San Dieguito Heritage Museum

To learn more about the area, pick up some history at the **San Dieguito Heritage Museum** (450 Quail Gardens Dr., Encinitas, 760/632-9711, www. sdheritage.org, Thurs.-Sun. 10am-4pm, free). Entertaining stories include how Moonlight Beach got its name during the Prohibition era.

San Diego Botanic Garden

Don't miss the chance to wander amid the unique and expansive **San Diego Botanic Garden** (230 Quail Gardens Dr., Encinitas, 760/436-3036, www. sdbgarden.org, daily 9am-5pm, $14 adults, $10 seniors, students, and military, $8 ages 3-12). A stroll through the gardens almost feels like a geography lesson. Plants and flowers range from desert cacti to a tropical rain forest plants, plus the nation's largest collection of bamboo.

Self-Realization Fellowship Retreat and Gardens

Tough to miss while driving along the Coast Highway is the **Self-Realization Fellowship** (939 2nd St., Encinitas, 760/436-7220, www. encinitastemple.org, Tues.-Sat. 9am-5pm, Sun. 11am-5pm, free). Its gold-pointed domes call attention to the spiritualist center, while just next door is the tranquil, manicured meditation garden (215 K St.). All of it sits high

Encinitas and Cardiff by the Sea

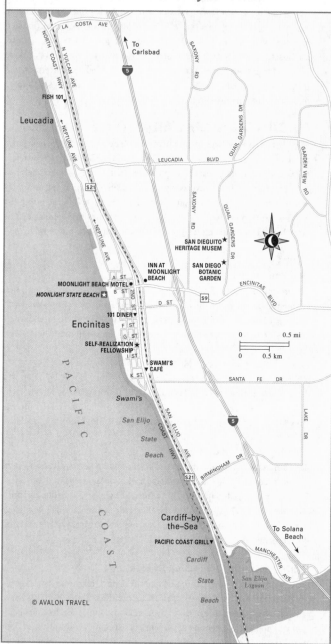

named **Swami's**.

Restaurants

Encinitas has become "coffee rich." The old train station building now houses San Diego's original coffee roaster, **Pannikin Coffee** (510 N. Coast Hwy. 101, 760/436-5824, www.pannikincoffeeandtea.com, daily 6am-6pm), with a lovely patio for drinking coffee or tea. Not far down the road is **Lofty Coffee Company** (90 N. Coast Hwy. 101, Suite 214, 760/230-6747, www.loftycoffeeco.com, Mon.-Fri. 6am-6pm). The organic specialty coffee roaster's shop manages to feel beachy yet design-savvy, with glass, steel, and wood panels housing a space that opens up in the summer, when a Kyoto-drip cold-brew iced coffee proves ideal.

Have some chocolate with your latte at this shop of renowned local chocolatier **Chuao Chocolatier Café** (937 S. Coast Hwy. 101, 760/635-1444, www.chuaochocolatier.com, Mon.-Thurs. 10am-8pm, Fri.-Sat. 10am-9pm, Sun. 10am-7pm). You will want to try everything—don't pass up the crackling chocolate bar infused with chili nibs and popping candy.

For breakfast with your coffee or candy, try local favorite **Swami's Café** (1163 S. Coast Hwy. 101, 760/944-0612, www.swamiscafesd.com, daily 7am-9pm, $8-15), known for its unique varieties of eggs Benedict (I'm partial to the avocado and Mexican chorizo sausage combo). For old-school diner-style grub, stop in at **101 Diner** (552 S. Coast Hwy. 101, 760/753-2123, www.101diner.com, daily 6am-10pm, $8-10) for traditional egg dishes along with apple-baked pancakes and stuffed waffles.

Named for U.S. 101, **Fish 101** (1468 N. Coast Hwy. 101, 760/943-6221, www.fish101restaurant.com, Sun.-Thurs. 11:30am-9pm, Fri.-Sat. 11:30am-10pm, $12-15) is a health-conscious seafood counter. The fresh grilled fish is outstanding, and even their fried fish uses light and heart-healthy rice bran oil.

To take advantage of this gorgeous coastline, reserve a patio table at **Pacific Coast Grill** (2526 S. Coast Hwy. 101, Cardiff by the Sea, 760/479-0721, www.pacificcoastgrill.com, Mon.-Thurs. 11am-4pm and 4:30pm-9pm, Fri.-Sat. 11am-4pm and 4:30pm-10pm, Sun. 11am-4pm, $25-45). Set on top of gorgeous Cardiff State Beach, this surf-and-turf restaurant lets you dine about as close to the ocean as you can without getting sand in your lap. In addition to the spectacular view, the kitchen provides a worthy dining experience, with strips of ahi tuna and a fillet you sear yourself on a sizzling hot stone. Follow it up with a fish perfectly cooked *sous vide* while you enjoy the sunset.

Arts and Culture

Rumored to be the first rural theater to show "talkies," you may still find first-run movies at **La Paloma Theater** (471 S. Coast Hwy. 101, 760/436-7469, www.lapalomatheatre.com). The best times to go are during premiers of new surfing films. Seeing great surfing and big waves on the large screen

top to bottom: Pannikin Coffee, Encinitas; the Pacific Coast Grill on Cardiff State Beach.

Sports and Activities

Beautiful Moonlight Beach is a great place to see true California beach living at its finest. But one of the great features of Encinitas is the presence of other state beaches and campgrounds.

Surfers book well in advance to reserve a space near the famous reef break at **Cardiff State Beach** (2500 S. Coast Hwy. 101, Cardiff by the Sea, 760/753-5091, www.parks.ca.gov), especially in the summertime. Adjoining **San Elijo State Beach** (2500 S. Coast Hwy. 101, 760/753-5091, www.parks. ca.gov) may not be as well known, but it offers its share of fun waves and uncrowded surf breaks—plus a campground. It doesn't offer much space, so you will hear your neighbors, but you'll fall asleep to the sound of crashing of waves and wake at the beach.

Between the campground and central Encinitas is **Swami's** (end of 2nd St., Encinitas), the sort of surf spot where you find local pros at play when it's really firing. Swami's is found right below the Self Realization Fellowship (which gives Swami's its name) and the cliffs above offer a terrific vantage point for spectators. On mediocre days the waves remain crowded with those looking to reach that top echelon someday. Due to its competitive nature, Swami's is not a place beginners want to try, but it can turn up some excellent days for visiting surfers with etiquette and skill who want a memorable San Diego surf experience.

Accommodations

For a good spot to spend the night, look no farther than the **Inn at Moonlight Beach** (105 N. Vulcan Ave., Encinitas, 760/561-1755, www.innatmoonlightbeach.com, $150-250). This lovely bed-and-breakfast puts you within walking distance of great beaches and restaurants. You can also find a good, clean stay at the charming and central **Moonlight Beach Motel** (233 2nd St., Encinitas, 800/323-1259, www.moonlightbeachmotel.com, $145), which seems to complement the feeling of this laid-back beach town.

For roughing it next to the ocean, reserve a campsite at Cardiff's **San Elijo State Beach** (2500 S. Coast Hwy. 101, Cardiff by the Sea, 760/753-5091, www.parks.ca.gov, $35-70). Car camping and RV spots line the cliffs overlooking the beach. Designated spaces are close together but fill up fast; reservations are available seven months in advance at the first of each month.

Practicalities

Cardiff by the Sea is just five miles north of Del Mar via U.S. 101 or I-5; Encinitas is just 1.5 miles farther north. From Downtown San Diego, plan on the 25-mile drive to take about 35 minutes. From I-5, take the Birmingham Drive exit for Cardiff by the Sea or the Encinitas Boulevard exit for Encinitas.

The **Coaster** (North County Transit District, 760/966-6500, www.gonctd.com/coaster, $4-12) departs from the Downtown Santa Fe Depot (1050 Kettner Blvd.) or Old Town Transit Center (4009 Taylor St.) and stops at the Encinitas Coaster Station (25 East D St., Encinitas). Buses and taxis provide further options.

CARLSBAD AND OCEANSIDE

Carlsbad is a pretty huge place, large enough to have its own airport (though it only offers flights to LAX). The presence of Legoland has put it on the map, with increasing numbers of visitors discovering its seven miles of coastline. And that's before factoring in craft beer tourism. The surrounding area has been dubbed the "Hops Highway" for the high concentration of breweries.

Five miles north, Oceanside grew up next to the Marine Corps Base Camp Pendleton. Young marines and their families have lived here dating back to World War II.

Sights

Carlsbad's Flower Fields

Carlsbad's Flower Fields (5704 Paseo Del Norte, 760/431-0352, www.theflowerfields.com, Mar. 1-May 10 daily 9am-6pm, $12 adults, $11 seniors, $6 ages 3-10) are endlessly beautiful during the spring bloom, with more than 50 acres devotes to the Giant Ranunculus. Just check the online calendar before visiting to make sure you don't miss the flowers in bloom; otherwise, you'll be left to stare at empty fields.

Leo Carrillo Ranch Historic Park

Built within a 27-acre canyon is the historically preserved **Leo Carrillo Ranch** (6200 Flying LC Lane, 760/476-1042, www.carlsbadca.gov, Tues.-Sat. 9am-5pm, Sun. 11am-5pm, tours: Sat. 11am, 1pm, Sun. noon, 2pm, free). Hollywood character actor and conservationist Leo Carrillo bought the 19th-century hacienda in 1937, consciously preserving its historic buildings. Part time capsule, part garden preserve, the lovely grounds are worth exploring on your own, but you'll get a lot more history by taking one of the free tours offered each weekend.

Legoland

The biggest attraction in Carlsbad is **Legoland** (1 Legoland Dr., 760/918-5346, www.california.legoland.com, daily from 10am, closing hours vary, $85-109 adults, $75-99 ages 3-12). The building-block theme park features a miniature United States made of interlocking plastic, and offers loads of kiddie-friendly rides and games incorporating pirates and dinosaurs, and using laser blasters to recover stolen treasure. Base admission gets you in, with higher ticket prices adding park attractions like the Sea Life Aquarium and the splashy Legoland Water Park (spring-summer only).

Marine Corps Mechanized Museum

Located on the Marine Corps Base Camp Pendleton, the **Marine Corps Mechanized Museum** (2612 Vandegrift Blvd., Oceanside, 760/725-5758, www.themech.org, Mon.-Thurs. 8am-4pm, Fri. 8am-1pm, free) features all manner of armored trucks, all-terrain vehicles, and some very large retired ordnance. You'll need to present valid photo ID for each member in your party to gain admittance to the base; from there, it's a 15-20 minute drive to the museum.

Museum of Making Music

A stroll through the history of recorded music in the fascinating **Museum of Making Music** (5790 Armada Dr., Carlsbad, 760/438-5996, www.museumofmakingmusic.org, Tues.-Sun. 10am-5pm, $8 adults, $5 seniors, students, military, and ages 6-18) reveals hundreds of vintage instruments, and even a few modern ones. Trace the advent of modern instruments and listen to snippets of popular recordings made at the time of their inception. Along the way, a few "Play Me" instruments allow you to make your own music (or noise), including my favorite corner of the museum: an exhibit devoted to the electric guitar.

Oceanside Museum of Art

Stop in to enjoy the contemporary and conceptual art collection of the **Oceanside Museum of Art** (704 Pier View Way, Oceanside, 760/435-3720, www.oma-online.org, Tues.-Sat. 10am-4pm, Sun. 1pm-4pm, $8 adults, $5 seniors, free military and students, free 1st Sun. each month). A rotating calendar of programs and events complement a series of modern and contemporary art exhibitions.

California Surf Museum

The small **California Surf Museum** (312 Pier View Way, Oceanside, 760/721-6876, www.surfmuseum.org, daily 10am-4pm, $5 adults, $3 seniors, military, and students, free under age 12) has plenty to say about local surfing history. Exhibits depict the evolution of the surfboard as well as well-known riders, including soul surfer Bethany Hamilton.

★ **Mission San Luis Rey de Francia**

Oceanside's top attraction is the **Mission San Luis Rey de Francia** (4050 Mission Ave., Oceanside, 760/757-3651, www.sanluisrey.org, Mon.-Thurs. 9:30am-5pm, Sat.-Sun. 10am-5pm, $5 adults, $4 seniors and ages 6-18, free military), the 18th of California's 21 Franciscan missions. It was founded in 1798 by Fermín Lasuén, successor to Junípero Serra. Also known as the "King of Missions," it's maybe just a little more impressive than the first.

Restaurants

Beer drinkers have plenty to celebrate at the shared tables of **Pizza Port** (571 Carlsbad Village Dr., 760/720-7007, www.pizzaport.com, Sun.-Thurs. 11am-10pm, Fri.-Sat. 11am-midnight, $10-25). If thick-crust pizza turns you off, try the 48 taps instead at nearby **83 Degrees** (660 Carlsbad Village Dr., 760/729-7904, www.83degrees.net, Mon.-Sat. 11am-midnight, Sun. 10am-midnight, $15-20). A full 35 taps are designated local, featuring many of the San Diego's top breweries served alongside decent pub food.

A longtime fish counter hidden inside a bland shopping center, **Pelly's Fish Market & Café** (7110 Avenida Encinas, Carlsbad, 760/431-8454, www.pellysfishmarket.com, Sun.-Thurs. 11am-8pm, Fri.-Sat. 11am-8:30pm, $12-20) built a reputation on crab cakes and clam chowder, and serves grilled daily selections of fish a number of ways. For a bite on the go, grab a sub from local sandwich favorite **Board & Brew** (201 Oak Ave., Carlsbad, 760/434-4466, www.boardandbrew.com, daily 10am-8pm, $5-10).

Carlsbad offers a good opportunity to grab an **In-N-Out Burger** (5950 Avenida Encinas, Carlsbad, 800/786-1000, www.in-n-out.com, Sun.-Thurs. 10:30am-1am, Fri.-Sat. 10:30am-1:30am, $5-10). The legendary California burger chain makes an honest-to-goodness fast-food burger with a well-known "secret menu" of upgrades. Go "Animal Style" for a saucy burger with grilled onions, pickles, and everything else.

For seafood, eclectic hotel restaurant **Hello Betty Fish House** (211 Mission Ave., Oceanside, 760/722-1008, www.hellobettyoceanside.com, Sun.-Thurs. 11am-10pm, Fri.-Sat. 11am-11pm, $15-30) serves plenty of raw and shellfish cocktails, as well as fish cooked any way. Fans of diner chain **Ruby's** (1 Oceanside Pier, Oceanside, 760/433-7829, www.rubys.com, Sun.-Thurs. 7am-9pm, Fri.-Sat. 7am-10pm, $10-15) will find a particularly fun outpost at the end of the 1,954-foot Oceanside Pier.

In Oceanside, your best beer bet is Stone Brewing outpost the **Stone Company Store** (310 N. Tremont St., Oceanside, 760/529-0002, www. stonebrew.com, Mon.-Thurs. 2pm-9pm, Fri.-Sat. 11am-10pm, Sun. 11am-9pm), which gives you a taste of Stone's core offerings plus occasional limited releases.

Sports and Activities

North of Oceanside, one of the top surf breaks in the county is at the northern edge of Marine Corps Base Camp Pendleton, one of the largest military bases in the world. Only military personnel have access to the 16 miles of coastline and other land around the freeway, but continuing north, just as you enter Orange County, is **San Onofre State Beach** (Old Hwy. 101 at Basilone Rd., 949/492-4872, www.parks.ca.gov, daily noon-midnight, $15), home to Trestles.

Named for a trestle bridge that surfers used to cross underneath to reach the world-class breaks, **Trestles** is most easily accessed by entering the San Onofre-San Mateo Campground. A 1.5-mile nature trail connects the campground to Trestle Beach. While camping has its own merits, people come here to seek the surf, which remains crowded despite the complicated access.

An easier-to-reach stretch of surf sits farther south in Carlsbad. **Carlsbad State Beach** (101 Tamarack Ave.) offers some southern swell days when the rest of the county is flat. There's something fun to surf most days and the sandy beach is a great place to sit and relax; an optical illusion played by the slope of the sand makes the surfers seem a lot closer than they actually are.

Also known as The Strand, **Oceanside City Beach** (301 The Strand N., Oceanside, 760/435-4018, www.ci.oceanside.ca.us) runs straight for about 2.5 miles, from Carlsbad north to Oceanside Harbor. Most of the beach is free of heavy crowds. Surfers tend to stick near the harbor and pier at the center of town, but wide swaths of sand stretch the entire length, with shallow swimming areas good for kids and beginning surfers who want to practice without competing for waves.

Golfers will appreciate the challenging 18-hole, par-72 **Aviara Golf Club** (7447 Batiquitos Dr., Carlsbad, 760/603-6900 www.golfaviara.com, daily 7am-5pm), with 7,000 gorgeously maintained yards of fairway. Its rolling green hills seem so far removed from the rest of the area that you might forget where you are.

Hotels

Stay on the beach in Carlsbad at the **Tamarack Beach Resort** (3200 Carlsbad Blvd., Carlsbad, 760/729-3500, www.tamarackresort.com, from $250), or treat yourself to the **Beach Terrace Inn** (2775 Ocean St., Carlsbad, 760/729-5951, www.beachterraceinn.com, from $250). Each offers direct beach access and locations within easy walking distance of village shops and restaurants.

For a reasonable stay, try the **Carlsbad by the Sea Resort** (850 Palomar Airport Rd., Carlsbad, 760/438-7880, www.carlsbadhotelbythesea.com, $150-250), which puts you within reach of Legoland, the beach, and a short walk from the Flower Fields.

For top-tier hospitality, no one tops **Omni La Costa Resort & Spa** (2100 Costa Del Mar Rd., Carlsbad, 760/438-9111, $250-300). Located slightly inland, the terra-cotta luxury resort, spa, and gold-medal golf course is a vacation unto itself. Expect exquisite comfort and service, as well as swimming pools, tennis courts, fitness classes, and activities for kids and teens.

Beach campsites may be reserved in advance at the **South Carlsbad State Beach Campground** (7201 Carlsbad Blvd., 760/438-3143, www. parks.ca.gov, $35-50). Hundreds of cliff-side spaces are set up for car camping or RVs and trailers, with stairs leading down to a long, beautiful, undeveloped beach with plenty of swimming and surfing options.

Oceanside hotel options are limited, but a reasonable oceanfront stay may be found at the **Southern California Beach Club** (121 S. Pacific St., 760/722-6666, www.southerncalifbeachclub.com, $150-250), which offers clean studios and condos that include full kitchens and views, plus direct access to the beach.

Practicalities

Carlsbad and Oceanside are best accessed by car. Carlsbad is 35 miles north of Downtown San Diego via I-5, about a 40-minute drive. Carlsbad Village lies at the north end of town and is best accessed by exiting at Carlsbad Village Drive. Oceanside is 40 miles (45 minutes) north of Downtown via I-5. San Onofre is even farther north, close to 60 miles from Downtown San Diego and at least a 50-minute drive.

The **Coaster** (North County Transit District, 760/966-6500, www. gonctd.com/coaster, $4-12) accesses the region from Downtown's Santa Fe Depot (1050 Kettner Blvd.) or Old Town Transit Center (4009 Taylor

St.). Two stops in Carlsbad will drop you in at the Poinsettia Station (6511 Avenida Encinas) in South Carlsbad, or in Carlsbad Village (2775 State St.). At the end of the line is **Oceanside Transit Station** (195 S. Tremont St.), which deposits you within walking distance of the pier and beach.

VISTA

Carlsbad proves a good launching point to visit craft breweries on the so-called "Hops Highway," the cluster of beer companies lined up near Highway 78 in nearby Vista. You'll find terrific beers at **Latitude 33** (1430 Vantage Court, Suite 104, Vista, 760/913-7333, www.lat33brew.com, Wed.-Fri. 3pm-8pm, Sat. noon-7pm, Sun. noon-5pm), **Iron Fist** (1305 Hot Spring Way, Vista, 760/216-6500, www.ironfistbrewing.com, Wed. 4pm-8pm, Thurs. 3pm-8pm, Fri. 3pm-9pm, Sat. noon-8pm, Sun. noon-5pm), and **Belching Beaver** (980 Park Center Dr., Vista, 760/599-5832, http://belchinbeaver.com, Mon. 4:30pm-8pm, Wed. 4pm-8pm, Thurs. 4pm-9pm, Fri. 3pm-9pm, Sat. 1pm-9pm, Sun. 1pm-7pm), within designated driving distance of the coast.

Escondido and Vicinity

Said to mean "hidden water," Escondido has become the place of not-so-hidden beer. While there's plenty to see and do in Escondido, the presence of Stone Brewing probably inspires more 40-minute drives from San Diego than any other local feature. Once a rural outpost, the town has grown rapidly; within the center of the sprawl, a quaint downtown district still holds the most interest. An old section of Grand Street (between Civic Center Parkway and Ivy St.) features a number of shops and restaurants old and new to provide a few hours' worth of exploration.

The surrounding communities of Rancho Bernardo and San Marcos have some prominent area attractions. All are collectively referred to by San Diego residents as North County.

SIGHTS
★ San Diego Zoo Safari Park

One attraction might be the exception to the Stone rule. **San Diego Zoo Safari Park** (15500 San Pasqual Valley Rd., 760/747-8702, www.sdzsafaripark.org, daily 9am-7pm, hours vary seasonally, $46 adults, $36 ages 3-12) might be related to the zoo at Balboa Park, but it does things differently. Here the animals have a lot more space to roam, with the landscape made to more closely resemble the natural habitat of a number of African species, including lions and elephants. Options to see these creatures include riding around in a jeep and getting a close up look at some pretty majestic animals.

★ Stone World Bistro & Gardens

Stone World Bistro & Gardens (1999 Citracado Pkwy., 760/294-7899, www.stonebrewing.com, Sun.-Thurs. 11:30am-9pm, Fri.-Sat. 11:30am-10pm) serves as a monument to craft beer, presented Southern California style, with a large desert garden rolling off its generous outdoor patio and bar. You may opt for a brewery tour to see how these guys do what they do, stay for dinner, or fill some growlers. Mainly, you'll want to check out the huge tap list, and try some truly world-class beers.

California Center for the Arts

Set on a large property next to Escondido City Hall is the multi-faceted **California Center for the Arts** (340 N. Escondido Blvd., 760/839-4138, www.artcenter.org, Mon.-Fri. 8am-5pm, ticket prices vary). The voter-created cultural center stages musical and theatrical performances, hosts seasonal museum exhibitions, and offers performing arts classes for adults and children. The vast complex boasts three galleries and a sculpture court; a 1,500-seat concert venue; a 400-seat theater; plus art and dance studios. Check online for a calendar of events covering a wide variety of artistic mediums and genres.

Bernardo Winery

"Southern California's oldest operating winery," **Bernardo Winery** (13330 Paseo Del Verano Norte, Rancho Bernardo, 858/487-1866, www.bernardowinery.com, Mon.-Fri. 9am-5pm, Sat.-Sun. 9am-6pm) features a cluster of wine and gift shops, a tasting room, and a small vineyard. The old timey "village" delivers on charm, and can make a relaxing and fun stopover on the way back from the Safari Park.

RESTAURANTS

Dining at **Stone World Bistro & Gardens** (1999 Citracado Pkwy., 760/294-7899, www.stonebrewing.com, Sun.-Thurs. 11:30am-9pm, Fri.-Sat. 11:30am-10pm, $15-30) is a given. But if you make it into downtown Escondido, stop in at **Intertwined Bistro & Wine Bar** (113 E. Grand Ave., 760/432-9839, www.intertwinedescondido.com, Tues.-Thurs. 11am-9pm, Fri.-Sat. 11am-10pm, $15-30) for creative salads and gourmet entrées. Nearby Parisian-style bakery **Delight of France** (126 W. Grand Ave., 760/746-2644, www.adelightoffrance.com, Mon.-Thurs. 8am-3pm, Fri.-Sat. 8am-9pm, Sun. 8am-2:30pm, $8-15) serves up great croissants and baguettes, plus sandwiches, quiches, and pastries the locals love.

Other Escondido downtown favorites include **Kettle Coffee and Tea** (119 E. Grand Ave., 760/738-8662, www.kettlecoffeeandtea.com, Mon.-Wed. 6:30am-7pm, Thurs. 6:30am-8:30pm, Fri. 6:30am-8pm, Sat. 7:30am-5pm) and **La Tapatia** (340 W. Grand Ave., 760/747-8282, www.latapatia.net, Mon.-Fri. 11am-9pm, Sat.-Sun. 11am-10pm, $10-15), a Mexican family restaurant dating back to 1932. Take it up a notch at **Vintana Wine + Dine** (1205 Auto Park Way, Escondido, 760/745-7777, www.cohnrestaurants.com, Sun.-Thurs. 11:30am-9pm, Fri.-Sat. 11:30am-10pm, $15-30).

clockwise from top left: a cheetah at the San Diego Zoo Safari Park; a cyclist rides along the Coast Highway; Julian's Main Street

The upscale lunch, dinner, and cocktail-destination restaurant resides upstairs from a Lexus dealership; just walk through the showroom to find the way in.

HOTELS

Accommodations within Escondido are not always the most welcoming, but you can hit pay dirt close by in Rancho Bernardo at the **Rancho Bernardo Inn** (17550 Bernardo Oaks Dr., Rancho Bernardo, 855/574-5356, www.ranchobernardoinn.com, from $250). The upscale resort offers golf and spa services amid a beautiful, tranquil setting. If you prefer to stay close to town, look into the Italian-style B&B **Regina Del Palazzo** (602 S. Grape St., Escondido, 760/690-2883, www.reginadelpalazzo.com, $125). The quaint and friendly accommodations are a short walk from Grand Street in downtown Escondido.

PRACTICALITIES

Escondido is located in North County. From San Diego, take I-15 north for about 35 miles; Rancho Bernardo is reachable in about 25 miles. This is a heavily traveled commuter highway, so avoid rush hour and expect the trip to take an hour or longer.

The North County Transit District offers the **Sprinter** (www.gonctd.com/sprinter) commuter train from Oceanside through San Marcos to the Escondido Transit Center (796 W. Valley Pkwy.).

SAN MARCOS

With a nod to the centuries-old beer-producing abbeys of Belgium, **Lost Abbey** (155 Mata Way, Suite 104, San Marcos, 800/918-6816, www.lostabbey.com, Mon.-Tues. 1pm-6pm, Wed.-Thurs. 1pm-8pm, Fri. 1pm-9pm, Sat. 11:30am-8pm, Sun. noon-6pm) has a huge reputation for producing some of the better Belgian-style beers this side of the Atlantic. Its small tasting room is out of the way in a San Marcos business park, but aficionados fill it often.

Julian

An adventurous day trip takes you to this little mountain town that sprung up after Fred Coleman discovered gold in a creek running through nearby Santa Ysabel. The ensuing gold rush didn't last long, but by the time it faded Julian was established and the apple trees planted then literally bore fruit. While a little strip of Main Street still has the facade of a mining town, today's gold is made from apples. Julian apple pie is coveted countywide as a true regional delicacy. You can get it at lower attitudes, but it's less fresh and fun.

From Gold to Golden Delicious

While herding cattle back in 1869, Santa Ysabel rancher A. E. Frederick Coleman stopped to water his horse and recognized a glint of gold in the creek bed. Formerly enslaved in Kentucky, Coleman had joined the Northern California gold rush before settling in the rural outskirts of San Diego, where the majority of the county's black population lived at the time. The agricultural potential of the area held greater opportunity for the minority population found in central San Diego, which was just starting to move out of Old Town.

Coleman's discovery brought a new kind of opportunity to the African Americans in the community: business ownership in a new town. He immediately formed a mining company; when word got out, the boom was on, attracting prospectors and opportunists from around the country. Coleman City sprung up around his claim, but dissipated once the source of the gold was discovered farther east. Ironically, it was a pair of former Confederate soldiers who lent their name to Julian. The Julian brothers came west from Georgia to follow the expansion of the railroad to San Diego. Beating the track builders to California, their party came across the gold rush and began mining. Within a few years, the population grew from nearly nonexistent to more than 600 people, with hotels, restaurants, stores, liveries, and saloons opening around a newly formed Main Street. The Hotel Robinson, opened in 1887 by another formerly enslaved person, Albert Robinson, and his wife, Margaret, remains open today as the **Julian Gold Rush Hotel**, the oldest continuously operating hotel in Southern California, older than Hotel del Coronado by about a year.

Like Coleman City, most gold towns turned to ghost towns once the gold ran out. However, Julian endured for a couple of reasons: The sense of community that arose during the 20-30 years of the gold boom and the tightly knit bunch of men and women who'd met, married, and begun raising families. Even without the gold, they wanted to stay.

Fortunately, the favorable agricultural conditions that first brought people like Coleman to Julian were also ideal for growing apples. East Coast native James Madison planted some apple trees in the early 1870s, and by the early 20th century, large and firm Julian apples were winning blue ribbons at World Fairs around the country. Today, Julian apple pies and ciders are standout regional treats, and apple picking is a popular late-summer activity. The **Julian Apple Days Festival** (www.julianmerchants.org, early Oct.) celebrates the annual harvest that has kept Julian a happy little mountain town for nearly 150 years.

SIGHTS
California Wolf Center

With a mission to preserve the presence of wolves in California, the **California Wolf Center** (K Q Ranch Rd., 760/765-0030, www.california-wolfcenter.org, tours: summer Mon. 10am, Fri. 3pm, Sat. 2pm and 4:30pm, Sun. 10am; winter Mon. 10am, Fri. 3pm, Sat. 10am and 2pm, Sun. 10am, $15-20) provides a home to several packs of gray wolves, including animals from Alaska and Mexico. Regularly scheduled tours include educational presentations and guided observations of two wolf packs. Reservations are required.

Eagle Mining Company

Offering a glimpse into Julian's gold rush past, the Eagle Mining Company (2320 C St., 760/765-0036, www.theeaglemining.com, Mon.-Fri. 10am-4pm, Sat.-Sun. 10am-5pm, $10 adults, $5 ages 5-13, $1 under age 5) offers tours 1,000 feet into the mile-deep mine, as well as gold panning activities and insights into milling operations. Located close to the center of town, it provides a fun and educational couple of hours' worth of activities.

Julian Pioneer Cemetery

Dating to the 1870s and still in use, you'll find the final resting places of multiple generations of Julian natives at the Julian Pioneer Cemetery (Farmer Rd. at A St., 760/765-1857, www.juliancemetery.org). Perched on a hill at the north end of Main Street, the cemetery provides a beautiful if solemn vantage point to look out over Julian and the surrounding area.

Julian Pioneer Museum

The history of Julian is on display at the Julian Pioneer Museum (2811 Washington St., 760/765-0227, www.julianpioneermuseum.org, daily 10am-4pm, $3 adults, free under age 7), mostly in the form of 19th-century clothes, furniture, and mining equipment. You'll also find early photos of the people and town, as well as a horse buggy and information about the original Native American inhabitants of the area.

Santa Ysabel Mission

Technically an *asistencia,* this sub-mission was built in 1818 to serve those who could not regularly make it to the Mission Basilica San Diego de Alcalá. About eight miles northwest of Julian, Santa Ysabel Mission (23013 Hwy. 79, Santa Ysabel, 760/765-0810, www.missiontour.org) actually had a greater conversion rate among the Deigueño and Luiseño people. The original mission structure is long gone, with a more modern white-brick chapel built on the site in 1924 and a small museum revealing insights into the *asistencia*'s long history.

SPORTS AND ACTIVITIES

Apple and pear picking in the later summer and early fall can be a fun way to occupy your trip to Julian. There are more than 100 years of history behind Peacefield Orchard (3803 Wynola Rd., 760/765-0530, Sat.-Sun. 9:30am-4:30pm). Pears have made a strong showing in recent years, and they can be picked at O'Dell's Pear Orchard (1095 Julian Orchard Dr., 760/765-1174, Sat.-Sun. 11am-4pm). If you prefer organic produce, pick the apples and pears at Apple Starr Orchards (1287 Julian Orchards Dr., 760-305-2169, www.apple-starr.com, Sat.-Sun. 10am-5pm). Seasonal harvests vary annually but typically begin in late August. Picking opportunities tend to be on weekends only, though orchards may accept weekday appointments on a case-by-case basis.

RESTAURANTS

The **Julian Café & Bakery** (2112 Main St., 760/765-2712, www.juliancafe. com, Mon.-Thurs. 8am-7:30pm, Fri. 8am-8:30pm, Sat. 7am-9pm, Sun. 7am-8:30pm, $10-15) was built in 1882, but burned down in 1957. Nevertheless, this rebuilt structure from 1978 tries to capture that old-time spirit, complete with an extensive breakfast menu and apple pies. Just up the street, the **Miner's Diner** (2134 Main St., 760/765-3753, www.minersdinerjulian. com, Mon.-Fri. 10:30am-6pm, Sat. 8am-6pm, Sun. 8am-5pm, $8-15) has more of a 1950s look and feel, with burgers and malts, good coffee, and, of course, apple pies.

For a slice of famous Julian pie, try selections from the **Julian Pie Company** (2225 Main St., 760/765-2449, www.julianpie.com, daily 9am-5pm, $8-12) or **Mom's Pies** (2119 Main St., 760/765-2472, www.momspiesjulian.com, daily 8am-5pm, $35 for whole pie). Both offer traditional apple pies plus variations featuring local berries, including strawberry and boysenberry. If you're struggling to decide, get a slice from Mom's and a whole pie to go from Julian Pie Company.

Further satisfy your sweet tooth with a visit to the **Julian Cider Mill** (2103 Main St., 760/765-1430, www.juliancidermillinc.com, Mon.-Thurs. 9:30am-5pm, Fri.-Sun. 9:30am-5:30pm). The shop serves delicious cider as well as preserves and candy. It's pretty much a sweet tooth's idea of heaven.

The tasting room at **Julian Hard Cider Co.** (4470 Julian Rd., 760/765-2500, www.julianhardcider.biz, daily 11am-5pm) serves several adult cider flavors, as well as bottles to go. If your drinking interests skew more toward wine, visit the local station of **Blue Door Winery** (2608 B St., 760/765-0361, www.thebluedoorwinery.com, Thurs.-Mon. noon-4pm) or **Witch Creek Winery** (2000 Main St., Suite 106, 760/765-2023, www.witchcreekwinery. com, Sun.-Thurs. 11am-5pm, Fri.-Sat. 11am-5:30pm).

Beer fans should head to **Bailey Barbecue** (2307 Main St., 760/765-3757, daily 11:30am-8:30pm, $11-25). Not only does the restaurant serve tasty barbecue, but it doubles as the home of the Julian Beer Company. A short drive from the center of town is more Julian craft beer at **Nickel Beer Co.** (1485 Hollow Glen Rd., 760/765-2337, www.nickelbeerco.com, Mon. 3pm-7pm, Thurs. 2pm-6pm, Fri. 11:30am-6pm, Sat. 11:30am-7pm, Sun. 11:30am-5pm).

HOTELS

An overnight stay in Julian doesn't get more central than the **Julian Gold Rush Hotel** (2032 Main St., 760/765-0201, www.julianhotel.com, $150-250). The "oldest continuously operated hotel in Southern California" appears in the National Register of Historic Places, though it has been upgraded since 1897 to include amenities like air-conditioning and Wi-Fi. Only slightly less central is the more modern and dog-friendly **Julian Lodge** (2720 C St., 760/765-1420, www.julianlodge.com, $150-250), just a block off Main Street.

The highest-rated stay in Julian may be found at **Orchard Hill Country Inn** (2502 Washington St., 760/765-1700, www.orchardhill.com, from $250). Located just uphill from the center of town, the lodge rooms and cottages of this Four Diamond property are country hospitable, right down to the patchwork quilts.

A few miles outside of town in a quiet, natural setting, the **Observer's Inn** (3535 Hwy. 79, 760/765-0088, www.observersinn.com, $150-250) offers a comfortable stay with a bonus: astronomy. The B&B offers "Sky Tours," setting up telescopes for guests to stargaze at the dark night sky. **Wikiup Bed & Breakfast** (1645 Whispering Pines Dr., 800/694-5487, www.wikiupbnb.com, $150-250) doesn't show you the stars, but if you prefer a hot tub, massage, and carriage rides, this comfortable woodsy lodge might be for you.

PRACTICALITIES

You will need a car for the day trip to Julian, which is 60 miles northeast of San Diego and about a 1.5-hour drive. From San Diego, take I-8 east for about 25 miles (about 40 minutes), then head north on Highway 79 for 25 miles (another 30 minutes) to Julian. The mountain town is also doable as a side trip from Escondido; Highway 78 leads west to Julian in about 40 miles (one hour).

ALPINE

If you've made the drive to Julian, it only makes sense to detour through Alpine on the way back downtown, solely to visit **Alpine Beer Company** (1347 Tavern Rd., 619/445-2337, www.alpinebeerco.com, Tues.-Thurs. 11am-10pm, Fri.-Sat. 11am-midnight, Sun. 11am-9pm). The regional favorite is too small to distribute widely, so visiting may be your only chance to try it. Taste a couple of fresh pours and leave with a few bottles to take home, or even better—get a growler full of an incredible seasonal release not available anywhere else. If you're hungry, enjoy some great smoked barbecue.

Background

The Landscape

GEOGRAPHY

San Diego may be famous for its gorgeous Pacific coastline, but east of the city are the Laguna, Palomar, and Cuyamaca Mountain Ranges responsible for keeping those beaches sunny and welcoming almost year-round. Part of the Peninsular Ranges, which extend from central California south into Mexico, these mountains act as a buffer against the clouds, maintaining San Diego's almost constant sunshine.

Santa Ana Winds

In fall and winter, high air-pressure funnels through the mountain passes with such force that it dries out and warms up, forming what are known as Santa Ana winds. The Santa Anas account for some of the scorching-hot days San Diego sometimes experiences in November or even February. When the Santa Anas are blowing, the coast may actually be warmer than inland areas. The resulting offshore winds can carve some nice waves for surfers, but they also bring a lot of dry heat to an environment considered at high risk for wildfires.

Plants

The San Diego area is classified as semiarid. Aside from the mountains ranges, the landscape is dominated by chaparral, a drought-resistant and low-lying shrubland. Plants characteristic of chaparral tend to have evergreen leaves with oily skins that help retain moisture. Unfortunately, they are also highly flammable, making them fast fuel for wildfires.

Low-lying coastal sage scrub dominates close to the beach in environs typified by nature reserves such as the San Elijo and Batiquitos Lagoons, Peñasquitos Canyon, and Torrey Pines. The five-needle Torrey Pine is one of the rarest pines in the United States. This endangered species grows only in the Torrey Pines Nature Reserve, north of La Jolla, and on one of the Channel Islands, a loose archipelago off the California coast.

Much more common are eucalyptus trees, an invasive species that thrives in drought conditions and salty soil. The Australian native arrived in California with the Gold Rush, in an attempt to plant fast-growing hardwood for rail ties. Unfortunately, the soft wood was unusable, and instead proved to edge out native species. The heavily aromatic leaves and peeling gray bark are common indicators of their presence near canyons and parks.

Bays and Waterways

The original shifting course of the San Diego River proved too unreliable a water source for the growing city, A damn went up in the 1870s to form

---

Previous page top: sandstone cliffs overlook the coastline; **bottom:** a cactus from the Desert Garden at Balboa Park

the El Capitan Reservoir (about 30 miles east of Mission Bay) and a fixed river channel was made for the runoff. The San Diego River flows out to the Pacific Ocean between OB and Mission Beach, though it doesn't always look like much, particularly in the summer when dry conditions lower water levels to near wetland status.

Mission Bay used to be a vast system of wetlands known as False Bay; then 25 million cubic-yards of sand and silt were dredged from the marshy area in the 1950s. There are still plenty of tidal marshes, estuaries, and lagoons along San Diego's North County coastline; these low-lying bodies of salt water are not deep enough to be a bay or an inlet, yet not quite solid enough to form firm ground.

San Diego Bay is the city's most indelible asset. Large and outwardly protected by the partially overlapping Coronado and Point Loma Peninsulas, this naturally protected harbor is what ultimately molded San Diego into the city it is today.

CLIMATE

San Diego enjoys 150 sunny days a year, with approximately 130 "partly cloudy" days (more like partly sunny), and 10 inches of annual rainfall. Summers are warm with cool nights, while winters are warm or cloudy during the day with colder nights.

In late May and June, a marine layer often rolls in over the city—a blanket of clouds held low in the sky by the pressure of an inversion layer. Locals call this phenomenon May Gray and June Gloom. During cool nights in fall and winter, fog creeps in over the ocean and covers the city in a gauzy overcast that lasts most of the day. East of I-5, this layer may dissipate into cloudless sunshine—a perfect example of San Diego's regional microclimates. Temperatures may rise 15 degrees just a few miles from the ocean. On average, inland San Diego and North Country will be 10 degrees warmer on most days.

ENVIRONMENTAL ISSUES

California has been suffering from a historically severe drought for several years. While the drought has not had an immediate impact on San Diego's water supply, usage caps and cost increases require conservation measures to be enforced to keep waste to a minimum. For visitors, this means that hotels will launder towels and linens only by request; water is not served at restaurants unless specifically requested.

When it does rain, water runoff can pollute the beaches in and around the Pacific Ocean, making contact unsafe for up to 72 hours. Entering the water at this time puts you at risk of ear and throat infections, and the nastiest of all, staph infections. Anyone with an open wound or a weakened immune system is particularly at risk, especially children. To confirm water safety, consult the county of San Diego's **Beach Water Quality Hotline** (619/338-2073, www.sdbeachinfo.com) to find out which beaches may be affected.

San Diego at a Glance

- Average Annual Rainfall: 9.9 inches

- Average Daily Temperatures (High/Low): 70/57°F

- City Land Area: 325 square miles (842 km²)

- City Population: 1.36 million

- Coolest Months: January-February at 65/48°F (18/9°C)

- County Land Area: 4,207 square miles (10,900 km²)

- County Population: 3.21 million

- Hotel Tax: 10.5 percent

- Hottest Month: August at 76/66°F (24/19°C)

- Incorporated: 1850

- Median Age: 35.6 years

- Median Household Income: $63,990

- Population Density: 4,000 per square mile (1,544 per km²)

- Sales Tax: 8 percent

- Time Zone: Pacific time

- Wettest Months: January-February with 2 inches (51 mm)

History

THE MISSION PERIOD

When Spanish conquistador Juan Rodríguez Cabrillo led the first Spanish ship into San Diego Bay in 1542, he encountered the region's original Native American inhabitants, the Kumeyaay people. The Kumeyaay wore clothing made from animal skins, reeds, or woven bark, and they lived in small thatched huts. At that time, the Kumeyaay were spread out among 30 clans connected by trade; some lived near the coast and would canoe miles offshore to fish. They would then trade with inland clans, who built dams and used fire to clear land for agriculture. A particularly large and central clan grew as a trade center along the San Diego River where the more robust waterway of the time drained into Mission Bay. In 1769, the landing party of Franciscan friar Junípero Serra chose this spot to establish California's first mission; the location gave him the chance to convert the greatest number Kumeyaay people to Roman Catholicism.

The Mission Basilica San Diego de Alcalá was the first permanent European settlement in the expansive area that would become Alta California, claiming the region for Spain and opening the door to the establishment of 20 more missions throughout the state. Along with the Junípero Serra came a garrison of Spanish troops who established a presidio (fort) along with the mission. Within five years, the mission moved several miles inland, but the presidio stayed where it was. As the Spanish presence grew, some retiring soldiers began building homes at the base of Presidio Hill.

In 1821, after Alta California became part of Mexico following an 11-year war for independence from Spain, this cluster of adobe structures became the small village of San Diego. Its small population of ethnically mixed Californios developed the Mexican pueblo we know today as Old Town.

While Old Town survived for decades, it didn't exactly thrive. During the 1830s, the population fluctuated and the presidio fell into abandoned disrepair due to complications of transporting supplies from the nearest boat landing at Point Loma.

STATEHOOD

The Mexican-American War began in 1846 over border disputes in Texas and quickly encroached on California, which the United States coveted for coastal trade. The victory at the Battle of San Pasqual, in what is now north San Diego County, cemented the U.S. annexation of the territory. In 1848 Alta California was ceded to the United States, and in 1850 California became the 31st state. At the time, San Diego's population was around 650, which qualified it to become a county seat.

BOOM AND BUST

In the early 1860s San Diego suffered floods, drought, a massive earthquake, and a smallpox epidemic. However, the city's natural harbor gave it great potential as a port of call for ships making the long journey around South America. In 1867, used-furniture dealer Alonzo Horton arrived in San Diego from San Francisco and bought 800 acres next to San Diego Bay for $265. He would go on to spend $45,000 to build a wharf that finally established a permanent shipping port. He sold 500-square-foot lots in what was then New Town San Diego, and by 1870 the population had grown to 2,300 people.

During a time of incredible growth, the new city boomed in size to nearly 40,000 people. With a promised connection to the transcontinental railroad, speculators were eager to invest, and public works projects saw the installation of electric streetlights, street cars, and a flume that transported water from the Cuyamaca Mountain Range 35 miles away. However, this massive boom was followed by a colossal bust. As the railroad passage was rerouted, San Diego's spot on the map was relegated to a coastal spur line from Los Angeles. By the late 1880s, the population had dropped to 16,000 as the overzealous speculation failed to pay off.

THE PANAMA-CALIFORNIA EXPOSITION

Over the next 20 years the population would steadily creep back. Local entrepreneurs and philanthropists spearheaded a movement to host an exposition commemorating the opening of the Panama Canal, which would make San Diego a much busier shipping destination. The Panama-California Exposition opened in 1914 at the newly developed Balboa Park, effectively announcing San Diego's return to prominence. The city had

clockwise from top left: palm trees are found all over San Diego; the County Administration Building beside Waterfront Park, Downtown; one of San Diego's historic district signs

By 1920, the city was home to nearly 75,000 people as well as the U.S. Navy's Pacific Fleet. Soon, the Marine Corps Recruit Depot opened in an area known as Middletown. Within 10 years the population would double, and it has continued to grow ever since, becoming home to defense contractors and technology companies—and attracting nearly 30 million visitors each year.

Local Culture

It's tempting to peg San Diego as a surf spot, military base, or a bilingual border town. But a city doesn't become the nation's eighth largest by attracting any type of person; San Diego lures a variety of people from other parts of the United States and abroad. Some come for opportunities, some for the lifestyle, and some because their orders tell them to.

NATIVE AMERICANS

The Native American population in San Diego is estimated to be a little more than 1 percent of the total, or about 20,000 people; the number is roughly the same as when Spanish ships first sailed into San Diego Bay. Along with the city's original inhabitants—the Kumeyaay people—other nations include the Luiseño, Cupeño, and Cahuilla. During the late 19th century, a government executive order forced these nations to move to reservations on the outer boundaries of San Diego County, including Lakeside, Campo, Pala, and Valley Center. San Diego County has more reservations than anywhere else in the country (a dubious distinction), though only a small percentage of self-identifying Native Americans currently live on reservation land.

LATINOS

San Diego is home to a huge Latino population that makes up more than one-quarter of the population. Spanish is the city's unofficial second language, and in many pocket neighborhoods, it's the first. Most of the Latino community in San Diego runs several generations deep; some can trace their ancestry back to the original Californio settlers of Mexican Old Town. While some communities may not be fully or equitably integrated, the sound of Mexican folk songs and the flavors of Mexican cuisine reminds all San Diegans of home.

IMMIGRATION

While significant numbers of foreign refugees have moved to San Diego to escape political, ethnic, or religious persecutions in their native lands—including many Eritreans, Somalis, Sudanese, Vietnamese, Laotians, Burmese, and Chaldean Iraqis—other ethnic populations date back to the

Famous San Diegans

Many folks have contributed to the convoluted history of San Diego, but these names tend to show up around town on buildings, parks, and museums.

- **Juan Rodríguez Cabrillo:** During the 16th century, Cabrillo fought his way through Mexico and Guatemala with the Spanish conquistador Hernán Cortés. Following many years living and working in Guatemala, he led an exhibition to explore the coast of California. His was the first ship to enter San Diego Bay, though he apparently preferred the name San Miguel. Though he died before completing his expedition, Cabrillo Point in Point Loma marks the location he may have first laid eyes on California.

- **William Heath Davis:** Davis is credited with having the idea to move San Diego from Old Town to a "New Town" beside the harbor. In 1850, he gathered investors to buy 160 acres and build a wharf in what is now Downtown. However, a depression hit in 1851, which is blamed for dashing his plans. Aside from the house he built for himself (and never lived in), most of the buildings Davis and his investors built were torn down for scrap.

- **Irving J. Gill:** San Diego's most prominent turn-of-the-20th-century architect, Gill moved to San Diego in 1893 and enjoyed great esteem and a lengthy career that saw him design homes for statured residents like George Marston and Ellen Scripps, as well as small economic cottages for working class people. He's seen as a pioneer of the arts and crafts movement, and the effects of his influence may be seen in Craftsman homes throughout the city.

- **Alonzo E. Horton:** Horton managed to fulfill the "New Town" dream of William Heath Davis. In 1867, Horton took a steamboat from San Francisco to San Diego and wound up purchasing 800 acres at auction. He returned to San Francisco and diligently sold lots, sight unseen, to people inspired by the idea of the "American Riviera." He built a wharf and several buildings to cement his property next to the harbor as the new and permanent center of San Diego.

- **George W. Marston:** Marston moved from Wisconsin to San Diego in 1870 at the age of 20. He dusted the coats of guests at the Horton House Hotel, then worked as a bookkeeper for a general store. Within 10 years, he owned the city's only department store. He was instrumental in developing Balboa Park, and bought Presidio Hill in order to preserve

city's origins. Chinese immigrants arrived in the late 19th century to work construction and lay track for local railroad lines. Though the Chinatown that originally formed near the harbor was dismantled a century ago, ethnic Chinese people remain a part of the city's cultural makeup. Asian populations account for approximately 16 percent of the city's population.

Many African Americans came to San Diego along with the Spanish colonials as the original settlement developed. When California became a U.S. state in 1850, slavery was outlawed, and in the years leading up to and

A statue of Juan Rodríguez Cabrillo overlooks San Diego Bay.

and created the Natural History Museum at Balboa Park, among many other endeavors.

- **Junípero Serra:** Serra was a Franciscan friar who founded nine of the 21 California missions, starting with the Mission Basilica San Diego de Alcalá in 1769. He's credited with creating the first permanent European settlement in California.

- **Kate Sessions:** Known as the "Mother of Balboa Park," Sessions came to San Diego as a schoolteacher in 1884. In 1892, she leased land in Balboa Park to start a nursery, on the condition that she would plant 100 trees per year within the park and 300 more around the city. She is credited with introducing cypress, oaks, pepper trees, and jacarandas to a city that had previously lacked them.

the site of the city's original settlement.

- **Ellen Browning Scripps:** Scripps was a great philanthropist and San Diego was her chief beneficiary. When the British-born newspaper publisher retired to La Jolla in 1896 at the age of 60, she had a mind to spread her wealth to the region. She lived in La Jolla for 35 years and spent millions on schools, hospitals, and gardens, established the Scripps Institute of Oceanography,

- **John D. Spreckels:** Spreckels had a massive an impact on San Diego. After visiting San Diego 1887, he built a wharf at the end of Broadway. Over the decades, he would become the richest man in San Diego, owning the ferry, streetcar, and local rail systems, both San Diego newspapers, Belmont Park, and most of Coronado, including the Hotel Del. He built office buildings, theaters, dams, and contributed to the establishment of Balboa Park.

during the Civil War, the city became a destination for many freed men and women. During World War II, many African American servicemen and women stationed in the city also chose to stay. Today, San Diego's African American population hovers around 6 to 7 percent.

Portuguese and Italian fisherfolk arrived in San Diego in the late 19th and early 20th centuries and established communities in Point Loma and Little Italy, respectively. Little Italy retains its *tricolore* heritage, with many influences commemorating its history and culture. In recent years, a growing Brazilian and Portuguese population has mingled around Point Loma and Ocean Beach, though businesses in these neighborhoods do not represent this influence.

SUBCULTURES

Surfers

San Diego is home to hundreds of thousands of surfers—it can get pretty crowded out in the water sometimes. The classic image of a lean, bronzed, sun-bleached blond carving up the waves does exist, and you'll see it often, but surfers come from all ethnicities and walks of life. While the majority may be born-and-bred locals, many picked up the sport upon arriving in San Diego from elsewhere and became instant devotees. The lone unifying factor is the stoke they feel any day that a great swell hits.

Military

Up to 150,000 people move to San Diego each year from other parts of the country, and many are with the U.S. Navy and Marine Corps. Most are under age 30 and represent the diversity found in the military. Many are stationed at a huge North County base, Marine Corps Base Camp Pendleton, or, for a short time, at the Marine Corps Recruit Depot. Naval bases are also located in Coronado, Point Loma, Miramar, and National City.

Homelessness

By some counts, San Diego has the fifth-largest homeless population among U.S. cities. The vast majority of the city's estimated 10,000 homeless are found Downtown, particularly in the East Village, with a second sizeable population around Point Loma and Ocean Beach. Ongoing programs sponsored by the city aim to provide shelter and treatment for those in need, but progress is slow. Homeless help and services are available through **San Diego County** (1200 3rd Ave., 619/236-5990, www.sandiego.gov) and by calling the city's info line (619/230-0997 or 211).

FESTIVALS AND EVENTS

Spring

Earth Fair

One of the world's largest Earth Day celebrations, the **Earth Fair** (Balboa Park, 858/272-7370, www.earthdayweb.org, Apr.) is presented by San Diego EarthWorks and attracts ecologically minded individuals. Booths highlight products and technological innovations in the world of conservation and sustainability that are both educational and inspirational.

Ethnic Food Fair

The International Village in Balboa Park features 21 cottages representing a number of foreign nations. In May, they host the **Ethnic Food Fair** (HPR

Cottages, Balboa Park, www.sdhpr.org, May), offering traditional food from each host country in an afternoon sure to delight the taste buds and push the limits of your stomach.

Fiesta Old Town Cinco de Mayo

Cinco de Mayo is celebrated in Mexico as a day of national pride, and the **Fiesta Old Town Cinco De Mayo** (Old Town, www.oldtownsandiegoguide. com, May) is the "largest of its kind" three-day festival. You'll find food, music, traditional attire, costumes, shopping, lowriders, and if you look hard enough, some tequila.

Rock 'n' Roll Marathon

It's easy to think that the **Rock 'n' Roll Marathon** (6th St. and Quince St., Balboa Park, http://runrocknroll.competitor.com, May, $90-130) isn't serious, what with all the bands, costumes, and drinking. While it may be a good time for onlookers, the participants are running a 26-mile marathon, a 13-mile half marathon, and a two-person relay (6 and 7 miles).

Summer

La Jolla Festival of the Arts

Amid all the food, beer, wine, jazz, and folk music, one might easily forget that the annual **La Jolla Festival of the Arts** (UCSD, 3453 Voigt Dr., La Jolla, 619/744-0534, www.lajollaartfestival.org, June) is about the artists and their work. Providing an elegant atmosphere for hands-on appreciation, it gives art-lovers a chance to mingle with artists and enjoy a La Jolla summer day.

OB Street Fair

Up to 70,000 people gather in Ocean Beach for the kooky, boozy **OB Street Fair** (locations vary, Ocean Beach, https://oceanbeachsandiego.com, June, free). Live music, a chili cook-off, an art walk, and carnival rides and attractions are hallmarks of the occasion, while a beer garden keeps it lively. Each year, kids and amateur artists paint one square of a community mural, which usually results in a patchwork-quilt seascape. Murals from previous years dot the neighborhood.

San Diego County Fair

From the second week of June through July 4 the **San Diego County Fair** (2260 Jimmy Durante Blvd., Del Mar, 858/755-1161, www.sdfair.com, June) offers food, music, rides, animals, car shows, and one or two beer festivals. And if that isn't enough, it's held right beside the racetrack in Del Mar.

San Diego International Beer Festival

The West Coast's largest beer festival offers more than "400 beers" and "one glass." The **San Diego International Beer Festival** (Del Mar Fairgrounds,

clockwise from top left: surfers on the beach; Sunset Cliffs Natural Park; the Scripps Oceanic Institute Pier

Del Mar, http://sandiegobeerfestival.com, June, free with fair admission) brings together more than 200 breweries—local and international—to give more than 10,000 craft beer lovers a place to immerse themselves in fermented hops, yeast, barley, and wheat. Five separate sessions keep it from getting too crowded, but some people attend them all and still can't get to all the beers.

Shakespeare Festival

Reason enough for theater fans to visit San Diego, the **Shakespeare Festival** (Balboa Park, 619/234-5623, www.theoldglobe.org, June-Sept.) usually offers two or three productions, primarily the celebrated work of the Bard and occasionally a well-known modern play that lives up to the legacy of the English language's prolific genius. Hosted in the outdoor venue of the Old Globe Theatre complex, it's a special way to enjoy the evening air while nourishing your need for culture.

Art in Bloom

Balboa Park's Spanish Village combines the work of local artists and horticulturalists into a single event celebrating creativity combined with the showiness of nature. **Art in Bloom** (1770 Village Pl., Balboa Park, http://svacartinbloom.blogspot.com, July, free) features live paintings and floral sculptures that often prove the most memorable parts of the event, with awards given to standouts each year.

Comic Con

Year after year, **Comic Con** (111 W. Harbor Dr., www.comic-con.org, July) is the biggest event at the Downtown San Diego Convention Center. What began as a modest celebration of comic books has exploded into an entertainment juggernaut, drawing all manner of sci-fi fans, cosplayers, videogame buffs, and celebrities. More than 125,000 people descend on San Diego to attend 600 staged events and 1,500 exhibitor booths. Take note when Comic Con takes place; it sells out far in advance, as do most of the hotels anywhere near Downtown at triple their normal rates.

Over the Line Tournament

Possibly the most organized annual drinking game, the **Over the Line Tournament** (Fiesta Island Rd., Mission Bay, www.ombac.org, July, free) has been at it for more than 60 years. Teams of three gather at Fiesta Island in Mission Bay to compete (and drink) in this goofy miniature version of softball, while their friends watch and also drink. Of the 1,200 teams that competed in 2014, most had raunchy or suggestive names—all in the spirit of BYOB fun.

San Diego's gay, lesbian, bisexual, and transgender community congregates around Hillcrest, its de facto hub, to stage the **San Diego LGBT Pride** (University Ave. from Normal St. to Upas St., 619/297-7683, https://sdpride. org, July, free) parade to Balboa Park and back. Weekend festivities include live music, rallies, and a massive block party that attracts thousands of people from all orientations to join in the joy, hope, and pride of a civil rights movement that has made incredible strides.

SummerFest

Chamber music receives special attention when the La Jolla Music Society presents **SummerFest** (locations vary, La Jolla, 858/459-3728, http://ljms. org, July and Aug.), a number of special engagements in area venues, including a free "Under the Stars" performance held beside La Jolla Cove. Most shows charge admission to see some of the world's top talents perform some of classical music's most heralded pieces.

Bike the Bay

One Sunday in mid- to late August, half of the Coronado Bridge closes to cars for **Bike the Bay** (619/269-6873, www.bikethebay.net, Aug., $50-55), a community bike ride over the iconic arched bridge. The ride continues around the mostly flat Bayshore Bikeway and offers a great way for cyclists to see a bit of town (and the view from the bridge).

Stone Anniversary Celebration

San Diego's beloved Stone Brewing throws the **Stone Anniversary Celebration and International Beer Festival** (333 S. Twin Oaks Valley Rd., Escondido, www.stonebrewing.com, Aug., $45-85), a massive weekend-long birthday bash. Stone invites 60 or so of its favorite craft-brewing friends from around the country to participate. More than 100 beers are on hand; guests can opt to taste special releases from some of their favorite brewers or discover something new.

Fall

Festival of Sail

Labor Day weekend, San Diego Bay brings another era back to life with the **Festival of Sail** (1492 North Harbor Dr., www.sdmaritime.org, Sept.). A parade of beautiful vintage tall ships sails across the bay, firing cannon salutes and coming to dock. A lot of food, beer, and nautical-themed attractions keep the event family-friendly and engaging for everyone who likes boats.

North Park Music Thing

Similar to Austin's South by Southwest festival, **Music Thing** (locations vary, 619/381-8789, www.sandiegomusicthing.com, Sept.) takes over live music clubs all over town, setting feature lineups of local up-and-comers as well as a few better-known headliners. Music industry workshops and networking take place during the day, providing a chance for creative folk to mingle and music lovers to learn about show business.

San Diego Restaurant Week

During **San Diego Restaurant Week** (locations vary, www.sandiegorestaurantweek.com, Sept. and Jan.), restaurants all over town offer special pricing on selected menus, giving a chance for foodies on a budget to check out new restaurants they might otherwise miss. Prices and availability vary; check online to secure a spot at the city's best eateries in advance.

Halloween Family Day

Each Saturday before Halloween, selected Balboa Park museums open their doors for **Halloween Family Day** (Balboa Park, 619/239-0512, www.balboapark.org, Oct.). From 11am to 3pm, children ages 12 and under can explore spooky hands-on displays that complement the usual educational and cultural fare. Parents don't get in for free, but reduced rates are typically available.

La Jolla Art & Wine Festival

The **La Jolla Art & Wine Festival** (Girard Ave., La Jolla Village, www.ljawf.com, Oct., free) shuts down a portion of Girard Avenue for two days to exhibit local artwork, gourmet fare, and excellent wine, as well as local beer. Proceeds support arts programs at area schools.

MCAS Miramar Air Show

Federal funds permitting, aviators put on a dazzling show during the **MCAS Miramar Air Show** (Marine Corps Air Station Miramar, Miramar Way, http://miramarairshow.com, Oct., free). The event is held over the airfield at the Marine Corps Air Station Miramar, which is home to some of the world's best jet pilots. There are Harrier and Osprey demonstrations, vintage plane shows, parachute teams, and, of course, the headliners, the Blue Angels.

Día de los Muertos

Día de los Muertos (Old Town State Historic Park, 619/297-9327, http://sddayofthedead.org, Nov. 1-2, free) isn't a street-fair kind of festival but a celebration of the traditional Mexican holiday that honors the dead. Old Town becomes the site of 50 altars as well as enlightening booths dedicated to face painting and *papel picado,* offering an opportunity to engage in other traditional practices before a candlelit procession to the Campo Santo Cemetery.

San Diego Bay Wine & Food Festival

The **San Diego Bay Wine & Food Festival** (Embarcadero Marina Park North, www.sandiegowineclassic.com, Nov.) is a gourmand celebration of the city's local culinary scene, with a little beer thrown in for good measure. Special tasting events, celebrity chef panels, and cooking classes are some of many events staged during the weeklong fest.

San Diego Beer Week

The second week of November is a great time to drink beer—at least that's what we tell ourselves when **San Diego Beer Week** (locations vary, www.sdbw.org, Nov.) kicks up. Events are tailored around seasonal and special-release beers that could be the best new ale or stout in town. It's a great time for beer tourists to sample some of the best local brewing.

Winter

Balboa Park December Nights

Billing itself as the "largest free community festival in San Diego," the annual **Balboa Park December Nights** (Balboa Park, www.balboapark.org, Dec.) draws hundreds of thousands of people to Balboa Park. Holiday lights and decor provide the main attraction, though special performances, food, and free museum entry (5pm-9pm) help make this an every-year tradition for many locals. The event is usually the first Friday and Saturday evenings of December.

Big Bay Balloon Parade

The Rose Parade may be the best-known event associated with college football, but 100,000 people line up to see San Diego's **Big Bay Balloon Parade** (locations vary, http://sandiegobowlgames.com, Dec.) kickoff to the Holiday Bowl. "America's largest balloon parade" runs along Harbor Drive and features hundreds of floats and, yes, balloons. You haven't lived till you've seen a pneumatic Cookie Monster float past the tall clipper ships of the Maritime Museum.

La Jolla Christmas Parade & Holiday Festival

Even the Village of La Jolla loves a parade. In December it stages **La Jolla Christmas Parade & Holiday Festival** (Girard Ave., La Jolla, 858/922-4046, www.ljparade.com, Dec.), complete with floats, equestrians, vintage cars, beauty queens, and marching bands. The parade route moves down Girard Avenue before turning south on Prospect Street, where a decorated Christmas tree marks the spot of the festival, along with food, games, and entertainment.

Ocean Beach Holiday Parade

OB has a unique character, so it's little surprise that it has a unique holiday parade. The **Ocean Beach Holiday Parade** (Newport Ave., Ocean

Beach, https://oceanbeachsandiego.com, Dec.) features floats and marching bands with the occasional countercultural twist, whether it's a team of Roller Derby women or the parade of surf-car classics known as woodies.

San Diego Bay Parade of Lights

Some neighborhoods are popular every year for their Christmas lights. San Diego Bay is one of these, however instead of houses and lawns it's the festively decorated boats of the San Diego Bay Parade Of Lights (locations vary, 619/224-2240, www.sdparadeoflights.org, Dec.). The two Sunday evenings before Christmas, dozens of boats parade through the bay—from Shelter Island to Harbor Island, the Embarcadero, and all the way around to the Coronado Ferry Landing. Pick your spot on the bay, and let the lights come to you.

Essentials

Transportation

GETTING THERE

Air

Also known as Lindbergh Field, **San Diego International Airport** (SAN, 619/400-2404, www.san.org) is a centrally located urban airport a mere three miles from the city center. While the location makes it a little noisy for those living in neighborhoods under the flight path, it makes getting to and from the airport a quick trip from most parts of the city. The airport is split into two major terminals plus a small commuter terminal, hosting 20 airlines and subsidiaries.

The county-operated **McClellan-Palomar Airport** (CLD, 760/431-4646, www.sandiegocounty.gov) is served by United Airlines Express (800/864-8331, www.united.com), which operates a regular daily schedule of commuter flights between Carlsbad and Los Angeles's LAX only. It's a convenient option if you plan to spend a lot of time in North County.

The opening of a pedestrian bridge border crossing in summer 2015 promises to make **Tijuana International Airport** (TIJ, 52/664-607-8200, www.tijuana-airport.com) a much more convenient option for travelers visiting San Diego from cities without direct flights to San Diego, or those wishing to fly on more affordable airlines, including **Aeroméxico** (800/237-6639, www.aeromexico.com), **Interjet** (866/85-8307, www.interjet.com), **VivaAerobus** (888/935-9848, www.vivaaerobus.com), and **Volaris** (866/988-3527, www.volaris.com).

Bus

Greyhound Bus Lines (800/752-4841, www.greyhound.com) has its terminal (1313 National Ave., 619/515-1100) in Downtown San Diego's East Village, with the option to stop in Oceanside (205 S. Tremont St., 760/722-1587) or Escondido (700 W. Valley Pkwy., 760/745-6522).

Train

Amtrak (800/872-7245, www.amtrak.com) offers daily service to and from San Diego on its *Pacific Surfliner* route, which extends up the coast connecting to Los Angeles, Santa Barbara, and San Luis Obispo. Trains depart from the Downtown Santa Fe Depot (1050 Kettner Blvd.), with stops in Solana Beach (105 North Cedros Ave.) and Oceanside (235 South Tremont St.).

Some *Surfliner* trains also make stops in Old Town (4005 Taylor St.), Sorrento Valley (11170 Sorrento Valley Rd.), and at two stations in Carlsbad (6511 Avenida Encinas; 2775 State St.). Consult schedules online for these additional stops.

Previous page top: the Santa Fe train depot, Downtown; **bottom:** a mosaic depicts the Coaster, a commuter rail line

San Diego by Air

The following airlines provide service to and from San Diego:

- Air Canada (888/247-2262, www.aircanada.com, Terminal 2)

- Alaska Airlines (800/252-7522, www.alaskaair.com, Terminal 1)

- Allegiant Air (702/505-8888, www.allegiantair.com, Terminal 2)

- American Airlines (800/433-7300, www.aa.com, Terminal 2)

- American Eagle (800/433-7300, www.aa.com, Commuter Terminal)

- British Airways (800/247-9297, www.britishairways.com, Terminal 2)

- Delta Airlines (800/221-1212, www.delta.com, Terminal 2)

- Frontier Airlines (800/432-1359, www.flyfrontier.com, Terminal 2)

- Hawaiian Airlines (800/367-5320, www.hawaiianairlines.com, Terminal 2)

- Japan Airlines (800/525-3663, www.ar.jal.com, Terminal 2)

- JetBlue Airways (800/538-2583, www.jetblue.com, Terminal 2)

- SeaPort Airlines (888/573-2767, www.seaportair.com, Commuter Terminal)

- Southwest Airlines (800/435-9792, www.southwest.com, Terminal 1)

- Spirit Airlines (800/772-7117, www.spirit.com, Terminal 2)

- Sun Country Airlines (800/359-6786, www.suncountry.com, Terminal 2)

- United Airlines (800/864-8331, www.united.com, Terminal 2)

- United Airlines Express (800/864-8331, www.united.com, Commuter Terminal)

- Virgin America (877/359-8474, www.virginamerica.com, Terminal 2)

- Volaris (866/988-3527, www.volaris.com, Terminal 2)

- WestJet (888/937-8538, www.westjet.com, Terminal 2)

Car

San Diego is bisected by I-5, which provides access to the North County coast and Downtown San Diego and continues south to Tijuana in Mexico. From Los Angeles, I-5 is a direct shot 120 miles south to Downtown San Diego. The drive can take two to three hours in light traffic, but up to five hours in rush hour or otherwise congested traffic.

I-15 provides access to San Diego from the northeast, and runs to Escondido, Riverside County, and eventually into Nevada and Las Vegas. This freeway is the most direct route to inland North County; in light traffic, it can take 30 minutes to an hour to drive the 30 miles north from Downtown to Escondido. However, I-15 suffers from impacted rush-hour traffic as commuters return home to Miramar, Mira Mesa, Poway, and Rancho Bernardo.

I-8 connects east to El Centro before crossing to Yuma, Arizona, in about 175 miles. In Arizona, I-8 connects to I-10 south of Phoenix.

Car Rentals

Most car rental agencies operate near the San Diego International Airport. The closest are **Hertz** (3202 N. Harbor Dr., 619/767-5700), **National** (3280 N. Harbor Dr., 888/826-6890), and **Avis** (3180 N. Harbor Dr., 619/688-5000). All are a short shuttle ride way, so Thrifty and even farther-away Enterprise are accessible enough. From the train station, **Avis** (1670 Kettner Blvd., Suite 1, 619/231-7137) is within short walking distance.

GETTING AROUND
Public Transportation

San Diego's public transportation is operated by the **Metropolitan Transit System** (619/557-4555, www.sdmts.com), which includes buses, a trolley system, and the Coaster, a commuter rail line run by the North County Transit District that extends from Downtown San Diego to Oceanside. The **Coaster** (760/966-6500, www.gonctd.com, $4-5.50 one-way) is a great way to visit Solana Beach, Encinitas, or Carlsbad; operating hours and schedules vary. The **trolley** ($2.50 one-way, $5 day pass) operates daily, offering three color-coded routes that make a good option for visiting through Downtown (all lines), Old Town and Mission Valley (Green Line), or south to Tijuana (Blue Line).

While the bus system is extensive and runs countywide, it can be complicated and slow; the uninitiated should plan the trip in advance by visiting the **SDMTS** website (www.sdcommute.com).

The **North County Transit District** (760/966-6500, www.gonctd.com) operates the **Sprinter** (Mon.-Fri. 4am-9pm, Sat.-Sun. 10am-6pm, $2 one-way) rail line from Oceanside to Escondido, a bus system serving mostly suburban areas, and a reservation-based shuttle, **Flex** (855/844-1454, call 30 minutes in advance, $5), which may be a handy option for those looking to get around between Encinitas and Solana Beach.

Car
Driving

San Diego is a freeway town, but getting around will be a lot less frustrating—and safer—if you know where you're going and how to get there before you hop on the road. GPS navigation services help, but the city is constantly bisected by canyons and waterways; the quickest way to get somewhere is often not a straight line.

I-5 stretches through Downtown San Diego, from the Mexican border north to La Jolla and the North County beach towns. I-5 connects to Highway 163 north through Balboa Park to both I-8 and I-805, to I-805 again farther north in Sorrento Valley, and in Oceanside to Highway 78,

San Diego Trolley Map

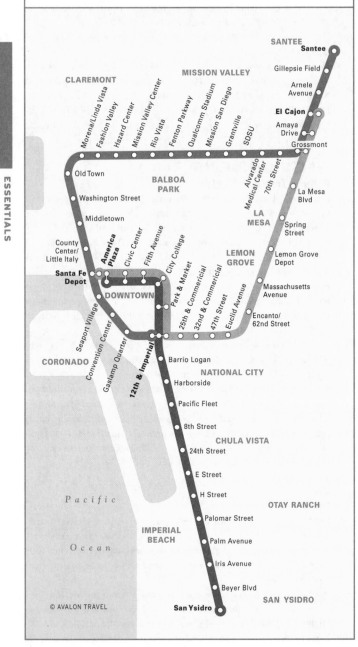

California Traffic Laws

In addition to typical traffic laws seen elsewhere, California stringently enforces a few less common rules with tickets and steep fines:

- **Do not phone or text while driving.** You may use a sanctioned hands-free device to speak on the phone, but if your are in any way holding a phone in your hand while you drive, you will be cited.

- **Wear a seatbelt.** This law applies to both front and backseat passengers, and it's mandated for safety.

- **Avoid car-pool lane violations.** Designated car-pool or high-occupancy vehicle (HOV) lanes require a minimum of two or three passengers to access (the exact number is posted). These are designed to ease traffic congestion and are especially enforced during rush hours.

- **Check car seat requirements.** Children under age 8 must be secured in a car seat in the back seat of a car unless they are taller than 4 feet, 9 inches.

- **No littering.** Tossing any trash out of your car will earn you a ticket worth at least several hundred dollars.

which leads east to San Marcos and Escondido. Driving the I-5 north of Del Mar can be a traffic nightmare during rush hour. Avoid traveling south in the morning or north in the afternoon.

Within San Diego, **I-8** offers east-west access to Ocean Beach, Mission Beach, and Mission Valley before connecting to I-805 and I-15 at its eastern points. Note that while I-5 crosses I-8 near Old Town, you cannot merge onto I-8 westbound from I-5 southbound; if you're heading to Mission Beach or Ocean Beach from the north, exit on Sea World Drive instead.

I-805 runs parallel to I-5 a few miles inland, passing through the North Park neighborhood in Uptown and reconnecting with I-5 just before Del Mar at Sorrento Valley. Take heed: Sorrento Valley is widely considered the city's tech hub and has the region's worst traffic during morning and afternoon rush hours (Mon.-Fri. 7am-9:30am and 3:30pm-6:30pm).

If you're unfortunate enough to see rain, drive cautiously. For one, San Diegans are not the best drivers in rainy conditions. Also, since we don't get a lot of rain, for a time after the first rain the road may be a little extra slippery.

Car Sharing Services

Alternatives to traditional car rentals are available. Several Web-based services rent cars to licensed drivers for short periods ranging from a few minutes to a few hours. These services require several business days to complete registration, so they must be planned out in advance.

Car2Go (877/488-4224, www.car2go.com) has a growing fleet of two-seat electric Smart cars throughout San Diego available for short-term use. Tracked by GPS, drivers use a computer or mobile device to find an

Navigating Surface Streets

San Diego has its fair share of dead-end streets, which can make getting from point A to point B a challenge. Following are some major thoroughfares to help you avoid them, and a few alphabetical schemes to keep track of which direction you're going.

Numbered streets run north-south and are numbered sequentially from west to east.

Alphabetical streets run east-west and start Downtown at A Street increasing as you head south, to L Street. Broadway replaces D Street and Market Street replaces H Street.

Alphabetized groupings reflect streets named after trees (Downtown, Balboa Park), birds (Mission Hills), and gemstones (Pacific Beach). Downtown, this grouping begins with Ash Street, which runs parallel with, and one block north of, A Street.

The San Diego airport is located on **Harbor Drive**, which runs south through Downtown and along the bay all the way to the Coronado Bridge. The road connects with a few key parts of town—Harbor Island, Downtown, the embarcadero—without too much cross-traffic.

Broadway is the major west-to-east thoroughfare through Downtown. There are a lot of buses and stoplights, and you may never be allowed to turn left, but chances are you'll need to drive it. Harbor Drive crosses Broadway at its western terminus.

Sixth Avenue is a one-way street that runs along the western edge of Balboa Park and is the most reliable passage through Banker's Hill into Hillcrest, where it meets University Avenue.

The wide, heavily used **University Avenue** runs east-west the length of the Hillcrest and North Park neighborhoods, with popular restaurants and bars scattered along the way. As University Avenue runs east, it crosses Park Avenue shortly east of the Highway 163 overpass.

The intersection of University and Park Avenues is the geographic center of Uptown. **Park Avenue** runs north through University Heights and south through Balboa Park to the East Village Downtown, the only direct route to do so.

University Avenue crosses **30th Avenue** in North Park; this intersection is sometimes referred to as Restaurant Row. As 30th Avenue continues north, it crosses El Cajon and Adams Boulevards, streets with increasing notoriety for shopping among younger generations.

available car in the vicinity. A member card unlocks the vehicle and users drive to another destination within the city. Best for short one-way trips, these cars are cheaper when rented by the minute, though they are also available by the hour. When done, park the car in any legal space within the service's vast operating area, which includes city parking meters.

While not nearly as extensive as Car2Go's fleet, **Zipcar** (619/546-9654, www.zipcar.com) has a number of multiple-passenger cars placed at key locations around the city for use as hourly rentals. Users must return the car to one of the company's designated spaces. This can be a viable option when you need a car to visit multiple places in a day.

Hired Cars and Taxis

While numerous taxis may still be spotted in populous areas, car-for-hire services operated by smart phone apps tend to be quicker, and often cheaper, alternatives. Services like **Uber** (www.uber.com), **Lyft** (www.lyft.com), and **Sidecar** (www.sidecar.cr) operate the same: drivers are recruited from the public and cruise the streets shuttling people around at the touch of a button. Simply pinpoint your location on a smart phone app to request a ride; the savvy GPS system will determine the nearest available car and send it your way. Rides tend to be clean and the drivers pleasant. Charges are processed to the user's credit card through the app, which means no money (and no cash tips) change hands.

For those wishing to stick with traditional taxis, try **San Diego Cab** (619/226-8294) or **Yellow Cab** (619/239-8061). For traditional limos and hired cars, contact **Flex Transportation** (619/796-3539, www.flextranspo.com) or **City Captain** (619/800-3515, www.citycaptain.com).

Ferries

San Diego has two major ferry routes—both run to and from Coronado. **Flagship Cruises** (619/234-4111, www.flagshipsd.com, $4.25 each way) operates the Coronado Ferry from two locations: the Broadway pier (between the USS *Midway* and Maritime Museum) and the 5th Avenue pier south of the San Diego Convention Center. The 15-minute trip runs daily approximately 9am-9pm, arriving at the Coronado Ferry Landing. The ferry ride can be a scenic activity in its own right, especially if you bring a bicycle to explore the opposite shore.

Travel Tips

WHAT TO PACK

The first thing you should pack is a swimsuit. Fancy attire isn't a priority unless you plan to attend a theater production, business event, or upscale restaurant. Most locals remain comfortable with warm-weather clothing, and you can do the same. Long shorts, short to mid-length skirts and dresses, short sleeves, and tank tops are common. In fall, winter, or at night, when temperatures cool, pack jeans, casual pants, and a long-sleeved shirt or light sweater to add layers.

Bring comfortable shoes for walking around and some sandals or flip-flops for the beach. Sunglasses are a must, preferably those with UV protection. Either pack or purchase sunscreen, especially if you're fair-skinned and haven't seen a lot of sun in a while.

Bring a valid ID for going out to breweries, bars, and clubs; local law enforcement cracks down on underage drinking and businesses will card even those in their 40s to avoid steep fines. If you're planning to hop across the border to Mexico, you'll need a valid passport to return.

clockwise from top left: Downtown at night; the San Diego Trolley; a pedicab offers transport around downtown

For in-person conversations and all the pamphlets you could ask for, stop by one of San Diego's many regional tourism offices: the **San Diego International Visitor Information Center** (1140 N. Harbor Dr., 619/236-1212), Downtown at the Embarcadero; **La Jolla Village Information Center** (1162 Prospect St., La Jolla, 858/454-5718); or the **California Welcome Center** (928 North Coast Hwy., Oceanside, 760/721-1101). Information is also available online at www.sandiego.org.

FOREIGN TRAVELERS

Foreign travelers entering the United States must have a valid passport, and most must have a visa issued by a U.S. Consular Official. Citizens of certain countries may be eligible to visit for 90 days without a visa pending the Electronic System for Travel Authorization (ESTA). To find out if you are eligible, consult the updated U.S. Customs and Border Patrol website (www.cbp.gov/travel/international-visitors).

The currency used in San Diego and the rest of California is the U.S. dollar ($), issued in paper bills with denominations of $1, $5, $10, $20, $50, and $100.

Tipping is a common and expected practice in the United States, particularly for waiters, waitresses, and others in the service industry. Standard tips range 15-20 percent for table service, $1-2 for bar or counter service, 15 percent for taxis, $1-2 to carry luggage, and $1-2 per day for housekeeping services in hotels or vacation rentals.

Standards of measurement differ from most countries as the United States in not on the metric system. Distance is measured in inches (1 inch is 25.4 millimeters), feet (1 foot is 30.48 centimeters), yards (1 yard is 0.91 meters), and miles (1 mile is 1.6 kilometers). Weight is measured in ounces (1 ounce is 28.35 grams) and pounds (1 pound is 0.45 kilograms). Volume is measured in fluid ounces (1 ounce is 29.57 milliliters), pints (1 U.S. pint is 0.47 liters); and gallons (1 U.S. gallon is 3.79 liters).

Electrical outlets in San Diego operate at 120 volts, 60 hertz, using a plug with two parallel flat prongs and often a third, round prong that functions as a safety ground.

English is the language spoken in San Diego, although a large number of locals are fluent or proficient in Spanish.

ACCESS FOR TRAVELERS WITH DISABILITIES

Travelers with special needs may require extra planning and may have to skip a few of the city's harder-to-reach attractions; however, there's more than enough to reward your efforts. A growing number of attractions have become compliant with the Americans with Disabilities Act (ADA), and the city itself is currently in the process of making sweeping upgrades to make it more accessible. For a comprehensive list of accessible sights and

ESSENTIALS
TRAVEL TIPS

assistive services, visit **Accessible San Diego** (619/325-7550, www.access-sandiego.org).

A few different transportation options may be available to those in wheelchairs or requiring assistance. Local transportation agencies offer ADA-compliant programs in San Diego, such as **MTS Access** (www.sdmts.com) and North County's **LIFT** (www.gonctd.com/lift). Each may require prior registration with **ADA Ride** (www.adaride.com). For private rides, contact **Cloud 9 Super Shuttle** (800/974-8885, www.cloud9shuttle), which operates daily 24 hours. Specially equipped van rentals are available from **Wheelchair Getaways** (800/642-2042, www.wheelchairgetaways.com) and **Better Life Mobility Center** (888/540-8267, www.betterlifemobility.com).

The **San Diego Central Library** (330 Park Blvd., 619/236-5800, www.sandiego.gov) includes the Oliver McMillan Center, which offers a wide range of assistive devices to help connect special needs individuals with computers and other technology.

Beachgoers may want to take advantage of **free beach wheelchairs,** available by calling ahead for a reservation at any of the following beaches: Coronado Beach (619/522-7346), La Jolla Shores (619/221-8899), Mission Beach (619/980-1876), Ocean Beach (619/221-8899), and Silver Strand State Beach (619/435-0126).

Mission Bay Aquatic Center (1001 Santa Clara Pl., 858/488-1000, www.mbaquaticcenter.com, daily 8am-6pm) operates an Accessible Watersports program that offers sailing, kayaking, and waterskiing lessons to people with disabilities. Activities usually involve adaptive devices or adjustments to accommodate different needs. Call ahead to reserve individual lessons (available year-round), or to find out about group events scheduled throughout the summer.

TRAVELING WITH CHILDREN

Many hotels and attractions in San Diego cater to children and families, often with reduced admission costs or kid-friendly programs. Several surf schools and water-sports rental agencies offer child-specific classes or even day camps that will keep kids active. In addition, these top playgrounds in the city should help:

- **Waterfront Park** (1600 Pacific Hwy., Downtown) lies between little Italy and the Harbor, with a playground, cooling water-jet fountains, and a pleasant view of the boats at the Maritime Museum.
- **Pepper Grove Park** (Park Blvd. at Space Theater Way, Balboa Park) is a scenic little park with a large playground split into areas for older and younger children.
- **Trolley Barn Park** (Adams Ave. at Florida St., Uptown) is a small grassy park with a large playground in the pleasant walking neighborhood of University Heights.
- **Kellogg Park** (6200 Camino del Oro, La Jolla) playground sits on a grassy park right behind the sand at La Jolla Shores beach.

- **Spreckels Park** (Orange Ave. at 7th St., Coronado) offers plenty of green grass, shady trees, a gazebo, and a playground for children.

SENIOR TRAVELERS

Travelers over age 65 (in some cases over age 60) may enjoy discounts and other benefits to attractions all over San Diego. In addition to discounted admission, hotel rooms, and public transportation fares, seniors may find dedicated spaces such as the **Senior Lounge** (Casa Del Prado, Suite 105, Balboa Park). Transportation assistance may be available by consulting the organization **FACT** (888/924-3228, www.factsd.org).

TRAVELING WITH PETS

San Diego loves dogs, and the city furnishes a number of off-leash parks, including several beaches. There are plenty of dog-friendly patios and even hotels that allow dogs, with some restrictions.

OB Dog Beach is the best stretch of sand in town, or try Fiesta Island in Mission Bay if your dog is less into playing with others and more about running around. If your socially fit pup would rather run on grass, head over to the **Grape Street Dog Park** in South Park.

Pet-friendly accommodations include Hotel Indigo and the U. S. Grant, Downtown; Porto Vista Hotel in Little Italy; the Ocean Beach Hotel in OB; Surfer Beach Hotel in Pacific Beach; La Jolla Village Lodge in La Jolla; the Hotel del Coronado (within walking distance of the Coronado dog beach); and the Grand Del Mar resort in Del Mar.

For an extensive directory of pet-friendly restaurants, hotels, and events—including a Surf Dog competition (Aug. or Sept.)—visit **San Diego Happy Dogs** (www.sandiegohappydogs.com).

Health and Safety

URGENT-CARE CLINICS

U.S. health care runs primarily on private insurance, meaning there are general-practice physicians and specialists all over town, but they are expensive without insurance coverage, and they are usually booked up weeks and months in advance. If you're traveling and in need of medical attention for minor illness or injury (sports injury, illness, digestive or skin problems), the best way to see a doctor is to visit one of these urgent-care clinics. Waits tend to be shorter than at an emergency room, and you may receive the treatment you need to keep your vacation going.

- **Sharp Rees-Stealy Downtown** (300 Fir St., Downtown, 619/446-1575, www.sharp.com, Daily 8am-8pm)

- **Rady Children's Urgent Care** (4305 University Ave., Suite 150, Uptown, 619/280-2905, www.rchsd.org, Mon.-Fri. 4pm-10pm, Sat.-Sun. 1pm-10pm)

- **Anderson Medical Center** (1945 Garnet Ave., Pacific Beach, 858/224-7977, www.andersonmedicalcenter.com, Mon.-Fri. 8am-8pm, Sat.-Sun. 8am-4pm, call for holiday hours)
- **Scripps Clinic Torrey Pines** (10666 N. Torrey Pines Rd., La Jolla, 858/554-9100, www.scripps.org, Daily 24 hours)
- **Carlsbad Urgent Care** (2804 Roosevelt St., Carlsbad, 760/720-2804, https://carlsbadurgentcare.com, Mon.-Fri. 9am-9pm, Sat.-Sun. 9am-5pm)

EMERGENCY SERVICES

If an immediately life threatening situation occurs, call **911** on any phone for emergency help, and an ambulance will respond quickly. If the ill or injured person is mobile enough to travel, you may also drive to the nearest of these emergency rooms:

- **UCSD Medical Center** (200 W. Arbor Dr., 858/657-7000, Hillcrest, http://health.ucsd.edu)
- **Scripps Memorial Hospital La Jolla** (9888 Genesee Ave., La Jolla, 858/626-4123, www.scripps.org)
- **Sharp Coronado Hospital** (250 Prospect Pl., 619/522-3600, Coronado, www.sharp.com/coronado)
- **Scripps Memorial Hospital Encinitas** (354 Santa Fe Dr., Encinitas, 760/633-6501, www.scripps.org)

SAFETY OUTDOORS
Swimming

Most, though not all, San Diego beaches post **lifeguards** during daylight hours; however, there may be some gaps in coverage around sunrise and sunset. When in the water, watch for **strong waves.** Even small waves can get the better of inexperienced swimmers, and it only takes six inches of rushing water to bring you down. **Rip currents** are a little tougher to spot. You might see a little ripple on the ocean surface, or spot a section on the edge of the waves where nothing is breaking. These may be indications a strong rush—or rip—is forming to suck water from the beach back into the ocean. If you find yourself caught in a rip current, don't try to swim against it; a deep enough rip could carry away a small elephant. Instead, try to swim across, perpendicular to whichever direction it tries to carry you. And try to signal a lifeguard.

Sharks may be the most feared creatures in the sea, but shark attacks in San Diego are very uncommon, and usually taking place in deeper water. More common dangers come from **jellyfish** and stingrays. The jellies are tough to see and may surround you before you realize it. Jellyfish stings hurt, but lifeguards know how to treat it. Further treatment should only be necessary in the event of an allergic reaction.

Stingrays hurt quite a bit more. Stingrays tend to shuffle along the sand in shallow waters. La Jolla Shores, for example, is a stingray habitat. When you step on one, the stingray responds by whipping you with a venomous stinger on its tail, almost like a giant bee sting. To avoid being stung, kick up the sand as you walk along the ocean floor; the stingray will feel you coming and get out of your way. If stung, seek treatment.

Sun Protection

The beaches get really crowded in the summer, but you can always spot those who forgot to wear sunscreen by their bright-pink faces and reddish-purple backs. Here's a tip: Use **waterproof sunscreen** on any exposed surface, SPF 30 or higher, and reapply it every two hours. Failing that, you may go from tanning to burning in 30 minutes; by the end of your beach day, you'll need to bathe in an aloe-based ointment, the only mildly effective treatment for sunburn.

Wildlife

There are a few natural predators in San Diego, but most aren't a danger to humans. **Hawks** occasionally swoop down to carry off small pets, and **coyotes** may group together to attempt the same. If you spot a hawk, pick up any dog less than 7 or 8 pounds. If you spot a coyote, corral your pets; there may be more coyotes lurking nearby. Coyotes can tease dogs into traps by appearing to be hurt or vulnerable. Coyotes fear humans, though, so make a loud or aggressive noise and they'll settle for watching you from a safe distance.

Rattlesnakes are a more formidable threat. Though snakes tend to hibernate in winter, in summer they may be found in any natural area and even residential ones. A heavy tread while hiking will help you avoid surprising a dozing rattlesnake; if they sense you coming, they'll usually slither out of your path. If someone in your party receives a rattlesnake bite, seek medical attention immediately. Bites may be lethal within 30 minutes.

Black widow spider bites can be quite dangerous. The shiny black spider with a bright-red hourglass on its abdomen lives all over San Diego, but the nocturnal creatures will do their best to stay out of the way and out of sight. On rare encounters, keep away from the spider and it will do the same. If someone is bitten, seek urgent care; if a child, an elderly person, or a pregnant woman is bitten, go to the emergency room.

CRIME

San Diego is one of the safest large cities in the country, but it's still a large city, and there are unsavory people who may try to prey on out-of-town guests. Use common sense: Avoid handling large amounts of cash in public and keep purses and wallets zipped or latched and close at hand. When driving, keep car doors locked; in hotels, keep valuables in a hotel safe. Do not bring hard-to-replace items to the beach—credit cards, electronic devices, jewelry, passports, or other valuables—it's impossible to keep an eye on your things while you play in the waves. If you do encounter violent individuals or theft, call the police by dialing 911.

Resources

Suggested Reading

Amero, Richard W. *Balboa Park and the 1915 Exposition*. Charleston, SC: The History Press, 2013. Delve deeper into the coordinated efforts of local civic leaders and philanthropists to produce the Panama-California Exposition, which effectively created Balboa Park and arguably put San Diego on the world map.

Carrico, Richard. *Strangers in a Stolen Land: Indians of San Diego County from Prehistory to the New Deal*. San Diego: Sunbelt Publications, 2008. The history of San Diego's indigenous Kumeyaay, Luiseno, Cupeno, and Cahuilla peoples, beginning long before the Spanish ever set foot in California, through the U.S. government's sometimes forced removal to outer-county reservations.

Castillo, Richard Griswold del. *Chicano San Diego: Cultural Space and the Struggle for Justice*. Tucson: University of Arizona Press, 2008. A recounting of San Diego's omnipresent Chicano culture and the ways it has manifested in the city throughout, and in some ways before, its civic history, including a detailed telling of the events establishing Chicano Park.

Davis, Mike, Kelly Mayhew, and Jim Miller. *Under the Perfect Sun: The San Diego Tourists Never See*. New York: New Press, 2003. A glimpse into behind the scenes political machinations of San Diego, where life ain't always sunshine, water sports, and beachwear.

Elwell, John C., Jane Schmauss. *Surfing in San Diego*. Mt. Pleasant, SC: Arcadia Publishing, 2007. A thorough and visually rich telling of local surfing history, dating back to the days of George Freeth, by longtime surf historian Elwell in collaboration with Schmauss, a founder of the California Surf Museum in Oceanside.

Engstrand, Iris. *San Diego: California's Cornerstone*. El Cajon, CA: Sunbelt Publications, 2005. A comprehensive history of San Diego written by a historian at UC San Diego, ranging from the earliest known human presence to the 21st century.

Hendrickson, Nancy. *San Diego Then and Now.* San Diego: Advantage Publishers, 2003. Primarily a photographic history of the city, juxtaposing vintage and current-day photographs of buildings and neighborhoods to highlight the changes over time.

Innis, Jack Scheffler. *San Diego Legends: Events, People, and Places That Made History.* El Cajon, CA: Sunbelt Publications, 2004. Engaging survey of the parade of politicians, religious cults, and larger-than-life characters that contributed to San Diego's development as a left-coast city.

Lee, Murray K. *Gold Mountain: A History of the Chinese in San Diego.* Virginia Beach, VA: Donning Co., 2010. Lee, Curator of the Chinese American History Museum, reveals the fascinating history of San Diego's Chinese and (once naturalization was finally allowed in 1943) Chinese American population, including a detailed account of the decline of Chinatown.

MacPhail, Elizabeth C. *Kate Sessions: Pioneer Horticulturist.* San Diego: San Diego Historical Society, 1976. Biography of local figure Sessions, the "Mother of Balboa Park," responsible for introducing a startling number of trees and plants to the once barren region.

McGaugh, Scott. *Military in San Diego.* Mt. Pleasant, SC: Arcadia Publishing, 2014. A photo-rich survey of San Diego's long-standing symbiotic relationship with the U.S. Military, written by a local military historian and curator.

McLaughlin, David J. *Soldiers Scoundrels, Poets & Priests: Stories of the Men and Women Behind the Missions of California.* Scottsdale, AZ: Pentacle Press, 2006. Compiled histories of the 21 California missions established by Spain in the 18th and 19th centuries, with the first three chapters devoted to Juan Cabrillo, Gaspar de Portolà, and Junípero Serra, three men who cemented Spain's temporary conquest of San Diego.

Internet Resources

Balboa Park
www.balboapark.org
Check out this Balboa Park site to keep up with museum special exhibits, find park day passes, and discover special events that happen in the park periodically throughout the year.

Bands In Town
www.bandsintown.com
Find updated concert listings and local music recommendations with the handy app from this company, which happens to keep an office in Little Italy.

City of San Diego
www.sandiego.gov
Providing information and access to all city departments, this city site's especially useful for researching the Parks and Recreation department, including specific rules, regulations, and amenities for all city beaches, including lifeguard information.

San Diego City Beat
www.sdcitybeat.com
One of the city's free alt-weekly publications, keeping up with relevant cultural happenings, including music and politics.

San Diego Convention and Visitor's Bureau
www.sandiego.org
Primarily a visitor information website, this group highlights goings-on at attractions all over town, including detailed explanations of cultural events and nice ideas for family activities.

San Diego Eater
www.sandiego.eater.com
A local food and dining blog, this site keeps up with new restaurant openings and foodie special events, and offers features relating to some top local chefs.

San Diego Golf
www.sandiegogolf.com
A useful place to look into all San Diego golfing opportunities, including help reserving tee times at in-demand courses around town.

San Diego History
www.sandiegohistory.org
A terrific resource for anyone interested in San Diego history, and representative of the San Diego History Center located in Balboa Park, as well as the Junípero Serra Museum on Presidio Hill in Old Town.

San Diego Reader
www.sdreader.com
San Diego's other free alt-weekly paper, with updated music, news and theater information, plus recent food reviews and coffee features written by yours truly.

www.signonsandiego.com

San Diego's long-established newspaper of note, the *Union Tribune,* of late rebranded *The U-T,* offers comprehensive news coverage of the region, as well as international stories contributed by the paper's news partners. The website is designed as a portal to local information and resources.

Taphunter

www.taphunter.com

Beer hunters will love this app, which keeps track of which terrific craft beers are currently on tap at nearby and popular restaurants and bars. Search by location or specific beer.

Thrillist

www.thrillist.com/san-diego

Probably the best way to keep up with the ever-changing trend of San Diego's nightlife, the San Diego branch of this global website covers food, music, cool happenings, and sights, written in Internet parlance by young people.

Uber

www.uber.com

Getting an inexpensive ride somewhere can happen in minutes with Uber's app. An Uber driver will locate you and get you where you're going. It's especially handy for beer tourists—think of it as a designated driver on demand.

Restaurant Index

Nightlife Index

Shops Index

Hotels Index

HOTELS INDEX

Photo credits

MAP SYMBOLS

▤▤▤	Expressway	○	City/Town	✖	Airport	⛳	Golf Course
═══	Primary Road	◉	State Capital	✖	Airfield	🅿	Parking Area
﹏	Secondary Road	◉	National Capital	▲	Mountain	▰	Archaeological Site
⋯⋯	Unpaved Road	★	Point of Interest	✚	Unique Natural Feature	♦	Church
------	Trail	•	Accommodation	🦘	Waterfall	⛽	Gas Station
··········	Ferry	▼	Restaurant/Bar	♦	Park	⬭	Glacier
▬▬▬	Railroad	•	Other Location	⬛	Trailhead	▨	Mangrove
══	Pedestrian Walkway	△	Campground	⛷	Skiing Area	▱	Reef
▥▥▥	Stairs					▱	Swamp

CONVERSION TABLES

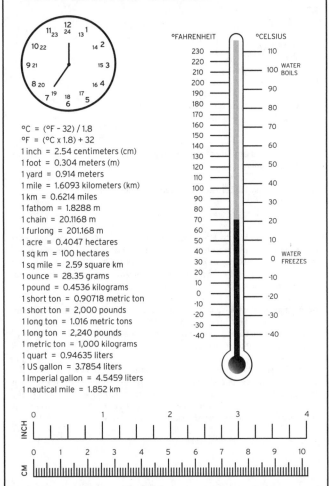

°C = (°F - 32) / 1.8
°F = (°C x 1.8) + 32
1 inch = 2.54 centimeters (cm)
1 foot = 0.304 meters (m)
1 yard = 0.914 meters
1 mile = 1.6093 kilometers (km)
1 km = 0.6214 miles
1 fathom = 1.8288 m
1 chain = 20.1168 m
1 furlong = 201.168 m
1 acre = 0.4047 hectares
1 sq km = 100 hectares
1 sq mile = 2.59 square km
1 ounce = 28.35 grams
1 pound = 0.4536 kilograms
1 short ton = 0.90718 metric ton
1 short ton = 2,000 pounds
1 long ton = 1.016 metric tons
1 long ton = 2,240 pounds
1 metric ton = 1,000 kilograms
1 quart = 0.94635 liters
1 US gallon = 3.7854 liters
1 Imperial gallon = 4.5459 liters
1 nautical mile = 1.852 km

MOON SAN DIEGO
Avalon Travel
a member of the Perseus Books Group
1700 Fourth Street
Berkeley, CA 94710, USA
www.moon.com

Editor: Sabrina Young
Series Manager: Erin Raber
Copy Editor: Christopher Church
Production and Graphics Coordinator: Lucie Ericksen
Cover Design: Faceout Studios, Charles Brock
Moon Logo: Tim McGrath
Map Editor: Albert Angulo
Cartographers: Albert Angulo and Brian Shotwell

ISBN-13: 978-1-63121-088-4
ISSN: 1941-6814

Printing History
1st Edition — 2008
3rd Edition — June 2015
5 4 3 2 1